CHICAGO MEDIUM RARE

By ROBERT J. CASEY

CHICAGO MEDIUM RARE

When we were both younger

By

ROBERT J. CASEY

Illustrated by ANN & JOHN GROTH

Publishers • THE BOBBS-MERRILL COMPANY, INC. • INDIANAPOLIS • NEW YORK

Grateful acknowledgment is made to the Chicago
Herald-American for permission to reprint material
originally published in that newspaper.

To HARRY . REUTLINGER

Without whom much of Chicago (Rare if
not Medium) could hardly have existed.

Contents

CONTENTS—*Continued*

PART I

EXPANDING CITY

Chapter 1

It Seems Like Chicago

CHICAGO, according to the experts, is a city that took root in a swamp about 1826, grew to noticeable size before 1890 and reached its ultimate magnificence day before yesterday. Some observers may take issue with this pronouncement on the ground that there is nothing ultimate about the magnificence, that the old town is going to be much more magnificent tomorrow. But nobody quarrels much with the troubadours who continue to sing a song about the old days having been pretty good.

Chicago today is truly an inspiring sight, although you may have a little trouble getting around in it. It is filled with tall buildings which most of the citizenry forget were the invention of a local architect. It has parks and playgrounds and grandiose boulevards. It is administered by a large choir of politicians of no doubt noble character, entertained largely by television, concerts, moving pictures and outdoor sports, and fed by thousands of restaurants which, one may admit, are just about the same as those of any other big city. As one looks back through a memory not too much strained, it seems to be more crowded than it was in the days when Lake View and Jackson Park were vacant lots. But its transportation system—which was terrific then—is terrific now.

It is difficult for even the most enthusiastic citizen to realize that Chicago was not always as it is now. Its earliest settlers were fired with the idea that they were founding a community that would be important enough to last forever. They aroused the laughter of the lake and river towns by their boastfulness. They were long the stock joke of New York's vaudeville. But anyway they passed along the idea of the city's permanence. The modern youth, as convinced as they were that Chicago *always will be,* may be excused for his belief that it *always was.*

But there were differences. As children we lived for a long time in what seemed to be a vast park some twelve minutes by steam train from downtown. Various circuses came every summer to perform in the vacant area just across our alley. There was little traffic in our front street except toy wagons and baby carriages. The days were usually sunny and quiet and peaceful. The silence after nine o'clock at night was something that no child nowadays has ever experienced. Residence districts like Hyde Park, Kenwood, Austin, Lake View, Ravenswood, Edgewater, had plenty of space, plenty of trees, plenty of birds and clusters of comfortable, hospitable, lamplighted houses. Transportation in those days didn't bother us much, but we had the idea that it was pretty fast. At any rate it was fast enough to suit the people who used it.

Those were the days of great newspaper characters like "Ten Dollar" Tom Murray, who sold suits of clothes for ten dollars a suit—"Good enough for me to wear, good enough for you to wear." As I remember what the males of the town looked like, it seems possible that he tailored them all. There was Heine Gebubler, who ran an interesting saloon; Charles T. Yerkes, who ran an interesting and almost permanent streetcar system; and a couple of rising young politicians in the first ward named Hinky Dink Kenna and Bathhouse John Coughlin. Shining stars of the populace were Eugene Field and Ben King, poets; Finley Peter Dunne, who was Mr. Dooley; Hamlin Garland, Elia Peattie, Opie Read,

12

Stanley Waterloo, Brand Whitlock, authors and reporters; Ben Reitman, Emma Goldman, Elizabeth Gurley Flynn and Bill Haywood, the world savers; Doc Sage, the talented dope peddler; Captain George Wellington Streeter, governor of the Deestrick of Lake Michigan; George Ade, the playwright; John R. Thompson, Billy Boyle, Jean de Jonghe, Jim Colosimo and Flapper Joe, restaurateurs; Alexander Dowie, the soul seeker who started the doctrine that the world is not round but flat; Warren Leland, Potter Palmer, John B. Drake, hotel men; George Pullman, proprietor of the indestructible Pullman Building.

There were some notable gamblers, just as now: Marshall Field, the Mandel Brothers, the Messrs. Siegel and Cooper, Schlesinger and Mayer, Charles Stevens, A. M. Rothschild, and some quiet Scotchmen named Carson, Pirie and Scott sold dry goods and such in the State Street trade. Still noticeable in the city's progress were Cyrus H. McCormick, P. D. Armour, Will Ogden, J. V. Farwell, James B. Forgan, George M. Reynolds, John P. Altgeld, Samuel Insull, Roger Sullivan, R. W. Sears and A. C. Roebuck. There were others, of course, but one forgets the names.

The most interesting public figures in my recollection were the lads who were seen every so often in parades. As a parade costume they wore flowing black frock coats and large, shiny top hats. Bobby Burke, the Democratic political boss, was one of the most ornamental of these. He was rather short and rather round, and his hat was incongruously high. It was a treat to see him.

Chicago people didn't have much money in the eighties. They probably had even less in the nineties. But they hadn't much trouble buying enough things to be comfortable.

You could get a top-flight straw hat for $1.25 in the spring of 1889. If you wanted to wait for a later sale—"before they fed 'em to the cows"—the price would be fifty cents, or maybe a quarter. You could get a pretty good suit of clothes at Ten Dollar Tom's for ten dollars, a shirt for seventy-five cents, a pair of shoes for $2.50, a necktie for twenty-five cents or less. There were also better types of clothing which, one is informed, cost more.

A streetcar ride cost a nickel. Sandwiches, ice-cream sodas, shoe shines, Sunday newspapers, a quart of milk, a loaf of bread, a gallon of gasoline, a yard of cheesecloth, a toy balloon, a sack of peanuts, a well-advertised cigar, a horse-racing tip, a glass of beer or admission to a "Nickel Show" were the same price.

A daily newspaper cost a cent. So did a stick of peppermint rock, two dipped caramels, a yard of licorice candy, a sugar bun, a peep show, illustrated books entitled *Red Riding Hood* or *Jack the Giant Killer,* odds and ends of fruit from a peddler's wagon, a good-luck charm from a gypsy, a song from the druggist's captive phonograph, a fine badge for the Fourth of July, a Christmas-tree ornament, a string of firecrackers, a dill pickle, a small block of paper, a beautiful picture (generally of ladies who seemed to be swooning), a spinning top, a peggoty, a fishhook, a doll dress, a chance on maybe $100,000 in a neighborhood lottery. Pennies are still circulating, but, apparently, you can't get as much for them.

I cannot say that people were better dressed in those days of Chicago's middle growth. Nobody among the males was interested in neatly pressed clothes because pressing was held to identify ready-made coats and pants. Looking at the counterparts of Beau Brummel that you saw in the streets, you were convinced that nobody at all ever wore ready-made suits.

Trousers all had one peculiarity which has always seemed strange to me. They generally had a wrinkle around the ankles, fitted tight on the lower leg and thigh and bagged generously at the knee. The wearer always seemed to be about to leap, and from certain angles gave the illusion of moving at a high speed. He had to walk carefully to avoid splitting his pants.

Women all wore long dresses with dragging trains which kept the sidewalks clean but did the wearer no good. The muck picked up in the shopping districts was hauled painfully home, along with the grippe germ or the diphtheria bug or the virus of the common cold. Nobody seemed to mind. An epidemic in those days might have wiped the town out. But God was good to us. There was a lag in epidemics.

There is plenty of argument that we managed to stay alive because Americans were a hardier lot in the eighties and nineties. I doubt that. I never felt particularly hardy and I can remember that *strong men*—weight lifters, hammer throwers and such— were one of the most popular features in museums, vaudeville shows and circuses. I am aware that then, as now, most people took a dim view of stairs when they got past the age of forty. It was man's aversion to climbing that made skyscraper construction stop with the tower of Babel, and a recognition of the aversion that made Chicago the first really modern city in the world.

Until about 1880 the bulk of the city's buildings were four or five stories high. They might have been stretched two or three stories higher without any changes in building method, but these extra floors would have been vacant. Five stories was about the limit to which any ordinary man could lift himself on a hot day.

Sometime just before the Civil War, Otis, or some other genius, had invented an elevator to help him lift iron parts for his factory. Shortly after the war he had added a device to keep it from falling, should the power cut off, and the world began to talk about a safe elevator for passengers. In the middle eighties it attracted the attention of the Chicago architects Daniel H. Burnham and John W. Root. Before 1890 they had built the Montauk Block, the Rookery Building and the first section of the Monadnock Block —all of them ten or more stories in height. Before Root's death in 1891 they had hung the twenty-one-story Masonic Temple to the clouds. For many years it was to remain the tallest building in the world. The elevators worked perfectly.

The building of the first skyscraper made changes not only in

Chicago but in all the growing cities of the United States. It made possible the concentration of hundreds of people over a ground space that twenty years before might have been crowded by a dozen. It gave quick access to the offices of people in associated professions. It slowed down the outward expansion of the original business district and made possible the Union Loop. And the hammering of steel and the piling of brick and stone has gone on ceaselessly ever since.

When I was a child you couldn't see any of the city above the trees in the middle of Lincoln Park. There were no lofty towers in your view from Austin or Kenwood. People used to go downtown and gaze for hours at the men who were lifting the new skyscrapers. The noise of the hammer men and riveters was the most inspiring thing in town. It was also the most unusual.

16

There were other major exhibits. Out on the near South Side you could view a life-size painting of the Battle of Gettysburg. In later years there was a fine cyclorama of the Battle of Manila, a spectacle filled with noise and smoke and splashing water.

On the site of the present Coliseum was Libby Prison—the real Libby Prison—which had been moved plank by plank and brick by brick from its original site in Richmond, Virginia. It was an uplifting place, filled with old soldiers, flags and guns, and old bullets and stirring messages. The World's Columbian Exposition of 1893 was another spectacle that gave the customers full satisfaction—at any rate I thought it was pretty marvelous. And before that there was a colossal, three-day pageant called the Chicago Fire.

There were splendid open-air concerts at some of the amuse-

17

ment parks. Creatore's brass band was big and boisterous and loud
—but none the less it was one of the finest brass bands in the
country. Creatore, who ran the organization and played a hot
trumpet, was glad to be an American. That is the message he
wanted to convey to his Sunday-afternoon audiences, and with
the aid of about 150 top musicians he seems to have done pretty
well at it.

With him—or with some of the other bands one met in the
parks—was a little boy about six years old, son of the manager or
something, who used to get riotous applause for reciting the
Gettysburg Address. I shall admit that he got no encouragement
from me. I was also six years old when I first heard him, and I
thought I could do a much better job of reciting the piece. But
nobody ever asked me to perform and I have now forgotten his
name. Very likely he went through life to become the greatest
reciter of the Gettysburg Address since Abraham Lincoln.

There were some notable singers around Chicago in those days.
It is recalled that May De Sousa, onetime musical comedy melo-
dist, got her start on the Sunday-concert circuit. The daughter
of a Chicago policeman, she might have gone on as a simple
housewife if somebody had not picked her to introduce a heart-
rending ballad by Bathhouse John Coughlin entitled "Dear Midnight of Love." The like of it was never heard elsewhere at any
time.

On a summer evening it was easy to get home from Sharp-
shooter's Park, or *Sans Souci,* or Chutes Park, or other haunts of
joy. You got aboard a leisurely horse tram or cable car and wandered off through the dark. In what seemed to be no time at all
you got home. Home, it seems, wasn't much farther away than
walking distance anyhow. And after 6:00 P. M. there wasn't
much of anything on the car track.

You'd alight at your own corner in the brightness of the coal-
oil street lamp and walk down the block to the salutes of the

neighbors who occupied the front porches. You'd sing out greetings to them and tell them proudly that you had just been to Whosit's Grand Auditorium Concert. And you'd mention, a bit smugly, that it was the finest performance you had ever heard—particularly the singing of "I Don't Want to Play in Your Yard."

The neighbors would nod approvingly.

Chicago was certainly a fine spot, you thought—strikingly beautiful, talkative, gay and friendly . . . and just exploding with wonderment.

Chapter 2

Dire Dangers

Much of what I have to tell you about the glories of early Chicago is admittedly hearsay. My grandfather had been here since they began to tear down old Fort Dearborn. But my immediate family did not move into the place till around 1891, at which period I was a year old.

It is not difficult, however, to reconstruct the adventurous beginnings of the city. For lack of better entertainment the pioneers of Onion Creek were given to conversation, and they talked about the things that interested me most. Some of the stories were fairly hazy. The account of the Fort Dearborn Massacre, for instance, was something that seemed to confuse most of these alleged eyewitnesses. They had all been hiding in dense shrubbery with others of their kind, and their vision was somewhat impeded by foliage, grass, warriors and such.

My grandfather gave me a better account of the first voyage of Will Ogden's railroad train, although he remembered the massacre with a lot of fine detail. Grandpa wasn't exactly an honored guest on the train trip. In point of fact, at that time he wasn't even in Chicago. He was somewhere up in Newfoundland on

account of his ship having run aground. But no matter. He was
a steam engineer, which made the Ogden line familiar to him
whether he had seen it or not.

The early chroniclers gave Chicago an important place in the
world—all of them. They also gave it tremendous historical
significance. Old Mr. Hennessy, an able boilermaker who lived
down the street from our house, advertised himself as a veteran of
the Mulligan Guards, and his Civil War reminiscences were so
vivid that I was convinced for a long time of Chicago's nearness
to the courthouse at Appomattox.

My childish mind had a little difficulty fixing the dates of the
momentous happenings that had marked the city's growth. They
all seemed to have occurred at once, and probably only yesterday.
But whatever the historical muddle of such thinking, it made the
march of Chicago vigorous and great and colored like a circus
parade. There weren't any hazy grays in what I knew about the
babyhood and adolescence of this great bourn. Even the days of
its advanced youth, which I came to know pretty well through
personal contact, may have seemed a little more gay and glorious
to me than to other people because I had had expert training as
an observer.

When I was five I could recite all the details of the Great and
Horrible Fire, which I somehow envisioned as a sort of pyro-
technic display, plus the destruction of one or two frame cottages.
Everybody in the neighborhood was a fire survivor, quite willing
to tell about his own danger and desperate loss, his own superb
heroism in getting out of the heat. The Great Railroad Strike and
the Haymarket Riot were similar living pictures. They had a
background of fire, too, plus a cast of snarling, embattled men
right out of the recollections of the old people who, perhaps,
didn't remember too accurately but weren't hampered by that.

I got to know all about the boom days and the days of the hard
times; the noise and dissension of the early Civil War days; the

rioting around Bridgeport; the announcement of peace; the cholera epidemic; the plans for better transportation; the entertainment of generals and opera singers and Presidents' wives. I was impressed by stories of how State Street had been lifted up out of the mud ten or fifteen feet so that the sewers would drain and the horses would be able to stand less than belly-deep in mire. I could see the beginnings of the metropolis that grew up after The Great Fire—a vivid picture—just as vividly as that of the city I saw torn down and replaced but possibly not quite so grand. I didn't know much about architecture or community planning then, but my grandmother had a book called *Cities of Europe* that might have given me some idea of what the constructors of the downtown district were actually trying to do. There were lots of pictures in the book that I thought were portraits of Chicago. But there was some misunderstanding about that because these vistas of fine structures were labeled "Paris."

That Chicago—the Chicago of the period before the elevator became popular—was a stately assemblage of four- and five-story edifices that would have looked quite natural on the Rue de la Paix. There was a lot of chatter in the newspapers about "the sunless canyons of the streets," and more about "the feverish hurry of the pedestrians." The pedestrians, it is true, walked as if they intended to go somewhere. They continued to have a fair speed until the crush of other speeding pedestrians slowed them down. But the "sunless canyon" stuff was a bit mysterious. To a child it seemed that the sun always managed to shine on one side of the street and most of the time.

Still the region that was about to become the "Loop" was a fascinating place—make no mistake about that. It was vibrant and active all the day. The constant movement of horses was like that of a county fair. There were the closed carriages and the ornate rigs of the rich, filled no doubt, with beautiful and handsomely gowned women. There were ordinary one-horse buggies, occupied by people in a hurry. There were unending streams of drays, hauled by steaming Percherons and directed by a cavalry of police. The air was filled with the nervous traffic's creak and hum, and by a sort of odd mélange of shouts, howls, swear words, the conversation between the truck drivers and the crossing cops.

The downtown district was filled with unbelievable things: men in clown suits advertising tailor shops; a lad in Scotch plaids who trailed up and down State Street calling attention to somebody's tweed clothes or somebody's tweed whisky; dentists' signs in which sets of teeth six feet wide opened and closed and clacked and clacked; opticians' signs out of which amazingly large eyes looked at you and winked; red-coated Hussars in front of hotels; oddly costumed sandwich men; hansom cabs; coachmen with fawn topcoats and high silk hats; bobtailed horses; brave bicycle riders; and, of course, the wealth of chinaware and leather and lace and cloth and ribbon and buttons and such inside the many stores.

But what part of the city was without its array of wonders? There was the Ferris wheel out on North Clark Street; and the La Salle Street tunnel; and the virtually motionless Chicago River north of Graceland Avenue; and the almost impossible equipment of the bathers who went into the lake at the foot of Diversey Boulevard. And, of course, to these you might add the grocer's sled, the ornate milk cart, the waffle wagon. Out in the residence districts there wasn't much traffic, but perish the thought that the streets lacked color and life—and clouds of dust.

When my parents brought me to Chicago we lived in a tree-shaded area near the Cuyler station on the North Western Railway. There was nothing about this location that seemed remarkable to me. But I learned afterward that we were pioneers in a sort of colony of pioneers. There were two or three parallel streets in this locality lined with two-story frame houses on broad deep lots. Not any of the houses was more than four years old. They were freshly painted, pert looking and comfortable—as comfort could be measured in 1891. Some of them are there yet. They don't seem to have changed much. Across the street from us was a two-story brick flat building. And that, in itself or in the thousands that followed it, hasn't changed much either.

The sidewalks were wooden affairs, the streets unpaved. The North Western track was separated from the customers by a simple three-strand wire fence. Three-year-old babies had no trouble crawling under the fence and frequently did. There were no streetcars, not even horsecars, in the neighborhood. If you were going anywhere, you went on the railroad or walked a mile or so to Clark Street and rode on a contraption called the "steam dummy." Ravenswood, which seemed like a thin settlement in a dense forest, stretched away to the north. A sparsely populated residence district, a couple of cemeteries and the lake were along the route to the east. Westward, across Lincoln Avenue, broad acres of grassy nothingness stretched on to the outskirts of town.

Our street was ideal for children. We could play all day in the middle of the dusty street. We could tour the whole neighborhood without thought of damages if we kept to our own side of the North Western fence. And save for the noise we made, the neighborhood was a shrine of complete quiet. I remember how it felt to come out through the front door, early on a sunny morning, and stand there listening to the silence which seemed less mysterious to me than it would now. It is a long time since quietude and Chicago have had any mutual relationship.

Life in this isolated retreat was far from dull. Everybody was always falling into the muddy ditch along the railroad track—and getting hauled out. Somebody was always getting lost and being found next door or across the street. There were odd little excitements such as visiting gypsy fortunetellers and hungry tramps and snowstorms and prairie fires.

At an early age I learned something about the principles of jet propulsion through my father's experiments with what he thought was a Roman candle. My father, who had lived a varied life in

24

urban centers, probably knew as much about pyrotechnics as any other man in the community. But when our second Fourth of July came around he discovered that he lacked information about an item called the "Rocket." Half a dozen of these things were delivered without warning at our door as part of Knoop's Spectacular Three Dollar Display and Firecracker assortment. He picked one up and looked at it with interest.

"A Roman candle with a handle" was his justifiable diagnosis. "What won't they think up next!" So he stepped onto the front porch, grasped the stick and lighted the fuse with a parlor match. . . .

So far as I know, that was the only cheap skyrocket that ever went off. My mother was quite angry with me. She thought I probably had something to do with it.

With good reason, your careful citizen of today goes abroad full of fear that he will be run over by an automobile or bashed by monkey wrenches falling out of airplanes. It is his unshakable conviction that the progress of civilization is mixed up with sudden death. Never, he thinks, has the life of man been so unpredictable and so cluttered with peril. But it seems to us that the *present* worries him merely because he has so little information about the past. He never was maimed by a runaway horse, tossed upside down by a cable car, set afire by a Christmas-tree candle or blown up by a celluloid collar.

The instability of the celluloid collar quite likely is now disregarded as a major hazard. Not for many years has anyone reported one simultaneously to the medical profession and the fire department. But it is a matter of history that while Chicago's best-dressed men favored such adornments, the casualty lists maintained a steady level. The last victim, so far as can be discovered, was registered at the County Hospital in 1903—a gay young blade whose name was Howard Elling. He lived at 1964 North Marshfield Avenue. (Old numbering.)

"It happened all at once," he told the examining surgeons. "And I do not know how. I was at the counter in the cigar store, and I leaned over to light my cigar at the gas jet . . ."

And that isn't all that we might report about the pitfalls of the quiet life when there was such a thing in Chicago.

Wooden sidewalks were undoubtedly a great improvement over weather-torn mud paths. But they had one unfortunate feature: the planks had a way of coming loose at one end. So when the hurrying pedestrian put a foot on the other end, they would leap up, trip him, break his leg or toss him into a ditch.

When the citizens escaped the sidewalks they found other hazards. Every night a fair percentage of the visiting yokelry got into trouble by blowing out the gas lights and getting properly asphyxiated. Never a night went by without somebody getting folded up in a folding bed. Sleeping was a much more serious business than anyone might have thought.

From the city's first days until the automobile came into general use about 1912, dealing with horses gave one's life a zest. Horses bit you, kicked, and ran away. They lay down casually and rolled on the cavaliers who were caring for them. They were notional and unruly. They would balk and sit down and tie up traffic with explosive effectiveness.

It is interesting to recall at this late date that no matter how frequently the good old steeds bit people, nobody ever accused them of spreading hydrophobia. The dogs came in for that honor almost exclusively. Never did a poor hound come home tired and dusty from his work of chasing wagons, sit down and wave his tongue in the breeze to cool it, but some hysterical housewife would send her little boy running for the police firing squad. We didn't have so much hydrophobia out our way, real or fancied. We had plenty of dogs, but we had to run too far to find a policeman.

The womenfolk with whom we had close association had persistent and awesome fears of gypsy kidnapers, and of voracious eagles that occasionally swooped down out of the blue—so we heard—to attack sleeping babies. I don't recall that any child in our vicinity ever fell victim to the gypsies or eagles, but it must have been worrisome for mothers in some parts of the town, particularly when upstairs front windows were left open at night.

Neither I nor any of my little playmates were ever allowed to go near Sheridan Road alone. That was another deadly menace. On occasion you might be allowed there in custody of your grandfather, who was the soul of wisdom and caution. If you held tightly to his hand, you might eventually cross this dreadful no man's land and watch the most optimistic of Chicago's citizens trying to catch fish from the breakwater. But even so, you recognized it as an extremely frightening and unprofitable effort. There was danger in the street—recognizable, throat-catching danger—for there were tides of bicycles rushing past at incredible speeds. . . .

You heard the oft-repeated cry from far off: "The scorcher's goin' to get you if you don't watch out!" Something was always goin' to catch you if you didn't watch out.

Hardly an adult lived through the days before electricity without at least one narrow escape from an adventurous ride on a horsecar in the winter. It was the occasional custom to strew the floors of such conveyances with straw to protect the customer's feet from chilblains that were worse than death. And it was to be expected that every so often the little stove at the front end of the car would ignite the straw. The victims, one is surprised to note in these days of the new "Old Look," were all women. Modes kept changing constantly between the Civil War and the Jazz Age, but in one respect they remained constant: women's skirts were always long and generally inflammable.

They were longer in the nineties and at the turn of the century than they have been since, and they were dragged through the slough and refuse of poorly cleaned streets like plows in reverse. And they yearned to take fire.

Along about the time of the Spanish-American War, some dressmaking engineer noticed the rising curve in female pneumonia cases and invented a remedy. Skirts were not shortened. That would have been too immodest a trick to think about. But a thing called the "dust ruffle" was attached inside the billowing train at the bottom of the hem. The idea was that the ruffle would act as a squeegee and relieve the skirt of the labor of sidewalk sweeping. The sidewalks got noticeably cleaner, but wet-legged women continued to die of penumonia at the same old rate.

Then came the trolley car with electric heaters under the seats. They were set well forward where they were most likely to touch the familiar bundle of skirt ends. The skirt ends would burn quickly and easily. So would the dust ruffles. One draws a veil.

This, admittedly, was one of the things about Chicago's growth that meant very little to us. The women of our neighborhood were like those of all other neighborhoods. They wore long skirts and "dust ruffles" in full accordance with the rules of style. Their skirts were just as inflammable as anybody's else. But when the danger was most imminent, and one boarded a streetcar in fear and trembling, we didn't have any streetcars.

Chapter 3

The City Rises

WHATEVER you may have been led to believe by tintypes labeled "Randolph Street looking East from La Salle Street in 1889," Chicago at the time of the World's Columbian Exposition had become a city.

It was experimenting with novelties in transportation—as, indeed, it still is—festooning itself with lights in bottles, spreading its wares in the most gaudy collection of bazaars since the days of Akbar the Great, talking loudly in a deep bass voice, and, thanks to the recent development of the elevator, tossing up towers higher than Babel.

Built as it was on a swamp, the bottom of which had never been located since the establishment of Fort Dearborn, Chicago was the least likely place on earth to have developed a skyscraper. Conservative capitalists, backed by the opinions of some of the best engineers in the United States, shied away from the idea of lofty towers rising out of a jelly of water and sand. If you couldn't find a solid bottom for your foundation, they said, your buildings would have to float in this semicolloidal mass—and such a project was obviously nonsense.

30

It turned out, however, that all the capitalists in Chicago at that period did not follow the same rules of conservatism. Some of them were hidebound, no doubt. But there were plenty of them with gamblers' wits. Daring had been the principal factor in making them rich, and they were quite ready to take a chance, silly or not.

There was no lack of architects and builders who had new ideas and daring—William Holabird, John Root, Daniel Burnham, Louis Sullivan, Dankmar Adler and William Le Baron Jenney. Some of them may not have had much money—particularly at the beginning of their drive to put a new face on local construction. But every one of them was ready to hazard his reputation to prove that the city's unstable soil would support a tall building. So eventually they altered the appearance not only of Chicago but of San Francisco, Lima, Shanghai, Rio, New York and, for that matter, most of the large cities in the world.

John M. Van Osdel and W. W. Boyington, whose impression was plain in the building trends that followed the fire, had made Chicago look something like a fairly raw Paris. There were stretches of four-story buildings along State Street with mansard roofs and chateau fronts, dignified lobbies and stairways that were grand to look at if not to ascend. The city was bowing with great dignity toward architectural tradition and was beginning to look uncomfortable.

Some newspaper engineer calculated in 1885 that an additional floor on each of the buildings in the downtown district would care for the growth of Chicago for fifteen years. But he admitted that the weight of an additional story would be a severe tax on the basic swamp. It might be better, he suggested, if Chicago were to move somewhere farther north—to Wilmette, for instance, or some place else where there wasn't any swamp.

The new architects, who had begun to raise a fine lot of argument about buildings of fifteen, seventeen and twenty stories—

31

fantastic conversation, their opponents declared—were uniformly a group that cared nothing for tradition. Until their coming, the foundations of buildings in the downtown area had rested on pilings or pillars of stone sunk deeply in the sand. Young John Root got the idea that taller structures could be erected on foundations that would have no stress to the sides, and as a sample, he invented a raft of railroad rails and concrete to be sunk considerably below the surface. The tall building, he argued, would be supported solidly by the raft.

His first venture with this construction was in Monroe Street. It was watched with leers and jeers by most of his contemporaries. A deep hole was dug with watertight wooden walls surrounding it. Steam pumps kept the excavation dry. A layer of cement some two feet thick was laid down as the construction's first step. Railroad rails were crisscrossed over it to a depth of a foot and a half, and cement was poured into the interstices. Another layer of concrete went in and another layer of crossed rails until the raft was some twenty feet deep. On top of it went the basement and ten stories of the Montauk Building, the first skyscraper that the world had ever seen.

Some of the skeptics remained, of course, and their voices were loud after La Salle Street and Michigan Avenue began to fill up with piles of masonry taller than most of the populace thought dignified, or safe, or even possible. Chicago was proud of new glories that brought astonished builders to its door from as far away as London, Paris and Berlin. But a large contingent of the citizenry continued to go around with chins pulled well down into the protection of celluloid collars, mumbling about the day when all these ungodly structures would tumble down into the street. In spite of which, the floating foundation became a standard in Chicago building for the next twenty years.

As the problem may be considered by one who has no buildings to put up and no insurance to pay, it would seem that the critics of the method may have had some slight reason for their uneasiness. The twenty-one-story Masonic Temple, for instance, arose on such a foundation and gave the architects plenty to think about. It was out of plumb during most of its existence—so much so at times that its overbalance could be observed from the State Street sidewalk. During the last twenty years, it was kept in safe equilibrium by a series of frequently adjusted jackscrews.

Louis Sullivan, who was a smart engineer as well as a genius of design, went through many bad moments in the construction of the Auditorium tower. Before his death he frankly admitted that he had more than half expected to see it one day spread out in Wabash Avenue. But he solved his problem by providing the tower with a special raft and erecting it as a unit separate from the rest of the building. It is still there.

In 1884 the nine-story Pullman Building was erected at Michigan Boulevard and Adams Street to demonstrate what could be done with pure masonry. Probably the finest structure of its time, it was built with brick walls several feet thick. It was one of the last great structures of pure masonry ever put up in Chicago. It is still standing. Catty rumor maintains that it might be replaced by a newer, more efficient pile save for the expense of breaking it apart.

Soon after the Pullman Building was completed, Burnham and Root, using similar construction, put up the nineteen-story Monadnock Block, probably the largest office building in the United States if not in the world. In La Salle Street rose the Rookery Building—and that, too, is still extant. Its designers declared that they were building a tower so far in advance of its time that it would endure as long as Chicago—and nobody so far can say that they were wrong.

Toward the end of the eighties William Jenney took an important step forward by introducing steel beams into the Home Insurance Building, which he put up next door to the Rookery. Such construction had never been used anywhere before. Despite the fact that the building rose faster than any previous skyscraper, and at lower costs, its importance seems to have been recognized only by other builders and architects. Nevertheless it marked the beginning of the modern steel-framed structure. Its basic features have not been altered much since.

Three years after the erection of the Home Insurance Building, William Holabird put up the Tacoma Building in La Salle Street, hanging the outer walls like a curtain on the steel frame. And this was the first building of its now familiar type to be found anywhere on earth.

The nineties covered the area now known as the Loop with a rash of office towers—the Ashland Block, the Woman's Temple, the Chamber of Commerce, Otis, Mercantile, Calumet, Rand-McNally, Manhattan, Monon, Commercial Bank, Mallers, Gaff, and Counselman buildings, among others. The massive Auditorium Hotel and the ornate Studebaker Building gave a new look to the sky line of Michigan Boulevard. A great many of these structures are still with us.

Contemporary writers were unbothered by bombast in their descriptions of these places. They sounded the loud timbrel, as well they might. Nothing like these palatial structures had ever been built before, they said. They had sprung from the city that made the way easy for magnificient thought. They lifted Chicago to heaven's gate—above the storms, above the clouds—almost beyond the stars—while dwellers in less gifted communities were still compelled to grovel far below "in the murk of unconcern and nonaccomplishment."

Recounting the glories of the new Chamber of Commerce Building, John Flinn, considerable authority on local glories, approached poetry. He said:

The new Chamber of Commerce Building is in many respects one of the finest commercial structures in the world, and certainly one of the grandest office buildings in the United States.

34

The property on which it stands cost $650,000 [he refers to the southeast corner of Washington and La Salle streets] and the building itself has cost the owners, Messrs. Hannah, Lay & Co., over $1,000,000.

Standing on the mosaic floor of the first story, throwing back your head and looking up [as was the custom of those days], you will see twelve balconies with their bronzed railings rising in symmetry above you. Away at the top, and crowning the grand central court, is probably the largest skylight in the world.

Through this mammoth window a perfect flood of light penetrates the central court so that the interior of the building is almost as brilliantly illuminated as the exterior during the day.

As you look up, if your neck will bear the strain, you will notice that not a post or a pillar is visible between the twelve balconies other than those of the north and south ends, the intervening stretch being entirely free from obstruction.

Looking down from the top, the people on the floor below seem like pigmies. The height makes us dizzy and we move away from the bronze railings fearful that the natural temptation to throw ourselves over it may gain mastery of us.

The Chamber of Commerce Building is a city within itself. There are more people doing business inside its walls than you would find in many a prosperous community. . . .

And more to that effect. Alter the names, and the same eulogy might have been written about any of a dozen tall buildings in the same neighborhood.

Flinn neglected to observe one important feature of the old Chamber of Commerce Building, however. Each balcony floor had its own individual design of mosaic. Anybody who had memorized these patterns was able to tell at a glance what floor he was on, which, at the time the building opened, was advertised as a remarkable assistance to tenants.

His fine praise for the style of the building seems to have been justified, though. For many years it was one of the most popular office locations in town. The waiting list of lawyers was another thing that the management bragged about when it wasn't discussing the mosaics.

It also found favor with the city's despondent who came into it to loiter and to examine the great central court with an eye to toss themselves into it from the top balcony. Special policemen used to chase these sad-eyed people from floor to floor. But leaps from the balconies went on just the same.

A few years before the structure was torn down the management installed a series of steel-meshed grids across the court to discourage would-be suicides from leaping. The cost of these gratings, along about 1923, was said to be about $650,000—just the sum that the original owners had paid for the land on which the building stood.

Using that as a basis, one might write an interesting essay on the subject of what happened to Chicago through the wild years of its growth. Along in the nineties you would buy land for a building and pay a price so high that it rated a gasp from the guidebook writers. Twenty-odd years later you needed a few simple gratings for the court, and they cost you as much as the land did. And nobody talked about it at all.

Either Chicago was getting wealthier or the value of the dollar was taking a sharp, quick slide.

Chapter 4

The Streetcar Comes

A LAD WAS in the office the other day with some samples of next year's Christmas cards. Unabashed by Congressional investigations and threat of dire things to come, the manufacturers of Christmas cards seem to work on the idea that all our tomorrows shall be as today and that there'll always be a lot of snowcovered English inns, stagecoaches and a plump citizenry that resembles Mr. Pickwick.

We looked at the holly-bordered scenery with growing nostalgia and some recollections of a youth in which a lithographer named Rafael Tuck had supplied all the Yule greetings decked out with blue-eyed blond angels and such. But admittedly the new samples of the old scenes failed to arouse any memory of preblitz English coaching houses and their holiday allure—no eye-catching boar's head and flaming Yule log, no smell of spiced wine and roast fowl, no sound of the festive sackbut, recorder and psaltery.

What came to our hazy vision was the Chicago equivalent of these antiquities—the streetcar transfer stations where there was always the same fascinating drift of eager travelers and you didn't need a holiday to maintain a spirit of high carnival. At least that's the way it seemed to me at the time. Maybe they didn't dispense boar's head and mulled sack, but they certainly had a fine supply of peanuts and soda water. As centers of social intercourse, the city will be a long time finding their like.

Like most of the institutions that have figured in Chicago's life, these came into being because of haphazard developments in the growth of the town. The cable-car system had begun to branch out of what is now the "Loop" sometime in the late eighties. It has always been a matter of argument whether the spread of population brought them about or they brought the spread of population. They turned out to be obsolete long before Charles T. Yerkes tried to make them a feature of Chicago with permanence like that of Lake Michigan.

The electric trolley car was a going proposition in outlying parts of the sprawling community in the middle nineties, and the populace was getting over the superstition that anybody who rode on it was in danger of being struck by lightning. But no matter how good they were, the electric car lines found themselves in a limited field. The cable lines controlled the approaches to the business district. The electric lines were compelled to confine their service to districts where there weren't any cable cars and, for that matter, the riding population wasn't very noticeable either. In spite of that, they laid their tracks out into the wilderness with a lot more imagination, or willingness to take a chance, than we have noticed in the traction business since.

Electric transportation was a new idea, and the men who supplied it seem to have been prompted by a spirit of youth. One of their lines went south to nowhere along Stony Island Avenue, starting from Jackson Park. Another rattled along in Evanston Avenue—now Broadway—from the old Lake View "Limits" to Evanston. From Wrightwood Avenue cable barns, rails and trolley wires were extended out Lincoln Avenue past the now vanished Bowmanville. And only the hardy souls had ever ventured

38

to learn how far the Milwaukee Avenue and Elston Avenue lines had plumbed the *bosque* to the northwest. Out west there were electrical connections through Oak Park, Maywood and numerous bourns that had been considered inaccessible except to horsemen with time on their hands.

The "transfer points" in the beginning were merely places where you alighted from one sort of streetcar and got onto another. You paid a second fare, of course, no matter which way you were going. "Free transfers" were still a long time in the future.

When the trolleys came in, the cable cars were already provided with terminal facilities on each run—generally a carbarn; if not that, some sort of turntable by means of which the grip car could be kept at the head of the three-car train.

The electric car, as everyone now knows all too well, can be reversed for its return journey merely by moving the motorman and little crank handle from one end to the other. But in the early days there seems to have been some disagreement about switching privileges in streets. There may have been some natural compunction about having the customers frozen to death while waiting out in the open for transport. But that was all a minor matter. Real estate in the electric-car zone was pretty cheap. The electric line engineers, copying cable technique, looped their track through a couple of vacant lots.

Not until later did the magnates discover the possibilities of making a parking lot out of the middle of a public thoroughfare by means of a simple switch.

The transfer points speedily became important trade centers which waxed steadily until the time the cable lines went out of business completely. Until the arrival of the electric cars the cable companies had offered prospective passengers no great comfort. Generally you stood in the barn—a great open shed which provided more protection against the snows of winter than you might expect to get on an open street corner, but in most seasons seemed to collect quite a lot of mud or slush. Then one of the trolley companies put up a waiting room in the vacant lot adjoining its loop, and a new feature came into the life of the harried traveler.

The pushcart merchants were the first to sense a new market at a point where the customers would have to loiter willy-nilly. Along the open loops they sold everything from bananas to shoestrings. Then the companies put up new buildings or revised old ones, and rented out stall space to the greatest collection of pitchmen that had been seen in Chicago since the World's Fair.

The cable companies, despite an aloof attitude toward changes for the better in equipment or service, moved some switch tracks in their barns and found space for waiting rooms, novelty stalls, grocery departments, penny-in-the-slot machines, soda fountains, hot-dog stands, cigar counters and tintype galleries.

In fact, as one historian has summed it up, Chicago's streetcar terminals very nearly attained the social status of present-day railroad stations—they no longer remotely resembled places where one might possibly board a conveyance to go somewhere else.

It has been said that the growing trade of these transfer points— far from the city's center—was what led to the planning of the Union Loop, which concentrated Chicago's big business for half a century. There may be a modicum of truth in the idea. Established business anywhere is always frightened by the popularity of competitive buying centers. It has also been said that downtown tradesmen, who swung considerable influence to promote the unification of traction lines, universal transfers and the electrification of the entire system may have been chiefly interested in getting rid of important rivals. This is less feasible. There have been neighborhood shopping districts in all large cities in history even before there was any automobile-parking problem, and presumably there always will be. It is certain, however, that a prosperous and picturesque institution which was a cross between a

40

French market and a county fair went out of business when the customers could get to town without having to change cars.

There were several of these enchanting places—one in Stony Island Avenue around Sixty-third Street, another at Madison Street near Harlem Avenue, a couple out on the North Side and at least two more somewhere out southwest. Basically they were the same —one-shot markets in the carnival tradition. To the customers all the salesmen were named George. To the salesmen the customers were just a succession of white faces without individuality, without identity. Except for one sad-faced woman who had possibly "seen better days" and presided gracefully at the hand-painted sofa-pillow stand in the Limits Terminal, there were no saleswomen. The day of the girl clerk was just dawning in the neighborhood grocery stores.

The general appearance of the arcades was pretty uniform. But they differed in stock, custom, prices and tendency toward good cheer, which was their principal charm. The Limits Emporium was the largest of the lot because it was the oldest and, from the beginning, catered to a larger number of people. It had a spacious waiting room where Lake View housewives met and loitered, as they came to do later in Loop hotel lobbies. The place after 4:00 P. M. was usually swarming with boys and girls from nearby academies, most of which have since moved farther out on the north shore. Between morning rush and 4:00 P. M. there was a steady rush of shoppers, few of whom came away unscathed.

Something of the same atmosphere filled the South Side Station. The little University of Chicago furnished some of the custom during the winter months, and in summer there were always mobs from the steel-mill districts flocking to Manhattan Beach.

The West Side spot, as one remembers it somewhat vaguely, was smaller, less noisy and less busy—probably because patrons had no great distance to travel to a well-established business center, which was Oak Park.

We gave our custom largely to the one at Lincoln, Wright-wood and Sheffield avenues, which was spacious and raucous and, save for the lack of clowns and elephants, much like a circus. It had the customary stalls putting out gum, crackerjack, flowers, fruit, novelty stuff, cigars, soda water and such. In addition to that, it offered a clothing store and a meat market which could be reached by glass doors from the waiting room.

You couldn't buy pickaxes, miners' lanterns or kerosene in it, but otherwise the Wrightwood Avenue Arcade had much the same appearance as a pioneer trading post, which in a way it was. Once, in an investigating mood, I ventured to inquire of another old-timer what had become of the Loop fruit stands that used to outnumber the saloons. And the answer was simple.

"Did you ever try," inquired my friend, "to take home a bunch of bananas on a Madison Street car during the rush hour?"

When one thinks the matter over it seems likely that the street-cars in the days of these transfer-point shops weren't so crowded as they have been since. One hesitates to admit that there was ever a moment when they weren't. But one seems to remember virtu-ally private rides out on the west end of Madison Street. And it was almost a matter of routine to lug bundles home from Wright-wood Avenue. Home delivery! Who ever heard of such a thing!

I wasn't much interested in the fruits and flowers that made a gaudy decoration for the stalls at the east end of the waiting room, except to notice that the orange peel trodden underfoot gave the place something of its aroma. The souvenir stand with its plush pillows and velvet-covered frames and silk-tasseled hair receivers didn't give me much uplift either.

But I recall that I had my first drink of root beer at the station soda fountain and bought at the candy counter the first taffy apple I ever saw. There was a gum machine in the corner near the cigar stand where a clown about the size of a Punch-and-Judy figure would bow his thanks for your penny and push your gum to you with a stick from the top of a pile. I have always associated him with the management of the traction company.

The toys were pretty good, too. The *pièce de résistance* of stock at all the transfer points was a green-coated tin monkey with a talent for climbing up and down a string. This specimen cost a quarter, which was a lot of money in those days but pretty cheap for mechanical toys. It ran as long as most devices of its kind. And when it stopped it defied fixing. Which shows how modern it really was.

There were troops of dolls, and every now and then a little table where you could buy patent can openers, glass cutters, pancake turners, potato peelers, bread knives and similar gadgets that cost a dime apiece. There were newsstands that sold *Farm and Fireside, Golden Hearts,* the *Family Magazine,* and other literature that I have never seen on sale anywhere else in this world.

On occasion you could buy patriotic buttons saying "We Mourn Our Loss," "Hats Off! Our Hero!" or "Remember the Maine!" Disasters were commemorated at the car terminals long after they had been forgotten by the country at large. And once I invested a regretted fifteen cents in a large plaster cow labeled—appropriately, no doubt—"Souvenir of the World's Fair."

All of these wayside marts are gone now. If people have to meet these days, they join the mob under Marshall Field's clock, or push the guests out of a hotel lobby, or stand on some street corner until friendship hardly seems worth the effort. If they want to buy plaster cows or string-climbing monkeys, they have to consult four clerks in a toy department. There is no longer any pleasant break in a journey to town. It's not necessary. You come to town nowadays in your automobile. And you find a parking place somewhere adjacent to South Bend!

"We Mourn Our Loss!" And maybe you think we don't!

Chapter 5

The General's Ghost

THERE was an authentic haunted house in Mayfair in 1898—
just as well-equipped and modern a haunted house as you will be
able to find anywhere in the world today.

It looked the part. It was a large, rambling stone building with
dark-gray walls, shuttered windows, a slate roof, and two cupolas
connected by a sort of widow's walk. It stood on slightly rising
ground a quarter of a mile from other habitation, and it was appropriately surrounded by a small forest of pines and gnarled oaks.

As for the resident ghost I cannot say much. I never met him
personally. But if hearsay has any status in a research such as this,
he was the restless spirit of a Confederate general who had come
north to live alone, far from his deserted homeland.

General or not, he had provided himself with all the customary
props—clanking chains, flitting blue lights and much unpleasant
laughter. Not many people had ever seen him, but that had
nothing to do with his social status. There weren't many people in
Mayfair. Alive or dead, he was still alone.

You'll be hard put to find the outlines of the 1898 district of
Mayfair on any map. Early cartographers depicted all that neigh-

44

borhood out toward the west end of Farwell Avenue with a blank space like the white spot of Arabia—a technique usually employed to indicate areas not yet explored.

Later maps showed a grid of streets in that area, but nothing to show the whereabouts of Mayfair, even as a whistle stop on the Milwaukee or the North Western. As nearly as I can recall its most interesting portion, it used to extend about half a mile east and about the same distance north from the corner of Montrose and Elston avenues.

I do know this: My grandmother's house, in which I was almost a permanent resident, was at Graceland Avenue and Perry Street (Irving Park Road and Greenview Avenue, as we know them now), six blocks north and about two miles east of Montrose and Elston avenues. It may have been farther east. And to get there—to Montrose and Elston—you had to take the Ashland Avenue horsecar to the cable terminus at Wrightwood and Lincoln avenues, ride all the way downtown, dismount and take a north-bound car on the Elston Avenue line to the end of the route. After a couple of hours travel you alighted at Montrose Avenue and completed the journey on foot.

There weren't any sidewalks once you left the streetcar line—hardly any indications of what you might call a road. There were plenty of trees among which the dirt trail wandered haphazardly. There were no street lights, telephone wires, footprints or other evidences of civilization.

The houses, such as there were, stood back out of sight beyond patches of woods. A stranger in this country had all the sensations of an explorer in the Indian country, which, to a certain extent, he really was. My Grandpa Wilson owned a house out in this hinterland. I have since concluded that he must have inherited it from somebody. He would never, of course, have bought it.

It was built somewhat on the plan of the manse haunted by the

Confederate general, but Grandpa had somehow managed to rent it to a family of recluses named Corman. He called on them once a month to find out why they were currently out of funds. As a matter of unvarying custom he would take me along. He didn't ride the streetcars to the business district and back again to Montrose Avenue and Elston Avenue. He used to rent a livery rig and drive out—which took just as long.

Thus I met Tom Corman, a lad about my own age, and from Tom I learned about the general and the haunted house.

We didn't visit it immediately. There wasn't time. But we laid our plans, consulted my grandfather and arranged for an all-day picnic in the woods to be held on the following rent day.

I was duly impressed by the finding of the haunted house. I didn't have to be told much of its gruesome history—all haunted houses, it seemed, were pretty much alike. This one looked haunted. And an eight-year old's imagination could read ominous messages into the creak and slam of the shutters stirred by a lazy breeze.

We looked around diligently for a place to get into the house, and discovered, somewhat to our relief, that it was sealed tighter than a drum. With a few backward glances we wandered out through the surrounding trees to a clearing that looked like a well-barbered park.

I have never forgotten the quiet beauty of that scene. Nobody had done anything to it since the Indians had moved away. But the grass was some unfamiliar variety that did not grow very tall, and we might have been standing in the middle of a broad lawn.

The surrounding trees were densely green, and ahead of us was a clear little river sparkling in the sunlight. The ensemble, as I know now, might have been part of any little-frequented section of the neatly beautiful English countryside. We sat down on the riverbank, listened to a chorus of birds and consumed a satisfying picnic luncheon of sandwiches and red pop.

Our conversation, naturally, concerned itself with the haunted house and its distinguished ghost.

"I'll get my grandfather to make a key for us," I promised bravely. "Then I'll come back and I'll get you and we can see what is in the house."

"The ghost probably wants something," said Tom. "They always do. They can't rest in their graves until somebody takes a message to their daughter or something like that."

"We'll see about it," I assured him with a heartiness that I didn't feel. "We'll ask the ghost what he wants when I come back."

But I didn't come back. The house was sold and I never saw Tom Corman again.

You'll find a lot of startling things on the map when you go about establishing the limits of Mayfair. It's a shock to be reminded of the fact that as recently as the beginning of the twentieth century great tracts of Chicago were still a reasonable facsimile of the original wilderness. At the time of the Cronin murder in 1889, Broadway ran through one lonely mile after another in a deserted region covered with shrubbery and sand. Wilson Avenue was just a passable crossroad. There wasn't a business house in Sheridan Road. Ravenswood, in the sector bounded by Irving Park Road, Ashland Avenue, Montrose Avenue (Sulzer Road) and Clark Street, was a dense oak forest in which my grandfather used to hunt rabbits. Over to the west of Ravenswood was Bowmanville, a sparsely tenanted farming district. Jackson Park, before they fixed it up for the World's Fair of 1893, was mostly tangled jungle.

Most of the district west of Crawford Avenue—now Pulaski Road—was uninhabitable prairie. And farther into town—on the corners of the occupied portions of it—were places like Mayfair that had not yet lost touch with the spirit of the pioneer.

Not so long ago I went to take another look at Mayfair. I could not even find it. East and north of the Montrose-Elston crossing I found a typical suburban development sprinkled with bungalows.

The woods were gone. The river was gone. My grandfather's old white elephant of a house was gone; so was the ghostly Confederate general and all that he represented. If his house was anywhere in this busy area, it was well concealed. One reason, it seems to me, why we have so few ghosts nowadays is that our ghosts can't find standing room.

Chapter 6

Gaslight

IT ISN'T so long since North Dearborn Street was lighted by gas lamps—only so long ago as the time when Sam Insull or somebody was trying to spread the gospel that "you can do it better with gas."

There may have been other important thoroughfares in Chicago, or in the rest of the world, that clung to such illumination—or to kerosene lamps, or the moon, or linkboys carrying torches—even though the popularity of electricity was taking a sudden surge in some localities. But none of these got the publicity that came to North Dearborn Street.

You know what North Dearborn Street looks like now, especially the last blocks of it that lead into Lincoln Park. Even to the eye of a stranger it presents all the usual marks of respectability and solidified wealth, plus a permanence something like that of the Great Pyramid and, perhaps, a greater antiquity. One might guess that it was inhabited solely by members of the Chicago Club, and he wouldn't be far wrong.

There are some modern buildings in the street, of course. They have a way of getting in everywhere. But they haven't done much to change the atmosphere of the district or to lessen the impression that this is a bit of Chicago embalmed as it reached the peak of culture in the nineties. There may be some new buildings, but there are plenty of brownstone dwelling places on fairly wide lawns with driveways leading to carriage houses—barns to you— now thinly disguised as garages.

One might think that gaslight would be safe in such a region until some of its denizens should prove some other illuminant better favored by tradition—tallow dips, for instance, or whale oil. But there is no accounting for heresy. Somebody around 1930— or was it 1940?—an interloper in the premises no doubt, got up a petition to change the street lighting. Surprisingly, he got quite a lot of signatures, and in the end his crusade for what he called modernization was successful, as anybody who rides along North Dearborn Street today can see. Its lighting is just as electric as that of any other street in Chicago and just about as bad.

There was a fight, of course. The old-time citizens held meetings and appointed committees and wrote pieces for the newspapers, decrying the change. Even the real graybreads of this transaction admitted that electricity had been successfully used in State Street, Jackson Boulevard and parts of Hyde Park for years. In many respects, they conceded, electricity was quite as good as gas.

That wasn't the point at all. The late Matthew Blackton, in one of numerous letters to the editor, made the position of the gaslight faction quite plain. The old residents of North Dearborn Street were not against change per se. What they unalterably opposed was "change without improvement." Wrote Mr. Blackton:

The gas lamps are part of the atmosphere of our neighborhood. Perhaps they may not be so bright as the electric lights concerning which we have been hearing so much. But they are mellower, and, perhaps because we have used them for so long, they seem friend-

50

lier. They have much warmth about them, particularly as they guide the traveler home on a snowy, winter night. They make this neighborhood something different from the rest of Chicago —something peculiarly our own. . . . And then, of course, we have to consider the future of the lamplighters. What will become of them?

There were some snide answers to Mr. Blackton's communiqué but none particularly to the point. The one most quoted was by George Hilf, a chauffeur, who sniffed at North Dearborn Street's desire to be alone—and different.

"Mr. Blackton says the lights of North Dearborn Street make that section different from the rest of Chicago," he observed. "But that ain't true. At night, with the gaslights on, Dearborn Street looks just like the inside of the La Salle Street tunnel or like the new Westchester subdivision where they ain't got no lights at all." He had an argument, at least enough of an argument to get himself widely quoted. But it was noticeable that he had nothing to say about Mr. Blackton's principal query: "What about the lamplighters?"

Unlike most historical specimens, with the notable exception of the buffalo, the lamplighter has been with us recently enough to have been known to thousands of people still living. Maybe you've been acquainted with one yourself, particularly if you've lived the past two decades on North Dearborn Street or in Winnetka. He was active in both those places until the end of the twenties—as quiet as the shadows he chased but never exactly anonymous.

Mr. Murray, who made the rounds in our neighborhood, might have served as a model for all the rest. He was a little man with a flowing black mustache, an earnest mien and a body as lean as a greyhound's. He was proud of his job and put everything he had into it, despite the fact that the public never seemed to realize his importance. He was willing to talk about it to anyone who would keep at his side while he worked, or join him on his own front steps in the twilight after the night's run was finished.

"It's a good position, boy," he would say. "But it's exacting. They don't give us uniforms like they give the policemen an' the firemen. They don't pay no attention to us unless we get sick an' nobody turns the lights on an' the city gets black, an' then the footpads come out to work. . . . An' what do you think of that?

"Some people know us because it's jest endin' daylight when we come around wit' the torch. It looks like an easy job to them. But that's because they never see how we got to git up at half past four or five an' go aroun' turnin' all the lights out agin. . . . An' always we got to have good legs an' keep in trainin' like them sprinters. . . ."

That, of course, was perfectly true. More lamplighters than athletes, in those days, died of athlete's heart. The rain or sleet or snow or other annoyances never stayed these messengers. You could set your clock by them. At 5:00 P.M. in winter, or along about seven in summer, the Mr. Murrays of Chicago would come around the corner on a dead run, each carrying a long-handled torch and a little short ladder.

Their routine was a perfect ritual of useful action. Years of experience in daily dashes against time had taught them all that was to be known about conservation of effort. *Clack!*—the right hand slapped the ladder against the bottom of the lamppost. *Whish!*—the left hand moved the torch to the "ready" position. *Wap! Tap!*—the lamplighter's rubber-shod feet mounted two steps and the torch unerringly speared the hole at the bottom of the lamp. One deft push turned on the gas in the Welsbach burner. One quick turn lighted it. And before the mounting glow had reached the top of the mantle, the lamplighter was down from his perch and running toward the next lamp.

What became of them? Well, what becomes of any professional performer when they take away his stage? They vanished. One

52

or two became track men, representing athletic clubs; but not many. Most of them died early—a matter of course in their occupation. But apparently enough of them survived to carry the torch through North Dearborn Street until the finish. Maybe some of the old clan now have sedentary jobs, pulling the switches night and morning in the plant that supplies the power for street lighting.

One suspects not.

M*ystery and Crime 1:*

Sundry Irish Activities

ONE of the fascinating features of Chicago between the Fire and World War I was that you could get out of it pretty easily. There were few signs of human habitation south of Sixty-third Street along Stony Island Avenue, or along State Street or Western Avenue, in the middle eighties. There were no connecting populations between the little West Side towns. Lake View, around our sector, was much praised for its agriculture until well into the nineties.

I recall a lush celery farm on Ashland Avenue that ran from Byron Street south to uncharted regions that I was not allowed to explore. There were little plots of cabbages and potatoes and such stuff west of us. And the main daily traffic in Lincoln Avenue was the parade of farm wagons to and from the downtown market.

There were few houses on Ashland Avenue then. There was a fairly thick settlement to the east of it. Marshfield Avenue, Paulina Street and Hermitage Avenue (then Commercial Street) were pretty well populated to the west. There was hardly anything along Graceland Avenue (as we then called Irving Park Road) except the cemeteries, Lake View High School, McDonald's printing plant and great quantities of whispering trees.

It is difficult to realize that the population of the city in 1891, when this vast loneliness was still a part of it, was somewhere

54

around 1,250,000 souls. Except for the bustling business district and the congested residence sections adjoining it, there was little evidence of such a growth. We had elbow room in those days and a sense of being somebody in a sparsely settled world.

As a six-year-old, I frequently took the mile-long walk to Grandma's house and back again without arousing much comment. The wandering gypsies and predatory eagles were still the subject of much conversation in 1896. But I gathered somehow that their field of operations was somewhere the other side of Ravenswood. Kidnapers seemed to be no cause of worry in our neighborhood. And of course there were no streetcars, no bicycles, no dashing horsemen or careening wagons on our unpaved roadways. There wasn't much to disconcert a child on a mile walk except that he might have a poor sense of direction and his feet might get tired.

It did not seem possible that anything of note could ever have happened in this idyllic setting, even on a dark and rainy night. For a long time I felt that harm came only to people who lived far away in some strange community. But it seems I was wrong about that. In point of fact, many Chicagoans looked upon our end of Lake View as a haunt of evil and made pilgrimages just to canvass our association with the "Greatest Murder of the Century." This murder, as Grandpa Wilson confided to me one day, was the Cronin Murder, which had come to pass in 1889.

"It was a matter of international import," he said. And I guess it was.

He pointed out the Carlson cottage, a little frame house that for a long time was the only building in Ashland Avenue between Graceland and Belmont avenues. It stood near Roscoe Street, and now, turned around, it is an ell of a structure passed by the Ravenswood "L." It is still intact, still recognizable and still unbeautiful.

As for the murder—well, Grandpa Wilson explained that he was coming home from a euchre party or a lodge meeting or something on the evening of Saturday, May 4, 1889, and reached the junction of Belmont, Ashland and Lincoln avenues just about midnight. He was about to turn north into Ashland Avenue, between the celery patches, when a buggy drawn by a white horse passed him headed south. As he proceeded along Ashland Avenue he was passed by an open wagon with a horse in the shafts that looked like it might be a bay. This vehicle, with one man in the driver's seat, was also headed south.

"It was very mysterious," said Grandpa. "Just too many people gallivanting around the streets at that time of night." He stood and watched the wagon turn west into Belmont Avenue, and so got to learn a lot about Lake View police procedure. Grandpa deserves no important place in history for this. There may not have been very many people living in Lake View, but those who did all seem to have been passing a restless night. All of them were up—and a good half of them saw at least one of the horses at various spots during the next several hours.

Those who saw made a mental note, for such traffic at such an hour was highly unusual. What made Grandpa Wilson's observation really important was that he counted not one man but three in the front seat of the wagon as it turned out of darkness under a street lamp on the Belmont Avenue corner.

That wasn't the end of the episode—not for him. As he neared Roscoe Street he was surprised to see a light in the window of the Carlson cottage. That puzzled him because, like everybody else who lived in the vicinity, he knew that the cottage had been vacant for months.

Because he was allergic to puzzles, he walked up the steps, pulled the bell and looked through the uncurtained window. He saw a table with a lighted lamp on it, a bit of carpet and a rocking chair—and nothing else. Nobody answered his ringing of the doorbell, which, he afterward admitted, was just as well.

Had he arrived a few minutes earlier he would probably have been a principal figure in this "puzzle of international import."

For while he had no reason to give much heed to it, this was the Carlson cottage; and in it, possibly half an hour before, Dr. Patrick Henry Cronin had been murdered.

"I have frequently been thankful that Fred Messig—or anyway I think it was Fred Messig—insisted on my staying for a couple more hands of euchre," Grandpa declared. "That's why I was so late getting to Belmont and Ashland avenues."

At eight o'clock that night Dr. Cronin, a highly successful physician, received a call at his office in the Windsor Theater Building, North Clark and Division streets, where he shared an apartment with Mr. and Mrs. T. T. Conklin. His visitor was a nervous and very excited stranger.

"I can hardly tell you, Doctor," declared this trembling man, "but one of the workmen in P. O'Sullivan's icehouse out in Lake View has been terribly hurt in an accident. If he doesn't get attention right away he may die."

"You'll have to wait till I get my buggy," demurred the doctor. But his visitor wouldn't hear of it.

"I have a buggy," he said. "We'll go in that."

He handed O'Sullivan's business card to the doctor, who left it on a table where it was later found by the Conklins. Dr. Cronin picked up a surgical kit and followed the stranger downstairs. At the curb was a buggy drawn by a white horse. Frank T. Scanlan, one of Cronin's old acquaintances, saw him take his place beside the nervous messenger and start north on Clark Street. Scanlan was the last person to admit having seen the doctor alive.

Grandpa knew none of this, of course. He got home and reported his adventure to Grandma as a matter of no particular mystery or importance.

"Guess somebody's moving into the Carlson cottage," he said. "I saw a light in the window and all sorts of traffic around the place." Then he went to bed.

At 7:00 A.M. a bloodstained trunk was found at Sulzer Road

(Montrose Avenue) and Evanston Avenue (Broadway), then little more than trails through a weed-grown wilderness.

At 10:00 A.M. Conklin reported to the police of the Chicago Avenue station that the doctor—a man of exceptionally regular habits—had not yet come home. Captain Schaack of the Chicago Avenue station telephoned to Captain Villiers of the Lake View Town Hall and the hunt was on.

The inquiry came to a dead end at the home of P. O'Sullivan, who lived near his icehouse, a few hundred feet from the back of the Carlson lot. O'Sullivan, the neighbors said, was out of town with his family. No one knew anything about the report of an accident to one of O'Sullivan's workmen. The Lake View police said that the whole business was probably a lot of silly gossip, that the doctor had probably gone someplace out of town on business and that they had best wait to see what else might turn up. And they would have waited, had it not been for the anguished cries of Chicago's Irish.

That brings us to another interesting part of Lake View's history. The region at one time had a large and vocal Irish contingent. Cronin had plenty of friends within calling distance of O'Sullivan's icehouse. They declared unanimously that there was plenty of reason to believe he had been killed—and by some of his own people.

For many years he had been active in the Clan-na-Gael, an Irish patriotic society which at the time had considerable strength. Recently the doctor had been suspended from this assemblage because he had accused the executive committee of dishonesty and treachery. But suspension had not ended his demand for a housecleaning. The avowed purpose of the Clan-na-Gael had been to free Ireland from British rule. Twenty-nine Irish revolutionaries had been sent to England on missions of sabotage and had been met at the docks by unsympathetic policemen. Deprived of their dynamite and useful friends, most of them had gone quickly to prison. Cronin, shocked by this constant loss of Irish rebels, took time to

58

study their connections in America and abroad, how they were financed, by whom and how they were dispatched from New York into the hands of Scotland Yard. His evidence showed that in almost every instance the men had been betrayed by Clan-na-Gaels at home who knew of their mission. Cronin charged that large sums collected to pay dynamiters had found their way into Clan-na-Gael officers' pockets.

"So," declared Patrick J. Fennessy, an irate Croninite, "our friend was killed by people who have led others to their deaths and who feared the retribution that was getting nearer and nearer to them every day that he lived."

The flaming indignation of the Irish was speedily caught up by other groups as the city went into a white heat. Chicago's detective force got no chance to rest for more than two weeks.

The mysterious wagon that Grandpa had seen turning west into Belmont Avenue had been noticed by some other people as it foundered in the mud near the Belmont Avenue bridge. It had been dug out of the morass and was gone by the time the police got there. But no matter. The search went on. The river was thoroughly—and unsuccessfully—dragged.

Squads of Chicago and Lake View police combed the brush around Sulzer Road between the lake and Clark Street. Other squads searched the weed plots of Graceland Cemetery. But no clew was turned up until the morning of May 22 when three laborers were sent to investigate complaints about the catch basin at Evanston Avenue and Argyle Street. They found the body of Dr. Cronin. His head had been badly battered, apparently with an ax.

Jonas Carlson, owner of the Carlson cottage, came to the Town Hall soon after that with his wife. They said that they had rented the house a month earlier to a man who became one of the sinister drama's most mysterious characters. Carlson said the man had disappeared. Mrs. Carlson said she feared something dire might have happened to him.

The police went home with them and examined the front room.

It was just as it had appeared to Grandpa Wilson except that the lamp had burned out and there were spots of blood on the floor that he had been unable to see from the window.

Carlson remembered then that the new tenant had been recommended by P. O'Sullivan, the ice purveyor. So detectives found O'Sullivan and arrested him.

Meanwhile the police were canvassing all the barns in Chicago in search of the white horse. They found him, eventually, in the livery stable of Patrick Dinan, a few doors from the Chicago Avenue station.

Dinan's information about the horse was lucid and startling. The man who had rented it with a buggy on the night of May 4, he said, was Detective Daniel Coughlin. So Coughlin was arrested on orders of Chief of Police Hubbard.

The coroner's inquest into the death of Dr. Cronin brought some of the affairs of the Clan-na-Gael into the open. As a result of that, Alexander Sullivan, lawyer, politician and director of the order, was also arrested. But he was never tried. One Martin Burke was identified as the man who had rented the Carlson cottage. He was picked up in Canada. Similar evidence indicated that the furniture in the room where Cronin was murdered had been bought by "Paddy the Fox" Cooney. He was never found.

John Kunze, a pal of Detective Coughlin, was pointed out by two witnesses as the actual driver of the white horse. He was indicted for murder. John Beggs, lawyer and a director of the Clan-na-Gael, had expressed enmity for Dr. Cronin. So he was indicted too.

If you read the old newspaper reports of proceedings against O'Sullivan, Beggs, Burke, Kunze and Coughlin, you realize the justice of Grandpa Wilson's comment: it was certainly a matter of "international import." And why not? The British, a bit concerned about plots to dynamite docks and factories and public buildings in London, were well represented at the trial. The

Irish—to wit, the Clan-na-Gael—were also well represented. So were lesser Irish patriotic societies shocked by the new perils that strewed the path of the eager saboteur. The state's case was presented loudly and effectively. Few local trials, before or since, have provoked so much oratorical bitterness. Beggs was acquitted, as everyone seems to have expected he would be. Nobody thought it much of a crime for an Irishman to speak ill of another Irishman. The others were sent to prison for life.

O'Sullivan and Burke died in Joliet two years after their conviction. Coughlin and Kunze served three years of their sentences, then were granted a new trial and acquitted. O'Sullivan's icehouse presently faded out of human ken. So, without much difficulty, did the Clan-na-Gael.

Coughlin came out of Joliet without appearing much the worse for wear. During the nineties he ran a saloon at 125 North Clark Street. For several years he was quite successful, but presently he was suspected of bribing a jury and indicted.

"I don't like indictments," he observed to some of his bar customers. "I don't like trials. You never know how they are going to come out."

And, apparently because of this belief, he left the country before his case was called. People interested in such things said that he went to South America. He was presumed to be dead in 1911 when friends and members of his family in Chicago ceased to get letters from him.

Nobody ever ventured a guess as to what had happened to "Paddy the Fox" Cooney. Grandma thought that maybe he had gone back to Ireland. But she wouldn't be positive about it.

"Ireland is the only country he would know much about," she said. "But I'm not so sure he would go there. He was friendly to the people in the Clan-na-Gael who were betraying the Irish heroes to those flinthearted English. And a whole lot of the Irish wouldn't have liked that—not a bit."

Grandpa was never quite pleased that his midnight visit to the Carlson cottage had received so little acclaim from the community. He had seen a buggy drawn by a white horse driven by one man. He had seen a bay horse drawing a wagon which in all probability carried the body of Dr. Cronin. He had seen three men on the wagon's front seat. He had seen a lighted lamp and other signs of tenancy in the Carlson cottage. But, a canvass of the district seems to show, so had everybody else in Lake View, although Grandpa sniffed at that suggestion. He thought he had been silenced by a sort of conspiracy.

"I saw what I saw and I know what I know," he said. "They were trying to protect somebody and they were afraid of what I might say. After all, this was an important case. Right there in the book I have at home it says—and I have memorized it—'Back of the crime was a conspiracy so cunningly contrived as to rival the diabolical plots placed at the doors of the secret societies of France, Italy, and Spain by the historians of the Dark Ages. In the United States, as an event of national importance, the crime may be said to rank with the assassinations of Presidents Lincoln and Garfield.'

"That's what it says. And that's what I believe."

PART II

TRANSPORTATION, PUBLIC AND PRIVATE

Chapter 7

The Clark Street Rope

No matter how far back you go in Chicago's archives—or how far forward—you keep running into what they call the traction problem. Reduced to its essentials, this means the trouble most people have getting from where they are to where they want to go.

It seemed to be almost finished—for a little while—until the customers started hanging to new enameled straps in twenty-cent cars instead of the old five-cent cars. The historians of this "reconditioning period," as some people call it, are going to find themselves with plenty to talk about. But shed no tears.

The voice of John Doe, complaining in 1952 about the speed and comfort and price of his transportation to Englewood, is like a phonograph record of the protest of John Doe's grandfather on similar subjects in 1850. There will never, apparently, be any permanent improvement. Ideal transportation for the people who need it would be a system big enough to give every customer two seats in the rush hours, fast enough to get him home in a matter of minutes, and priced at about three cents. The operating corporation, on the contrary, figures that it can make money by using equipment until it falls apart, operating at a crawl, and providing seats for nobody at a fixed price of twenty-five cents. There is nothing new about this. It is an argument that came to the

65

passenger-hauling business before the invention of the wheel. We need not go into the problems of Chicago's first days when horsecars and horsebusses were the traction system. We can skip the business of how the preposterous Charles T. Yerkes worked here and in Springfield to get perpetual franchises for what he said was a "company dedicated to providing transportation." Everybody who ever wrote a book about Chicago or ran for office at a municipal election has discussed it at suitable length. But it might be well to look into the situation of the Chicagoan who had to get home for supper during what we have called the city's middle years. Changes were coming in public vehicles. Cables, steam and electricity were threatening to replace the horse—as eventually they did. The weary customer was dreaming of a luxurious, rapid ride at the end of the day. His numbers were increasing and he was thinking of a home out in the country somewhere around Thirty-second Street or North Avenue. . . . Ah, yes!

Just before the World's Columbian Exposition, horses still furnished the bulk of the power for the local street railways. The cable car had gone into use in the early seventies in San Francisco. The first electric car had had a successful trial in Cleveland in 1882. But these innovations made little impression on Mr. Yerkes and other Chicago horse fanciers in the late eighties. Although a more or less experimental cable line had been run out to the South Side, there is some evidence that our traction system might have remained unchanged throughout the years had it not been for the rising price of hay.

Along about 1890 some interested statistician figured out that it cost eighteen cents to run a horse a mile and that even at this expense the total daily run per animal averaged fourteen miles. As against that, this expert declared, it cost only about six cents to run a cable car a mile, and the cable car would run all day and all night.

So, by the end of 1891, both cable and electric cars were operating in the Chicago area and the horse was relegated to a short haul in La Salle Street, where he remained until well into the next century.

By that time the Chicago City Railway Company was running out from the river to Fifty-fifth Street via Wabash Avenue, State Street and Cottage Grove Avenue. The North Chicago Street Railroad was in business from a terminus at Wrightwood and Lincoln avenues and another at the old "Limits," near Diversey Avenue and Clark Street, to the business district via the La Salle Street tunnel.

If you wanted to get farther north, you could still take a horse-car, although for a time a steam-propelled "dummy" car was in service in Clark Street between the "Limits" and Graceland Cemetery.

The West Side was served by the Madison Street line, which had two branches—one in Milwaukee Avenue and a second running in Madison Street from downtown to Fortieth Avenue.

Probably referring to the North Side line, an eager newspaper editorialist of this day declared:

There is no finer machinery than this anywhere. Nothing has been spared that could possibly add to the efficiency of the company's service or the comfort of the patrons. Those who first were prolific with adverse criticism have become just as lavish in their encomiums of praise. And the entire system is now recognized by the unprejudiced as being without equal in the country, and, as one is forced to admit—vastly superior to the horse-drawn cars and buses.

The Washington Street and La Salle Street tunnels were open at that time. A third tunnel which crossed the river between Jackson and Van Buren streets was completed a year later. And that wasn't the only cause for rejoicing. The Lake Street elevated structure had been completed from Market Street as far west as Union Park.

The construction of the South Side "Alley L" road was being pushed southward "to the southern limits of the city," and actually

67

got out to Jackson Park for the World's Fair. Both of these lines ran trains of cars pulled by little steam engines.

In the general enthusiasm over these accomplishments there was considerable talk about an elevated road to parallel the Chicago, Milwaukee and St. Paul Railroad tracks as far north as Wilson Avenue, another to run from the river to Waukegan, and a third to tap the West Side via Randolph Street. For quite a time this was merely talk.

It is interesting to note that none of the loud cries directed toward Yerkes was transferred to the "L" builders. It is also *odd* because some of these amateur engineers had been targets for the press in other financial fields. The treasurer of the Lake Street line, for instance, was one Mike McDonald, onetime part owner, with Cap George Wellington Streeter, of the Apollo Theater, and later operator of big-time gambling establishments. He is said to have coined the phrase "A sucker is born every minute" long before it was credited to P. T. Barnum.

Chicago, willing to believe any magnate who promised better transportation, was boastfully proud of the new elevated roads and immensely pleased with cable cars that traveled twelve miles an hour. But there were still plenty of people in town who figured that these novelties would never really supersede the horse. Conservative journalists still had a lot of good words to say about the Russell Street-Carette, which was fast, comfortable and trackless.

The Russell Street-Carette Company was organized just as the cable cars were beginning to operate. It started with vehicles that had been well designed for an omnibus service, it was backed by plenty of capital and it promised to stay in business indefinitely, no matter how successful the cable car might prove. In 1893 the company had thirty-five carettes and 300 horses to transport passengers from Ashland Avenue over Adams Street and Michigan Avenue to the Rush Street Bridge and thence to Lincoln Park. It planned to have 260 more vehicles and another 3,000 horses in

68

service by 1894. In his *Chicago Guide Book* John Flinn wrote:

This is the only line that transports passengers directly and without change between the West and North sides. The Russell Street-Carette is the most comfortable vehicle yet introduced to meet the demands of the public for a conveyance that can be operated on streets without tracks. It is much larger and moves much more easily than the customary omnibus.

It is provided with a rear platform which is as low and as convenient for elderly persons as the street-car platform. The carettes are nicely upholstered, contain spring seats with backs covered with Wilton carpet. The interior is finished in natural woods, ash and cherry being used for the doors. All trimmings are bronze.

The Russell Street-Carette Company operated a couple of years with many passengers and much promise. But it had troubles, particularly in winter. The well-upholstered busses weren't much warmer than the vehicles of odd design that had preceded them. There were a few mudholes en route, and the horses contrived to get stuck just as they had always done. The expansion program with which the corporation started involved the outlay of a lot of capital that presently wasn't there. Along about 1896 the cable car seemed to be the answer to the city's problem. There were lots of these lines in operation. They contrived to be cold in winter and damp when it rained. They were speedily just as crowded as any horsecar ever had been. They had accidents and they had delays. And, when the starry-eyed straphangers got used to them, they had no end of criticism.

Bert Leston Taylor, of the Chicago *Tribune,* enlivened their struggle with a ringing battle hymn:

> "For I am the guy with the fishy eye
>   And the think-tank filled with dope.
> My work is to watch the beautiful botch
>   That is known as the Clark Street rope."

It was, of course, just a song—not a factual record. The cable-car riders knew that no one was assigned to watch "the beautiful botch" that was the cable. The cables broke and continued to break. And cars piled up and the passengers walked home, as they had always walked, until the day these vehicles quit running.

The first electric line of the Chicago district was the Calumet route running between the South Chicago rolling mills and Stony Island Avenue and Ninety-fifth Street. It had one innovation, an overhead trolley line, for which the operating company made an apology in all the newspapers. Said this announcement:

As soon as possible, the line will be extended to Washington Heights and Morgan Park. The overhead system will be removed at an early date—as soon as an economical and otherwise practical storage battery appears. So far there is none to be found, and the trolley line is a necessity for convenience and safety.

The electric car came along in a few years. It still had the over-head trolley. It was still in most features the same little leaping, goatlike thing that had startled the natives of the Calumet district. But it had one thing which the Calumet operators had forgotten to advertise: it had greater speed than the cable car. It could make as much as seventeen miles an hour if there weren't any wagons on the track. Electric cars were a little bigger than those they superseded, and they got bigger at intervals through the years. They were more easily heated and just as readily crowded. But the straphanger contrived to get home late for dinner just as he always had.

There were a few regrets when the cable cars went away. They may have lacked speed, but none of my friends was much interested in speed anyway.

They ran in trains—a grip car in the lead and anything from one to three trailer cars following. The grip car was the choice

70

location for traveling kids. The gripman stood in the middle of
its front platform, facing a group of levers which he operated to
get a grip—or release it—on the cable under the street. Inasmuch
as the gripman and his apparatus occupied most of the car's floor
space, there were two seats—long wooden benches—parallel to the
sides of the vehicle and facing outward over the street. I recall that
we piled into this dubious shelter in all sorts of weather—in driving rain or in winter blizzards. We could see everything that was
going on, and we certainly felt in tune with the great outdoors.

Somebody had thought of the seasons in the cable car's operating office. The winter trailers were like all other cars we had ever
seen—closed, stove-heated if at all, and generally stuffy. But one
of the most encouraging signs of warm weather was the "summer
car" that they dusted off and hooked to the grip car along about
the middle of April. It too followed previous car designs pretty
closely. But its sides were open and the cool breezes, if there happened to be any, blew across it with many an interesting effect.
Ladies lost their hats—and sometimes their money. There were
shrieks and tears and imprecations. Rain blew down the starched
necks of starched shirtwaists. Bundles of female hair came loose.
Escorts looked embarrassed. Volunteers tried to lower the curtains at the sides. The grip car rattled on with its cheery load of
soaked little boys, and ancient dames fainted and old men got
their feet wet.

It is interesting to note that if you dropped an umbrella off the
inner side of the car, it would do you no good to hop off at the
next stop and run back after it. Such things were about the only
prizes that ever came to the hands of the worthy wagon drivers.
These men were diligent, constantly alert, and quick on the snatch.
It seemed to me that they must have acquired great quantities of
umbrellas.

We lost the summer car when electricity began to push the
trams about. Some of the trolley lines continued the old cars for

a few summers. But these fine vehicles came finally to the end of a racketing life and were not replaced. There were other losses that no child of the period will ever forget. There were peddlers of toy monkeys who could spring aboard a summer cable car, canvass the customers and spring off again before they could be reached by the conductor. There were interesting gents who would pay their fares, recite a rhymed greeting and beg for whatever they could get. There were sprightly young men who used to throw things at the gripman—not because they disliked him particularly but because he was the sort of target from which there couldn't be any retaliation.

There were also the boys who found out how to hook the cable with a kinked wire dropped down through the slot, the other end of the wire attached to whatever the ingenious lads wanted to fasten on. So it became a fascinating experience in Chicago to see bundles of paper, wheeled carts, baby buggies and such like touring down the middle of the car tracks at fourteen miles an hour. There was something almost miraculous about them then, as there would be today.

Chapter 8

The Bicycle Menace

I T WOULD appear that the time has come to say a few words about bicycles.

The fact that so many historians have ignored the significance of this interesting conveyance in the life of the eighties and nineties may have led you to believe that Chicagoans failed to recognize it socially. Well, maybe you should have lived in those joyous days.

The town at the time of the Columbian Exposition had a population of 1,208,669. It also had 2,000 miles of streets, some of which were paved. There was no reason—no reason at all—why it should not have been able to support about 50,000 bicycles. So presently it did.

Admittedly, despite their bid for popularity in Europe during the seventies and early eighties, the first bicycles were nothing to arouse confidence or bring about a popular demand. All of these pristine models had a six-foot wheel in front, with pedals on cranks attached directly to the axle along with the handle bars. The saddle was set forward on a thin frame which curved over the big wheel to a second wheel—about eighteen inches in diameter—behind.

The first one of these things to appear in the United States was imported in 1876 and was ridden by an acrobat. All subsequent riders of these devices finished up as acrobats, whatever they may have been to start off with. It was a job of talent to get to the saddle of a high-wheeled bike. And a job of greater talent to stay there. The physical equipment required by the operator was of no great moment except for a stout skull.

Willie Kress, who lived in the flat above us in part of my early childhood, owned one of these things and performed on it with considerable skill. I observed at the age of five that he could make it run faster than our dog, whose speed I took to be a sort of universal standard. When he came off the bicycle—frontward, with the rear wheel rocketing up to wallop him as he descended—he moved even faster.

Willie had a special costume for his performance, even when he was only taking practice rides around the block—tight-fitting knee pants, brilliantly striped stockings, blue silk blouse, rubber-soled shoes and a red cap with a long bill. He also wore long, carefully combed mustachios which I have somehow associated with the riding of high-wheeled bicycles ever since.

Willie made the trick look easy—which was natural enough, considering that he had been working at it for ten years or so. He didn't have to climb up on a box or ladder as some practitioners did. He could flip himself into the saddle from a standing start on the ground. And perfection in such a technique as that was very rare indeed.

Once aboard, it seemed that he was moving along on a cloud, and I longed to try such a journey myself. But I never did. My legs were too short, for one thing, and by the time they got long enough the high-wheeled bicycle was on display in the Field Museum.

Also, Willie wouldn't let anybody play around with his bicycle—not anybody. He informed us that it was a very delicate and complicated mechanism which the touch of an amateur might throw completely out of kilter. Such a disastrous development might cause him to take a long fall—on his head. We never told him, but that was the sort of performance we were aching to see. He had a few mishaps, which I greatly enjoyed, but he was good enough, somehow, to escape the mortuary. I never could see how.

The tires on this gadget were of hard rubber, which at the time seemed to be a matter of no importance. Our street was surfaced— if you care to call it that—with uneasy sand, through which protruded, now and then, a considerable rock. Despite his skill, it was Willie's misfortune every so often to run afoul of one of these immovable lumps. Most of the kids of the neighborhood waited days on end for this contretemps. The vigil eventually paid off.

It was the nature of these tall front wheels that they couldn't get over an obstruction very easily. Whenever they hit a rock they stood still. The rear wheel kept on traveling. The rider moved in

a graceful arc across the handle bars and put his face into the road. And that is what happened repeatedly to our Willie. The spectacle was something lovely to look at and educational to hear. But we might have known that chances for looking at it were diminishing.

By 1895 the town was getting overrun with "safety" bicycles—which is to say, machines with two wheels of the same size. In general those bikes didn't look much different from the modern ones. It was discovered that you didn't need to be an acrobat to ride on one of them. You could romp along fairly well on dirt roads or, failing that, on the sidewalks. So Chicago considered them with a keen and practical interest.

Inasmuch as anybody could ride these swift and fascinating carriers, everybody did. Some riders were skillful. Some were not. Life for anybody who had to walk became a serious mistake.

One of the oddities of people who dash about on two-wheeled conveyances is their obvious unwillingness to be alone. Present-day motorcyclists preserve the tradition by taking over the roads in small mobs. They haven't the numbers of the early bicycle enthusiasts, but they give you some idea of the chaos you can achieve if the crowd instinct is strong enough.

In the good old bicycle days the first thing you did after buying your bicycle was to join a cycling club. You had a wide choice. There was, for instance, the Chicago Cycling Club.

("Take Illinois Central train, foot of Randolph or Van Buren Street, or cable car on Cottage Grove Avenue line. *And bring your own bicycle.*") There were also the Kenwood Cycle Club, and the Sheridan Road Wheelmen's Association, and the North Side Touring Club . . . and a couple of dozen others.

"The membership," reads the prospectus of the Chicago Cycling Club, "consists of about three hundred wheelmen from all parts of the South Side, their runs being on the beautiful boulevards and avenues of the South Park system."

76

I do not know when bicycles first began to be called "wheels" or bicycle riders "wheelmen." But there it is. I might have looked it up sometime save for the more stirring problem of how, or why, you operate a club of bicyclers. What 300 associated "scorchers" in close formation could do to a beautiful boulevard or quiet avenue of the South Park system is something that nowadays one can only try to imagine. I may not know when these gay bloods came to be called "scorchers," but I think I know why.

Something over fifty such clubs came into existence in the year before the World's Fair and must have been a great help to people who wanted to take buggy rides to Jackson Park. Very nearly a thousand such organizations were listed in 1896, not counting the "associations" and "councils" of clubs that had representatives in all parts of the country. One of them announced:

The objects of this organization are to secure harmonious and concerted action in all matters of general interest to wheelmen in Chicago and vicinity, particularly in such matters as municipal legislation, improvement of the streets, the prevention of the theft of wheels, to spread a knowledge of the rights and privileges of wheelmen, to promote track and road racing, to foster club intercourse and, so far as possible, to aid the state and national organizations of The League of American Wheelmen.

The Vikings' Bicycle Club, whose address unfortunately is lost, was a little more blunt in its statement of purpose.

"This club and its associates control 1,500 political votes and will support those candidates favorable to wheelmen and wheeling."

It is hardly necessary to mention that every politician in town, regardless of age, experience or weight, was an avid "wheelman." I hoped at one time to see all these devoted characters riding their bicycles in frock coats and top hats in the annual parade. But they failed me. Walking, they decided, is more simple and dignified in a parade.

It was the privilege of any worthy person as a member of the Calumet Swamp Bicycle Club or the West Wheeling Wheel Club to appear in an athletic costume like my friend Willie's. It was spectacular garb. And it was speedily discovered that an alderman in a spoon-billed cap, peering over a fine handle-bar mustache, was always considered a remarkably good subject for newspaper art. So maybe the politicians were sincere in their ruling to support dignity and simplicity in parades. Or maybe the members of the rules committee couldn't ride their bicycles very well.

Of course there were bicycle lobbies in the city council and state legislature. There was a brisk black-market trade in stolen bicycles. There were bicycle accessory shops and bicycle repair shops and paint shops and tire shops. There were bicycle artists and bicycle art. And there were plenty of stirring songs about bicycles. One, in keeping with the musical trend of the day, was heartbreaking and a bit mystic:

"For I ride alone to the distant blue,
    My bicycle gliding away
    To the fields of green where my loved ones lie
    Awaiting the judgment day."

Everybody thought it was quite a nice song—and topical. There was also one which said, "For you'll look sweet upon the seat of a bicycle built for two." There need be no further discussion of that.

In the field of art there was one popular piece—the picture of a girl in bloomers saying good-by to her horse because she had transferred her love to her bicycle. This was revived and altered some years later when she tossed her heart to an automobile. But it was really bicycle art at its very best.

The bicycle hasn't yet gone from us, as you will admit after dodging two or three dozen of them while you are trying to get out of your garage.

Bicycles, it seems, continue to be popular in Europe. When the

78

Germans invaded Holland not too long ago they gathered up a pile of millions of bicycles—somewhere around two for every inhabitant. The bicycle supply in France and Belgium was enough to cut down the German steel shortage for a couple of years. If you are old enough, you might sit down and think what such a bicycle population may mean to these worthy countries. Their wars are temporary and sporadic. Their bicycles, one judges, go on forever . . . and at a price! Have no doubt of it, at a price!

It is unlikely that many aging Chicagoans remember much about bicycles except that they ran on sidewalks when they should have been in streets, and that they knocked you down every now and then and broke your legs. Other, more important things have come to plague us such as athlete's foot, shovel thumb, pink toothbrush, five-o'clock shadow, housemaid's knee, whisky tenor, straphanger's wrist, cigarette cough, writer's cramp and Chinaman's chance. Currently we get upset about airsickness, motorist's fatigue, cinemagoer's psychosis and television squint.

Always we look upon these things as something new and different. They aren't, of course. The deadly diseases of today's advertising columns are merely those of another vogue and another generation altered to meet the modern demand. In 1896 nobody had halitosis, or B.O., or housewife's fatigue, or shell shock. But the medical authorities, who today view with alarm in the thirty-five-cent magazines, were deeply concerned about the ravages of *cyclist's crouch, handle-bar cramp* and *head-lamp eyestrain*.

The worst of these ailments, oddly unrecognized now despite the continuing presence of bicycles among us, was *cyclist's crouch*. It seems that the scorcher, hunched over the handle bars to cut down wind resistance and give an illusion of great speed, was cramping his insides dangerously. Something would have to be done about this, the experts declared in sepulchral tones, something drastic. The wheelman would have to give up wheeling except in a genteel, upright position, or the United States would

79

presently be filled with a race of men incapable of eating or breathing and able to stand up only when supported by short crutches.

It was horrible to contemplate. But that wasn't all. Even before there was any agitation for laws that would compel people to sit up straight on bicycles the dermatologists set up a cry that women cyclists in America were developing a complexion known as *scorcher's flush!* There was one that really brought the populace up with a shock.

The charm columns of the daily newspapers were filled with recipes for lotions, pomades, skin soaps and smears "to keep the American Woman as beautiful as she was before the coming of the bicycle." One species of unguent, rubbed into the skin before the user went out for a spin, was supposed to furnish "sure and pleasant protection against the flying particles of sand, cinders, grit and other abrasives," while minimizing "the destructive effect of the sun." Usually a second cosmetic was required after the finish of the ride to remove the first. The customary claim for this was that it didn't do any harm.

At the height of the bicycling craze the people selling "machines" were disturbed at scientific research into the connection between pedal pushing and girlish beauty. Secretaries of trade associations wrote letters to newspaper editors protesting what they called a biased attitude on the part of beauty-hint writers. These harangues about red-faced, rough-necked, unlovely wheelwomen, they said, were simply ruining the bicycle business.

But apparently nobody cared any more about the back-page epidemics in those days than they do now. Maybe the women bought the cosmetics recommended for lovely cyclists—maybe they didn't. But they continued to ride bicycles.

Late in 1896 a Boston anatomist named Marcus Edwards sounded a warning that made the vocal worries of the cosmeticians seem trivial. Bicycling, said this learned professor, was going to make

80

over the underpinning of the human race. In three or four generations, he believed, the torso of the bicycle-riding American was going to get thinner, not to say emaciated, because in bicycling it did no work whatever, and therefore got no exercise. Legs, on the other hand, were being worked as they had never been worked before. Muscles that had played no part in ordinary leg movements were now a prime factor in peddling. The results might be easily foretold, he declared. Muscles subjected to exercise become strong and hard, but while in use they take on no permanent shape. They grow to meet the demands placed on them.

So, he mentioned, it was only a matter of time until bicyclists and their offspring would have wonderful legs—large, strong and powerful—and out of all proportion to the body they adorned.

The first bicycle fad died out before anybody had a chance to prove him right. But with a few unimportant alterations, his theory is with us still. His name was easily recalled about 1910 when some scientists stated that the leg on the brake side of an automobile driver was bound to grow twice as large as the one on the clutch side.

There were other little fancies that no longer seem remarkable in the spread of the bicycle cult. Of course there was a lot of legislation. Each municipality and state had rules about where you could ride a bicycle and how fast, what you could wear while riding it (divided skirts were considered not only ugly but a public scandal in some sections of Alabama), what extras you had to hang on it in the way of bells and lights.

Parking, you may be surprised to learn, was a constant problem. When a rash of wheelmen came rolling into a community there was never sufficient place at the curbs for them to leave their machines. And natives held that bicycles piled promiscuously on sidewalks, as they sometimes were, constituted a menace to navigation. Racks capable of holding a hundred bikes at a time had been invented, but they were never in the right places. So the problem went as it seems to have been going ever since. It was never solved.

Public protest against the craze fell into familiar patterns. There was the customary cleric who loudly voiced the fear that the bicycle would carry people away from church services on the Sabbath. There were shopkeepers who declared that the bicycle, by permitting shoppers to canvass a greater area, was rushing them to bankruptcy.

"The bicycle sounds the death knell of the small town," warned John M. Foster of Odell, Illinois, as early as 1897.

Keepers of livery stables found themselves in a depression that seemed likely never to end. Saloonkeepers, of all people, averred tearfully that they now spent most of their time unprofitably taking their lonesome ease in their inns. Wheelmen shot past their doors in thousands but never seemed to feel the need of beer, wine, whisky or free lunch.

As against this, Charles Whittlesey of Princeton University has since declared that all the businessmen who became successful between 1910 and 1925 did so because of the energy they had acquired riding bicycles.

College athletes got their start in bicycle clubs, he said. They strengthened their muscles and their perceptions. They were made strong and they learned to be quick.

And he closed with the observation that he didn't think driving an automobile could be classed as exercise.

Chapter 9

The Wonderful Hansom Cabs

Hardly a man is now alive in our community who has ever seen a hansom cab, much less ridden in one. It is possible—or was until recently—for a nostalgic or merely curious experimenter to board one of these interesting vehicles in Central Park, New York City, and take a spin in it, much as he may ride in a Roman chariot on a merry-go-round. And until shortly before the late war, hansoms were still being put to practical use in Sydney, Australia. But, for all that, they have been gone a long, long time. The present generation, which stares in awe at the infrequent sight of a horse, probably never heard of them.

The hansom, as imported by Chicago straight from London in the late eighties, was primarily a two-wheeled cart drawn by a single horse. The double seat was permanently enclosed in a box remotely resembling a modern coupé body except that it was entered through twin doors of glass in the front. Once past the doors the passengers sat down to look through a sort of picture window at the broad rump of the horse and such bits of the city as might happen to be visible beyond.

The driver was mounted on a sort of perch like the cupola of a caboose on the top and back of the passenger's box. He guided the horse by means of reins that came to his hand across the roof. He communicated with the passengers by means of a trap door. The passengers communicated with him by opening the front doors and screaming.

There was a considerable demand for these conveyances in the city right after paved roads became worth mentioning. They were faster—even with one horse—than the old-style four-wheelers because they were lighter. They were cozier, too. But mostly they were cheaper. For short hauls they continued to be popular until the collectors of Americana came around to garage them in museums.

It is interesting to note that long service in London did not reduce the suspicion with which Chicago riders greeted the first hansoms to appear on downtown streets. Drivers of other cabs complained that these "upended coffins" frightened all the horses in town but their own. There was agitation in the city hall, as usual, for some sort of new control. Alderman Kelly of the Fourth Ward contended in 1889 that hansoms should pay twice the hack license required of other cabs because "two-wheeled vehicles can do twice the business of four-wheeled vehicles at half the cost."

Some other lawmaking genius, now forgotten, wanted hansoms abolished altogether, just as a matter of precaution. He is quoted anonymously in the *City Guide Book* for 1889:

The balance of these vehicles is wrong. They may yet become one of Chicago's most serious menaces to life and limb. Should a shaft break or a strap come loose, there would ensue an accident that would surely beggar description. The whole carriage would trip over backwards. The driver would be crushed beneath his cab and the valuable lives of his passengers would be snuffed out by concussion.

Probably something might have come about to make the hansom cab conform to the rigid etiquette of life in Chicago, but before any laws could be put through the city council—that is to say, before the economic worth of such a law (to its promoters) could be established—the hansom had come so far in public favor that it seemed likely to stay. The dissenters retired, which was just as well. In the first seventh of the new century the hansom cab went out of business unassisted.

The taxicab was making a bid for Chicago's traveling trade in 1910, but the horse and the hansom, with occasional improvements, plodded along for three or four years. There are still thousands of people in Chicago who remember the dim view that bright members of the populace took of the struggling taxicabs on the streets around 1908. There was still some question about how far they could run. And up to 1908 no hansom cab had justified the prophecy of the 1889 *City Guide Book* by tumbling over backward.

The progress of the automobile in the 1900s was undeniable. Along about 1910 it was freely forecast that the gasoline vehicle would have a future. There were some people in the 4200 block of Jackson Boulevard who had actually made a trip in their "machine," a Benz, from their home to Milwaukee and back in a single day with virtually no mishaps on the road.

"It won't be long now," said my Grandpa Wilson after reading this piece. "You'll be seeing these automobiles all over the town. They'll be as thick as bicycles are today. You mark my words!"

So I thought maybe that's how things were going to be.

One thing that Grandpa didn't consider in his calculation was the social aspect of the cab business. The horse-drawn carrier for quite a long while still had something that the gasoline taxicab lacked.

There was the item of battered elegance, for instance. The brass on your livery rig always looked a little mildewed, the black paint a little gray and dusty. And no private coachman on the growing Gold Coast ever had a plug hat like that of the red-nosed hackie who came around to take you to funerals or weddings. These things were the touches of honored use, which the cab-riding people of Chicago had grown used to through a long number of years.

It seems that folks who hired taxicabs felt the criticism of the unfortunates who were still following horses to cemeteries and such. There was little elegance about the gas conveyance to justify its use if one lost one's friends. It was noisy, drafty, uncomfortable and unpredictable. It ran into things and it frightened horses. Yet it might have languished and the horse might have gone on lugging high-minded Chicagoans here and there but for one thing: the taxicab was faster.

Taxicab companies in the beginning of such transport were small, the financial condition of most of them precarious. Because of this, their rates were high—another feature of the trade that enabled the hackmen to look cheerily into a bright future. But the speed remained. Taxicabs began to travel quickly to distances that a horse never could reach. Then one day John Hertz painted the taxicab yellow—so that it could be recognized instantly as a taxicab—and he rented it out for purposes of transportation instead of swank.

In a way this is what the hansom cab had done to the four-wheel trade, but the taxi's effects were more widespread and more permanent.

The last stand of the hackmen was courageous but not too bright. A few of them accepted the inevitable, sold out their horses and buggies to rural undertakers and turned their livery stables into garages. But not all.

A heated four-wheeler, horse-drawn as usual, made its debut along about 1900. The heat was furnished by a charcoal burner hitched behind it. The lure of color was tried the same year, long before pink iceboxes and blue washing machines came onto the market. For a while the streets were filled with horse-drawn carriages finished in maroon, walnut brown and navy blue—an "unheard-of novelty," the papers called it. The horse cabs followed the trend, but it began to appear that the disagreement between such vehicles and taxis was something more than a matter of color.

A "two-horse hansom cab" was given brief notice in the newspapers around 1910—the forerunner, no doubt, of "super power." But the ultimate battle chariot of the hackmen came, as such things always do, with a surplusage of invention. At long last somebody— he was later identified as George H. Gurnee of Momence—got around to put the cart before the horse.

Combining the best features of the old hansom and the horseless carriage, this inventor produced a cart which the horses pushed rather than pulled. The passengers, whose view was no longer obstructed by the rear elevation of the horse, got their first view of what a road actually looked like. The hackman, still seated in a coop up on top, no longer had to bother with reins. He controlled this remarkable vehicle with a whip and a steering wheel.

What happened to this thing? Well, nobody seems to be exactly certain. Somehow it ran off a bridge approach in Jackson Park and, thanks to the angle of descent, upended. The accident proved, too late for practical use, that in the delicate balance of a hansom cab a horse may be tossed aloft as well as a passenger. The driver was unhurt. He said that he had been trained to light on his feet.

Chapter 10

The Horn Was "Extra"

O NCE in the days of my youth a high-pressure salesman named Tom Sweeney extended himself to sell me a saddle.

"Just the thing for you," he said. (Or maybe he said, "Just the ticket!") "It's made of genuine saddle leather from tough range bulls, hand-sewed and hand-fashioned by the best saddle makers in the West. It's expertly tooled and amply cut—not a thing skimped in it anywhere.

"And, as a special trade inducement, this week only we are throwing in a set of stirrups, stirrup leathers and cinch—all for the single price of seventy-five dollars."

This piece has nothing at all to do with Mr. Sweeney, but it is interesting to recall at the moment how smartly he anticipated salesmen in other lines—such as those who put out automobiles. The auto peddlers didn't offer you any stirrups or cinch straps as a special trade inducement—nor lights, tools, top, bumpers, horns, bells nor whistles. All they gave you was conversation plus an engine in an unequipped buggy. Presumably you paid a couple of thousand dollars for this basic attraction, for that's the way prices went in those days. Then, after you had learned to drive it, you used it mostly for transportation to and from the accessory shop.

Some of the gadgets that now seem to be as much a part of an automobile as the carburetor or clutch never appeared in the original inventory, but they weren't greatly missed. Current necessities, as well as sales techniques, were different. You needed a bumper, for instance, just as much as you needed spats and a top hat. You weren't likely to meet another car in the road, and if you happened to run into anything else, you wouldn't be going fast enough to bend it.

You didn't need a horn either—not even one of those honk-honkers that you worked by squeezing a rubber bulb. You could get pedestrians out of your way by yelling at them. And in the country the blast of your squawker was likely to frighten livestock and arouse whole communities to murderous frenzy.

You didn't need a windshield because you never raised any wind. Perhaps in storms it might have been expected to furnish some protection. But in rain or sleet it had to be removed. Otherwise you wouldn't have been able to see where you were going.

Junius B. Wood once observed that the most important part of the motorcar of this period was the jack—a highly sapient judgment. But you didn't get that free either. You submitted to the approved blackmail and bought it before you dared drive away from the display rooms.

"And this jack that we recommend for the Flopmotor Four car is the Ajax," came the dulcet voice of the honest salesman. "We can supply the Ajax for only nine dollars and seventy-five cents. It is made of nonbending, tinlike tool steel and is sold with a three-day guarantee.

"Of course you may never need this jack. The rubber that goes into our special tires is special hand-rubbed rubber. It is perfectly durable, and motoring roads are improving rapidly—but if you should run into trouble out in the country somewhere, it might be nice to have a jack."

That may not be a stenographer's report of the talk, but it isn't too inaccurate. Those were the days when the automobile and the palaver that went with it were both continuing miracles.

If a customer could bring himself to believe that one of these horseless carriages would run at all, he had no trouble accepting the rest of the credo outlined by the salesmen. It would run virtually without fuel, they said. And what was so wonderful about that? It would never need any repair, they declared, and the tires would last to the end of time. Well, once you had taken a ride in one of the things you could believe all that without a strain.

That motor transport retained its popularity and eventually remade the social and economic life of the United States is something that a continuous observer has a bit of trouble explaining. I suspect that the cause lies not so much in the automobile's fulfillment of its promises as in the simple persistence of the lads who believed that it could be made to take them from here to there. Those people were pioneers in the true sense. They suffered untold hardships, they tossed away their money like drunken sailors, they laughed at all discouragements and they listened to siren voices far beyond the horizon, until at last they got from here to there.

After the first few years' experience with tires "guaranteed for a thousand miles," nobody ever thought of going anywhere without a jack and a patching kit. The second thing every motorist learned was how to mend a tire. "Time out for puncture repair" was a calculation that figured in every travel schedule. But such annoyances were accepted like the rain or the bumps in the road as part of the price you paid for going places without walking.

Early clutches had a way of grabbing, slipping or burning up—so much so that most of the trade magazines carried advertisements for new ones designed to replace whatever brand you got with the car. The change-over was universally expensive, but a lot of the customers tried it. Then they squirted castor oil into this new improved specimen, or benzene, or "clutch dope." Until George Borg made a good one out of a couple of pieces of tin and a spring, the clutch was something more than an automobile part. It was a fascinating mystery.

In the futile scramble for improvement, few enthusiasts were ever content to leave a car in the shape in which it came to them. The world was suddenly filled with trick carburetors and gas injectors and mechanical vaporizers—and an army of carburetor sharks to keep them in adjustment. Gasoline had gone as high as ten cents a gallon, and people were beginning to talk about the economy that they somehow never got.

Basically the early engines must have been pretty good. After their fashion they ran, protestingly perhaps, but they ran, and with considerable regularity. This is pretty remarkable when you consider the jobs they were set to do and the kind of fuel that was fed to them. About the time the cracking process was introduced in oil refineries, the gasoline that you could buy for ten cents a gallon from the corner grocer was virtually noninflammable.

All the early cars were of the open variety—*touring cars,* as, in our ignorance, we referred to convertibles. That a passenger might find it uncomfortable to sit in one in cold weather made no difference. Passengers were amazingly weatherproof—as they had to be—and anyway, most cars were set up on blocks for the winter.

When engines got hardier, so did the drivers. Cars were seen running around until late in the fall—sometimes later. The supply houses began to do a fine business in foot warmers, ear muffs, pocket flasks and blankets.

Some of these robes were more expensive than Oriental carpets—some of them *were* Oriental carpets. A good camel's-hair blanket sold for as much as $150, and such prices were paid readily because there wasn't any penicillin for the treatment of pneumonia.

So you bought these things, and then you went out and bought yourself some thiefproof rug holders with which you could lock the bedding supply to the back of the front seat. The rug holders, one must confess, were not too good. Most of the thieves had a set of keys. Those who hadn't found it fairly easy to take down part of the front seat and remove the whole business to a shop where he could find a file.

Motors improved a little. You went farther afield. You bought ratchet cranks—"they make starting easier"—hood ornaments, shock absorbers, patent magnetos, chains, tools, two ropes, shimmy stoppers, rattle eliminators, one-man tops, antiknock charms, rearview mirrors, electric bugles, brake improvers, fuel filters, auxiliary water pumps, thermometers, cigar lighters, gas gauges, trunk racks and special baggage, water buckets, compasses, charcoal-burning heaters, a library of Automobile Blue Books, a spare wheel and holder, and finally a speedometer, a new headlight system and a Prestolite tank.

The nonworking automobile clock made its appearance about the time the manufacturers decided to put on a free windshield as standard equipment. It wasn't so enthusiastically received, this free gift. It's only attraction seemed to be that it didn't cost anything. It was simply a pane of ordinary glass set in a frame. It could not be slanted to let a little breeze into the car. It was set staunch and solid against the rain. And gravel and bits of rock that traffic might throw against it wouldn't do it any good. So presently it was improved at no increase in price. It began to appear as two horizontal sections which could be moved independently or taken out altogether.

The nonworking windshield wiper came along soon after the nonworking windshield. So did the permanent top, the never-used window shades, the cut-glass flower holders and the rear-seat notebook-and-pencil set.

You still had to buy such things as shock absorbers and swank trimmings. It was a long time before most of a car's gadgetry came as part of the original purchase. But still one yearns for the days that are gone. Maybe you had to shop for a windshield in 1900. Maybe the needless bumper cost you an extra fifty dollars. Maybe you had to pay through the nose to surround yourself with speedometers, compasses, canvas buckets, horns, cigar lighters and gas gauges. But anyway you got the car. It ran as well as you expected it to. And you were able to pay for it.

Mystery and Crime 2:

Where Are They Gone?

ONLY the other day a graybeard with rheumy eyes mentioned the possible vote of honors to Mrs. Patrick O'Leary for promoting the greatest surge in Chicago's growth. And a fine young man, who was seven or eight years old when the first bombs fell on London in World War II, looked up to inquire:

"Who was Mrs. Patrick O'Leary?"

"She had a cow," replied the graybeard.

"I seem to remember something about that," said the boy. "But I don't know exactly what."

"That's the trouble with so many of us," mentioned the graybeard.

It's not surprising that lads of a wartime generation should not be wasting memory on Mrs. O'Leary's cow. Granted that the cow, if the legend is true, was responsible for one of the greatest accidents in history. One kick against a lantern, a stream of burning coal oil in the barn refuse, and Chicago, the city of sham and shingles, was on its way out. But a city rebuilt has little reason to laud, or even to think about, the city it replaced. Certainly in the lore of Chicago—from the cow to the factual bootleg extravaganzas of the roaring twenties—the fire is just as startling and just as easily worth remembering.

94

Growing as it did, independent of precedent or pattern, the city contrived to produce characters more fantastic than Paul Bunyan and folkways as odd as any ever recorded in Baedeker. First to put up skyscrapers—and first to tear them down again—its geniuses were among the world's earliest experimenters with traction devices. Their success in such matters has been taken over by the politicians. Chicago inventors gave the world its first automatic agricultural machines, moving-picture dramas, compartmented ships, assembly-line sausages, Coin Harvey, needle beer, the vacuum tube and the 26 dice game.

Few of us who are finishing the cycle that began with the first world's fair are willing to be classed as ancients. But in our not unusual span of life we have seen Chicago present the greatest miracle of transportation since the invention of the wheel—the electric trolley car. And it is significant of the city's astonishing development that we who saw the trolley car begin will live to see it end.

Who is likely to forget the little steam engines that carried the customers to the World's Columbian Exposition over the "Alley L?" And what veteran of the nineties trained to think kindly of horse-drawn vehicles can fail to recall the amazing comfort—and speed—of the early cable cars?

Where save in Chicago was there ever such an assemblage of characters as Peter Hoffman, Diamond Joe Esposito, Allan Pinkerton, Joe Medill, Dwight Moody, Bill Haywood and Ortie McManigle? As some forgotten philosopher observed: "It takes all kinds of people to make a world, and they're all here. . . ."

At any rate, they all have been here . . . and some trace of them still is left. The town they built or harried, the town they lived in, was one of roominess, a place of determination and an eager friendliness—a place where there was noise without good reason.

None of these people was compelled to take his meals as we do—in some factory of mass-produced food, with an elbow in somebody else's soup. Their restaurants had elbow room. And, whatever their occupations, so had their lives.

Amusements were simple but plentiful and inexpensive. There were theaters all across the town. There were picnics, kirmesses and carnivals in the parks, neighborhood choral societies, the electric fountain in Lincoln Park, Manhattan Beach in Jackson Park, winter bobsledding, sports events at Tattersall's. For more robust practitioners there was also the annual First Ward Ball which, at the moment, we shall barely mention.

And what of the bicycles that made our parents shudder at the mention of Sheridan Road? What of the gay costumes and the generous mustaches of their riders? What of the long-suffering part of the population that was always being taken for rides in "livery rigs?" . . . I refer, of course, to the women.

What became of the "hourglass girl," and the "bloomer girl," and the well-wrapped "bathing girl?"

What ever happened to Heine Gebubler's electrified saloon, and Hooley's theater, and five-cent beer, and the Masonic Temple Observatory, from which "on a clear day you could see clean across the lake," and Newsboys' Alley, where you could get a substantial meal for three cents? Have you forgotten these places? Could you forget?

Where are they now—the old German beer gardens that covered Chicago from end to end, and the old Whaleback, and the Carlson Cottage, and the Relic House, and Libby Prison, and the Mysterious Mr. Dove, and Cap Streeter, and Middleton's Museum? All, all are gone—and you won't find much about them in the guidebooks.

The passing of old landmarks, and of the people who made them landmarks, is something that we view with a wistful regret. Some of them, in the course of events, just had to go. The historic barn of the lad who insured an outlet for his cow into what is now the Loop probably would have been sadly cramped in the middle of a group of twenty-story buildings. The cow wouldn't have been too comfortable either.

Studying the pictures of the city as it stood before 1871, we find it easy to say a word for that other famous cow—Mrs. O'Leary's. And we have become practiced in the art of holding back the tears every time progress blots out another architectural monstrosity bearing the label "General Grant Slept Here." But we do think it would have been a nice thing if somebody had thought of preserving the "Holmes Castle" at Sixty-third Street and Wallace Avenue. It would have taken status as a sort of municipal shrine—a haven of meditation for complacent police officials and overinflated detectives.

Dr. H. H. Holmes, who during his sojourn in the city in 1893 and 1894, turned out to be a sort of exterminator who may well have averaged a murder a week. That, of course, did not affect his position in local society. He was hanged, eventually, because he had made a traceable error in Philadelphia.

Holmes came to Englewood in 1887 while it was still a separate municipality, and he got a job as a pharmacist in a drugstore owned by a woman who appears in the record merely as "Mrs. Doctor Holden." He was young, handsome, courteous and well liked by his employer. In a year he had boomed business to such an extent—particularly with the women customers—that he was made manager of the store.

In 1891 a beautiful young woman named Julia Conner came to Chicago accompanied by her husband and her eight-year-old daughter. She was looking for a job which, thanks to her encumbrances, seemed difficult to get. But Dr. Holmes wasn't fussy. He hired both Julia and the spouse, who turned out to be so negligible that his name never got into public prints.

In 1892 the doctor was involved with "Mrs. Doctor Holden" in a litigation over his accounts. There was a settlement. "Mrs. Doctor Holden" went away—nobody knew where—and Dr. Holmes took over the drugstore. Shortly thereafter, on a corner opposite the shop, Holmes set about building the Castle which he said was to be a hotel for the service of visitors to the World's Columbian Exposition, due to open the next year.

It was several years after the end of the fair that some historians interested in the antiquarian status of the place first saw the inside of it. They reached Sixty-third Street and Wallace Avenue after a long safari via horsecar, cable car and walking, much too late to make any firsthand study of its peculiar uses. But it was still a worth-while pilgrimage. There was yet a gruesome and mysterious atmosphere about the building—although that, of course, is something the investigators may have brought along with them. We might have seen the advertised phantom flitting past the upper-floor windows if there had been any upper-floor windows. We clustered in the main entrance for a spine-chilling moment, and then trooped hastily across the street to the blessed haven of the old drugstore. We gazed back at the Castle with an awe that could have been inspired by no other building in Chicago except, perhaps, the big vault in Graceland Cemetery. Somehow it seemed to resemble the big vault as, indeed, it had a right to.

Even without its fearful history it would have made a fine memorial to gloom. It was a dingy pile of brick, three stories high, 150 feet long and 50 feet wide. Bays and enclosed balconies, that seemed never to have had an opening to the light, jutted promiscuously from its blank walls. What windows it may have had above the ground floor were tightly shuttered and dead. Memory brings it back as the sort of house that the cartoonist Charles Addams might have designed as a model home for ghouls, which is what it was. It may have had some patronage from World's Fair tourists, but it is difficult to be sure. Lots of people were seen to go into the place, but there is no certain record of those, if any, who came out.

98

Holmes financed the construction of this monstrosity by processes that lead one to doubt the mental balance of his contemporaries. He cashed bad checks. He floated loans on nonexistent properties. He doctored the books of the drugstore. Then, after transferring it from one dummy titleholder to another, he mortgaged it in the name of the last fictitious owner. The liens on the Castle were so numerous that he was in constant trouble in the courts. But he went steadfastly on to the achievement of his ambition: he was determined to be a Bluebeard—the sort of Bluebeard the world would remember.

Julia Conners' husband disappeared almost on the day the building was completed. The broad-minded police thought they saw an explanation for that. Julia moved into the Castle with Holmes.

From the Tobey Furniture Company the doctor ordered and received enough movables to outfit a hotel—beds, chairs, parlor fittings, pictures, crockery, silverware, linens, hardware, carpeting, curtains, tables, portieres, stoves, kitchenware and what not. Tobey's deliverymen carted it in. A few weeks later, when Holmes's check turned out to be no good, they sent out squads to repossess their wares. But they never got anything back save some dishes.

The Castle had been closely watched day and night, and the watchers could swear that nothing had been taken out. But when Tobey's workmen searched the premises nothing was there.

The doctor, it seems, had stored all the furniture in a ballroom. After that he had sealed up the entrance with a brick wall which he painstakingly plastered and papered.

At this period Holmes was married to a girl in New Hampshire. He had deserted her and attached himself to another woman in Wilmette. He went on from there. Without thought of Julia he brought into his ménage one Minnie Williams, a Texas heiress. Simultaneously he opened one of the Castle's stores in Sixty-third Street as an office. Through this headquarters passed, in groups of five or six, some 150 stenographers, clerks and typists, all of them female, all of them at one time or another occupants of windowless rooms on the building's second floor. Even without the World's Fair trade, the place seems to have been somewhat overpopulated.

In June 1893 Minnie Williams' sister, Anne, came up from Texas on a visit. She disappeared.

A few months later Dr. Holmes married Georgie Anna Yoke in Denver. Minnie Williams was a witness. What she thought she was doing has never been explained. The wedding party returned to Chicago and then Minnie disappeared. So did Julia and her child. The press later charged that a considerable group of his payless stenographers also stepped out into the blue at the same time. But that may not be true.

The most fantastic feature of Dr. Holmes's activities was not his genius for providing death traps in what looked much like an ordinary apartment building but in collecting prospects for murder who had no friends or families. It appears that he managed to take them out of places like Denver or Des Moines without leaving anybody an inkling of where they were bound for. Estimates of the total of his murders have never been verified. The local police closed their records by writing him down as a one-man scourge.

In this period the doctor did a fairly active business selling articulated skeletons to hospitals. But his expenses were still pretty high. He went into business with a trusting crook named B. F. Pitzel, took him to Philadelphia and insured his life for $10,000. So Pitzel died and Holmes collected.

Three of Pitzel's five children then disappeared. Maybe Mrs. Pitzel would have disappeared too, but just about that time the Philadelphia police exhumed Pitzel's body. The remains of two more Pitzel children were discovered in the basement of a house Holmes had rented in Toronto.

Chicago police belatedly made a search of the Castle. The like of it had never been seen before in Illinois or any place else. The second floor, where Holmes had maintained his private apartment, was a rabbit warren crossed by secret drops and passages, concealed stairways, trap doors and movable walls. There were numerous rooms without windows—several that could be entered only through hidden doors.

A chute led from the doctor's bathroom to an asphyxiation chamber below. In the basement were vats of acid, a dissecting room complete with instruments, and a gas-fired crematorium. In conveniently placed quicklime vats the horrified searchers found oddments about which nothing could be told except that they were "the bones of women." Some investigators, who may possibly have been a bit eager, said that as many as two hundred victims were represented in the pile.

The doctor was hanged at Moyamensing prison in 1895. His memory was green in Englewood—particularly on wintry nights when there was no moon.

PART III

PRIMITIVE, OR PRETELEVISION, LIVING

Chapter 11

Housekeeping or Something

IT SEEMS to us that what the well-equipped housewife of Chicago's middle years lacked in the way of tools was quite a lot. She didn't have such things as oil mops, patent cleansers, frozen foods, vacuum cleaners, canned biscuit dough, electric toasters, mixing machines, adjustable-temperature stoves, specialized grills to make twelve-egg omelets, meat slicers, roast basters, percolators, pressure cookers, dry ice, cherry pitters, lettuce cutters, electric refrigerators or garbage-disposal units. She had a broom, a cake of soap, an egg beater, a range, a coffeepot, a sack of flour and a coal hod. And she didn't complain much.

Over the little kitchen sink hung the device that was one day to give her a new place in the world—namely, the can opener. Few yet realized its importance to the cause of women's rights.

As yet it was virtually an untried invention because there wasn't anything to try it on except canned corn or now and then, perish the thought, canned oysters. Good old salmon and the enterprising sardine were among the first dainties to get into tin containers, and were a sort of emergency ration in nearly every local home by 1890 or earlier. But their cans came equipped with a key that theoretically pried them apart. The can opener, therefore, doesn't come into this discussion of nineteenth century labor-saving devices. For the moment it was just a luxury, like the iron dog on the front lawn.

There has been a tradition in the United States that Mother was always a better cook than Mother's daughter, and that Mother's mother was a better cook than Mother—and so on, and on and on. Like most pleasant generalities this is difficult to prove, but the evidence supports it in part. We don't know exactly how good a cook Mother was, but there is no doubt whatever that Grandma was one of the best chefs who ever fluted the edge of a pie. I have frequently thought that the women of those days had to be good cooks because they had such a lack of raw material. I am still inclined to believe so.

Our grandmothers didn't get much assistance from anybody outside their own kitchens. It was a matter of pride with them that they were able to make anything. Recipes and culinary techniques were the themes of arguments beyond count and generally beyond settlement.

Baker's bread, or, as it used to be called, "boughten bread," is a convenience of fairly recent adoption in the Chicago area. There were bakers in town, of course, long before the Big Fire; and during the rebuilding period there were shops in nearly every neighborhood. Large, dusty men, generally Germans, would make no bones about selling you a pound loaf for a nickel or the large economy size for seven or eight cents. But old-school housewives would have none of such business.

"In the first place," was the dictum of one grandma with whom I once had close association, "no baker ever knew how to make a loaf of bread. In the second place, I can save about a penny a loaf making it myself. And in the third place, women who go running out to bakeshops are lazy no-goods who don't care anything about the health of their families. And, what is more, everybody knows them for what they are."

So the baking of bread and buns was a routine in most homes
two or three times a week. That didn't mean, it should be noted,
that there was any vacation period between bread days. Pies had
to be made, and cakes and cookies. There had to be a fire in the
stove all day anyway, Grandma would argue. Well, then, it would
be a sin to waste the heat. So she mixed and kneaded and baked
and thereby established the reputation that she certainly deserved.
How she did it is a mystery unsolved and engrossing.

If you wanted to do some baking today, you'd consult the cookbook and get out the specified ingredients and mixing gadgets.
You'd break a couple of pounds of prepared dough out of the tin,
add butter and sugar and salt and what else as set forth in the
book. You'd blend it all in a growling mixer. Then you'd set your
oven regulator, slip your pans into the stove, shut the door and
turn on the soap opera.

On the same job Grandma, who didn't have any cookbook but whose head was filled with an understanding of such accurate measures as "half a small cup of sugar," "butter the size of a walnut," "a small pinch of salt," "a moderate portion of chocolate," et cetera, would proceed in a sort of mechanical ritual. She would take a handful of something and a dash of something else, plus a couple of scoops of flour and a knob of dough saved from some previous batch. She'd mix it and knead it with her bare hands and eventually get it into an oven whose temperature might be anything from a hundred degrees to five hundred and would never stay the same for five minutes. Her product was good—at any rate her customers made no complaints. Grandma wasn't exactly a cook. She was a magician.

What with the tides of immigration pouring into the United States there wasn't any help shortage, and the "hired girl" was an institution in large numbers of homes. She was generally Swedish or German. Her wages were three or four dollars a week. And her term of service was dependent on how long it took her to learn enough English to qualify for a better job.

She was nearly always a willing worker and once in a while knew something about the care of a house. But, despite the availability of such assistance, plenty of Chicago housewives, then as now, did their own chores.

Women hadn't yet made any inroads into business and hadn't much to occupy their time outside their homes. So every day they swept vast areas of Brussels carpets without the benefit of vacuum cleaners. They removed soot from innumerable shelves with a feather duster. They repaired the household linen, darned socks, sewed on buttons, cleaned suits and made their own underwear. They did all their own laundry work, leaning over a washboard in a wooden tub. Their supply of hot water was probably just what they had been able to carry a kettleful at a time from the kitchen range.

They scalded their washing in a boiler on the same range, put it through a wringer clamped to the end of the sink, starched it, deposited it in a wicker basket, carried it into the yard and hung it on a clothesline to dry.

They did their own marketing and cooked three meals every day. They went to bed early for good reason.

Once or twice a year a woman identified as the "dressmaker" came into the house to make clothes for all the family but father. The "dressmaker" ceased to be an institution in Chicago households when the big stores began to stock ready-to-wear garments in a variety of styles and sizes. But while she lasted, her influence was widely felt. What survivor of that period does not remember her arrival—the deferential greeting of the lady of the house, the pleased curiosity of the clustered kids, the general upheaval of the established routine?

For a couple of weeks the place was cluttered with large sheets of Butterick patterns, scraps of cloth, braid and findings. The sewing machine kept running far into the night. The results were never quite in accordance with the specifications because the "dressmaker" was always an individualist who didn't like the way the patterns were made.

On account of the numerous things that went into the manufacture of a gown—the fluting, the piping and the insets of whalebone—the "dressmaker," no matter how much overtime she put in, never finished her work on schedule—if any. Eventually she packed her little grip and went away, and the house seemed normal again. The housewife turned out proudly in new clothes, and everybody was happy. The "dressmaker" was expensive. She got ten dollars a week and her keep. But all in all she was worth her price.

Boys weren't so much concerned with the "dressmaker." They

weren't particularly fond of the trousers and waists she made for them. But they deeply appreciated the confusion she brought into their uneventful lives. Generally they could be fitted out with "ready-to-wear" raiment at a lot of little shops that their fathers would have scorned. Along toward 1900, when the "dressmaker" was just fading away, you could get a pair of knee pants for a quarter at some of these men's stores. Aside from her other homework, the lady of the house had to take care of this matter, too.

The housewife's recreational program was simple. She was likely to attend a couple of church affairs in the course of a year, or play euchre or cinch every now and then with some little neighborhood association. Sometimes she managed to take the children to see a circus or arrange for a picnic in Lincoln Park. She couldn't have got away to visit the movies if there had been any movies— and there weren't.

Apparently there were no women's clubs in those days either. . . . It seems easy to guess why.

Chapter 12

How to Cure This and That

THERE is no doubt that they were a hardy race—the people who filled up Chicago during the middle ages. And, come to think of it, they had to be. Chicago seems to have been a tough place to live in.

If you were able to read in the nineties, you may remember an interesting and useful feature of the daily journals—a one-column box printed, as a general rule, beside the weather report. It showed a series of little flags, sometimes white, sometimes black and sometimes in varying combinations of black and white. Each bore the label of a pumping station supplying the city with fresh water—Rogers Park, Lake View, Chicago Avenue, Jackson Park— and an expert could tell just by looking at them what percentage of typhoid he might expect to get that day with the water that came out of his tap.

If the flag bearing the label of your district was black, you boiled your water. Otherwise you probably took your chance. For typhoid seems to have been rated in the public mind right alongside dandruff as a scourge too common to cause any worry.

Out in the lake there was still a limitless supply of good water, and no one will criticize the engineers who put in the original pumping systems for their belief that no typhoid germ could possibly swim out to the intake of the system at a five-mile crib. But the town had outgrown its sewage-disposal facilities—it was constantly outgrowing its sewage-disposal facilities—and that made all the difference. Plagues of one sort or another from the sixties had come to be looked on as a sort of heavenly visitation and were just as much a part of the town's routine existence as riot, mayhem and arson.

The day was presently to come when the opening of the drainage canal would end the necessity for the daily flag display. Meantime, such books as *Home Remedies* and *What To Do Till the Doctor Comes* were continuous best sellers.

One day your observer was sitting in his office—to wit, a desk in first grade of the old Red Building of Ravenswood School—when little Frankie Oliver, aged six, arrived a bit late. Children as a rule aren't much concerned with scents and attars, but there seemed to be an atmosphere about Frankie just as definite as it is difficult to describe. That Miss Weedon, the teacher, also noticed it was quite obvious.

"Where have you been, Frankie?" she inquired by way of preliminary. "Why are you late?"

"I have been sick," said Frankie. "My mamma told me to tell you that I have a cold."

Miss Weedon clucked sympathetically, sniffed and gave him a careful look.

"Have you something around your neck?" she inquired.

"Yes," said Frankie proudly. "My mamma put it on. It's an asafetida bag which is going to cure my cold."

"Very nice," commented Miss Weedon. "Just the thing for it. But I don't think you should take any chances on a cold. I shall write a note to your mother, and you can have a little vacation stay at home until you are all well again. . . ."

So she wrote the note and gave it to Frankie, who seemed to be very pleased. He went out, and then Miss Weedon opened all the windows and we all played a game called "Running around the Room."

I related this charming incident to my mother when I went home for luncheon and she seemed unimpressed. She said that asafetida bags were a superstition and that a child might just as well wear a necklace of rabbit's feet. But maybe she was wrong. In view of recent studies on the subject of the communication of disease, much might be said for the asafetida bag. Certainly nobody was likely to come sufficiently near to the wearer to contaminate him.

There were other pleasing theories of medication in those days that now, unfortunately, seem to have gone out of vogue. If, for instance, you got bitten by a dog—which, considering the ratio between the canine and human population, wasn't hard to do—you were in for a glorious day. Amid excitement that brought panic to everybody in the neighborhood you were rushed off to the nearest doctor's office, which usually entailed a ride of a couple of miles in a fascinating horsecar. The doctor was always a placid person who said "There! There!" in soothing tones to your mother but unfailingly showed a great deal of enthusiasm for your dog bite.

He didn't shoot you full of rabies serum, as I understand is the custom in these decadent days. He washed out your wounds with something that smelled like horse liniment, applied a coating of brown gook that the woman next door would identify as "yarbs" and finished off the operation with a bandage that you would certainly be proud to show your friends. Then you were led across the street to a drugstore, fed a couple of ice-cream sodas and escorted home in triumph to look for another accommodating dog.

Not quite so profitable but only a little less interesting were croup and whooping cough. Your parents had long-standing instructions about what to do with such things. You had to have a good case of croup to get a dividend. A minor-league case was treated with applications of camphor and goose grease right in your own home. And there was no percentage of profit in that.

When you had a bad case you were wrapped cozily in blankets, hoisted into a livery rig and hauled over to the gashouse on Clybourn Avenue.

I was a little disappointed on the occasion of my first visit to discover that I was not going to be allowed to wander around the big gas tank. But it didn't spoil my day. With a couple of dozen other kids I was given a place on a long bench in an adjoining shed that was gassy enough to suit anybody. And there I sat for a wonderful hour, looking at picture books provided by the management.

I got a bag of gumdrops on the way home. The gift was pure lagniappe. And just for the record, I might say that the cure seems to have been pretty good too. I got rid of the croup eventually and lived to take a similar treatment for whooping cough a year later.

Sulphur and molasses, as a spring tonic, was falling out of favor in the late nineties—a scientific disaffection that can be recalled without noticeable regret. In its place came a concoction of cream of tartar that tasted something like lemonade and did nobody any good.

In our house, for some unrecorded reason, the fear of tetanus ran pretty high. So our injuires from rusty nails and mishandled firecrackers were always given quick treatment with a carbolic-acid wash, one bit of our pioneer pharmacopoeia that seems to have remained with us to the present day. We consumed great quantities of Beef, Iron and Wine. Fever of any kind promptly brought its quinine. And once I took a course of gin—in small quantities for scarlet fever. The gin, possibly, should not be mentioned in connection with the home fight on disease. It was administered on a doctor's prescription and called "spirits of juniper." I never found out why.

There were other wonders in the curing of ills besides asafedita bags, trips to the gashouse and gin. Most of them, I regret to say, weren't too good.

You'd wonder, when you hear about penicillin and streptomycin and the sulfa drugs, how an improperly medicated world stayed in existence long enough to discover them. Modern men and women—all of them no doubt perfect physical specimens—presumably know nothing about the ravages of any disease worse than halitosis or athlete's foot. It seems a bit gratuitous for them to prate with an air of proprietorship about a miracle-working pharmacopoeia that has eliminated (or has it?) all bacteria from the world, grown hair on the bald, repaired broken legs and fixed up cases of dandruff once considered "too late for Herpicide."

People who know no pain certainly are not qualified to discuss remedies. What can they say about the fine, glowing healthy life in Chicago in the nineties when the neighborhood crones with their kitchen simples knew more about medicine than Aesculapius and were present at every sickbed to keep the family physician from making any serious errors. Now that nobody gets sick any more—thanks to vitamins, diet, sulfadiothynosamil, sobriety and the laying on of hands—the populace has probably forgotten that a first-rate illness in the good old days was a matter of social importance. We may have had aches and pains in the nineties, but there were compensations. We never were very lonesome.

You came home, possibly, with a headache, and if you couldn't eat your chocolate cake at luncheon, you were sick. Your mother looked at your tongue. She never revealed what she saw on it or what she expected to see, but the opening of your mouth never failed to remind her of an accepted routine. As a precautionary measure or merely as a bit of ritual—like locking the barn door or searching the cellars of Parliament for Guy Fawkes—she would administer a large-economy-size dose of castor oil.

The ostensible explanation for this was that if it didn't cure you, it would certainly do you no harm. And who can say that that wasn't fair enough!

You were then put to bed while your little brother was sent on the run for a doctor. Then ensued a state of dire suspense while you lay comfortably in the sheets and everybody stood around looking worried and glum, for the business of getting the doctor would take little brother on a long run.

It is a matter of record that calamities such as this always befell the household on days when the iceman had to go to a picnic at Beugelbaum's Grove and the local box was empty. So some other member of the family was shagged out to the Milwaukee Railroad siding at Swarzchild and Sulzberger's branch plant to salvage a chunk of ice out of a refrigerator car. But right about there the family's part of the physical labor then required in the treatment of disease came to an end.

The neighbors, led by Old Mrs. Goeltz and somebody we thought was called Mrs. Anaesthesia Ryan, rival practitioners but both as good as could be found in any community, moved in. How they found out that anybody was "under the weather" at your house is one of those things that nobody has explained any more than the homing talent of pigeons. It seems to have been instinctive—like their quick awareness of what herb would cure what.

Anyway, they always arrived as soon as Old Dr. John Stone— sometimes ahead of him. He accepted their presence as he did other natural phenomena, but he never seemed to be completely reconciled to it.

"He's got the croup," (or bronchitis, or whooping cough, or measles or mumps or a touch of the sun) the doctor would announce. "Get this prescription right away and give him a teaspoonful in a half glass of water every hour till the fever breaks. . . ."

At which the visiting angels would sniff.

"Croup!" would come the dissenting chorus. "It's obviously *mal de mer* or the blight or the vapors. And what the boy needs is a good dose of camomile tea, mandragora root and wampum weed."

Then they would wrangle over techniques of treatment: was it better to administer decoctions of herbs or a series of hot poultices "to draw the poison out?" The question never was settled. The doctor, generally, was reduced to incoherence.

As for the lady of the house, it was her theory that if goose grease and camphor wouldn't cure an ailment overnight, well then, nothing would do it any good except prayer. So when the tumult and the shouting died you got the medicine that the doctor prescribed for you. It always tasted like cardamom seed, but that's all anybody except the doctor seemed to know about it. In addition you got rubbed with goose grease and camphor, and every once in a while you got a dividend in the shape of a tablespoonful of honey and lemon juice, which rated high locally as a cough medicine.

All about you ranged bottles and jars and boxes of unidentified weeds gathered by the neighborhood herbalists from the gravel buttes and clay holes along Western Avenue. Mostly, they seemed to be there just for ornament and to maintain the community tradition that "everybody was a real help whenever there was sickness in the house."

You recovered eventually, and for a day or two you were allowed to sit up in a chair amid scenes of great rejoicing. All the healers came back again to claim their share of credit for the miracle and to recount other wondrous cures wrought by Old Extract of Henbane (or lettuce-and-dandelion plaster) for Cousin John's boy and that Flatzheimer child. These recitals were generously larded with stern criticism of the doctor.

When they had completed their discussion without a fight, they began to give advice on how to recoup one's energies. The rules, like the remedies, were many and varied:

(A) Sleep with your window closed and avoid the night air.

(B) Eat nothing but good, easily digested food such as oatmeal gruel.

(C) Wear a copper finger ring "to absorb the poison."

(D) Take a daily dose of sulphur and molasses.

And more to the same effect.

I do not wish to give you the impression that Chicago's residence districts were populated by folks recently arrived from darkest Africa or the Australian bush. They were, in the main, just as bright as most people of their period.

Every housewife had a list of sure-fire remedies, the recipes for which had come down through believing generations from a source somewhere back in the Stone Age. She gave them freely to everybody, whether she was petitioned for this service or not. Some of her ancient lore had a hint of modern influence. You still ate handfuls of quinine. And your taking it was in accord with the women's attitude toward medical practice. Nobody knew exactly why you were taking quinine; you just consumed it, no matter what was wrong with you, unless some arrant disbeliever in your family succeeded in cutting off the supply. It was the theory that if quinine wouldn't cure malaria (which it wouldn't), then it ought to be able to cure something else. And so it was with the other formidable drugs in the cabinet, from Nux Vomica to Paregoric. They were kept because they were certain to be useful some day. No housewife ever threw away anything, and the populace developed a remarkable resistance to doses that should have filled the graveyards.

All in all, an amazing period, my brothers. The people you meet today don't look much different from those old-timers. But men used to survive traps that would ruin the town today. Perhaps it was because of the good scientific thought that a man ought to eat a hearty breakfast of ham and eggs and pie "to keep up his strength" during the work of the day.

It is interesting to note that the same diet was given him if he was about to be hanged.

Chapter 13

And These Were the Modes

IF YOU want to know something of what has happened to Chicago in, say, fifty years, take a look at State Street in 1895.

The street, looking north from Van Buren Street, is paved with Belgian block, granite cobbles that have worn round on top, hurt your feet through your thick-soled button shoes and make high heels a deadly hazard. Women in long skirts traverse the crossings gingerly, their eyes on the ground, unmindful of the threatening horsecars. There are no traffic lights, traffic signals, pedestrian's rights or traffic cops.

The few policemen in sight wear long blue coats, luxuriant mustaches and coal-scuttle helmets. They twirl their night sticks—attached to their wrists with leather thongs—with all the skill of drum majors.

As you view them from this side of the calendar they remind you of the old Keystone comedies. But they have had plenty of experience with the top thugs of the country during the recent World's Fair and, by and large, they aren't such bad police.

There are no automobiles in the mass of vehicles crawling around the corners. There won't be any for another ten years. But already the good townsfolk are complaining about the congestion.

If you are a visitor, your relatives will smile a little proudly as they protest about the difficulties of walking in this street—the avenue of famous stores.

"You probably have noticed," they began hopefully, "that everybody in Chicago seems to be in a hurry. Nobody takes it easy any more. My goodness, you'd think the town was going to a fire! Everybody seems to leave his manners at home."

At the time, most likely, you would have agreed with this criticism, particularly if you came from some village where you had room to saunter and no reason to do anything else. But, just between us, the speed of pedestrian traffic in State Street in 1895

wasn't much better than that of the snails' parade you can see today.

The female modes of the nineties were not adapted to sprinting. The men, in tight-fitting pants that bind at the knees, are not likely to take the risk of splitting a seam just to get to the other end of the block a little sooner. Out in the street the traffic moved at the speed of a leisurely horse, and there really is some congestion.

All day long the pavement creaks to the unhurried procession of brewery trucks, ash wagons, horsecars, phaetons, barouches, closed carriages and plain buggies that somehow managed to get into jams at the street corners—just as wheeled vehicles have been doing ever since.

The people who jostle you on the sidewalks in what is known as a hurry may seem an odd lot—not the women, perhaps, for they had what was briefly resurrected as the "new look." This is to say that they wear a costume embracing them from neck to sidewalk level. The superstructure is tight-fitting, with a row of buttons down the front. High lace collars extend out of them on props of herringbone. Waists, pent up in corsets, are infinitesimal, and beams are correspondingly broad, their extent accentuated by artificial back porches known as bustles.

Skirts trail enough to keep the sidewalks clean. Hair is piled forward on the head—and there is quite a lot of it. The feathered hats fit precariously on the top of this mass and look, somehow, familiar.

The men are all of a pattern in their modish, tight-fitting trousers, gaudy vests, ready-made four-in-hands, chin-cutting collars and little round derby hats.

To say that the ensemble looks like something out of a Mae West movie is to offer no criticism. This fascinating raiment is not going to look very quaint for another ten or fifteen years.

Pay some attention to the buildings along the avenue. They aren't going to be here much longer. For the most part they are low, dark structures with columned fronts and retiring roofs. Somebody has already noticed that they give Chicago "a sophisticated Parisian look." And maybe they do. Anyway, they are worth your inspection. Their uninspired sameness gives the street a unity that it is never going to have again.

State Street is already proclaiming itself "The Most Complete Shopping District in the United States If Not in the World." Perhaps it is. It certainly looks like it. Both sides of it are lined continuously with shops, from Marshall Field's to Siegel, Cooper & Co. At every street crossing there is a pushcart peddler selling apples, oranges or hot roasted chestnuts.

You miss the red fronts of the ten-cent stores—because there aren't any ten-cent stores. They have not yet come this far west. Neither are there any blazing electric signs on the flamboyant fronts of moving-picture theaters—for the same reason.

Electricity is being put to an increasing use all over town. But at night State Street is still lighted by the moon—if any—and by gas lamps set on standards spaced four to a block.

If you want to go anywhere from State Street, you can always pick up a hansom cab in front of the aging Palmer House at Monroe Street. If your destination is a railroad station, you can go inside and arrange with the porter for a seat on a Parmalee omnibus. But if you are in a hurry, wherever you are going, you will probably walk. It's quicker.

Long blocks of cement sidewalks are studded with little glass bull's-eyes which provide a problematical amount of light to salesrooms below. They are dangerously slippery when wet. Sprained ankles and broken legs continue to be a prime civic hazard. These reaches echo hollowly as the shopping crowd mills over them.

In the windows of offices above some of the lesser stores, advertising is showing signs of progress. Eyes two feet wide wink at you to indicate the atelier of an optician, and supersets of snapping white teeth apprise you of a waiting dentist. But there isn't much of this sort of appeal. What there is of it doesn't seem to draw many customers.

Art, as we have been taught to understand the word, was a long time getting to State Street. Even the display windows of the big shops seemed to have been filled by some hurried shipping clerk with a shovel. Scabrous wax figures that looked like recent arrivals from Graceland Cemetery displayed the dresses for women and the ready-made suits for men. Each of these exhibits was labeled with a large hand-lettered ticket: "In this style, cheap at $8.80." There was no attempt to provide a background for the windows that might possibly be restful to the eye. There was nothing about the whole display that was either eye-resting or eye-catching. So many "bargains at $8.80" were jammed into the window that nobody could look at them without getting a case of "tourists' fatigue." There was no harmony of shape or color, and little attempt to classify the goods. The backgrounds were rosettes and stripes and rainbows of crepe paper. They were definitely the world's farthest south in aesthetic appeal.

You may have noticed that the pants on the dummies supposed to represent the "man about town" were neatly pressed, while those of the men beside you gazing at the presentation were somewhat askew, wrinkled and baggy at the knees. This little difference was thought to distinguish between tailor-made clothes and ready-mades, although ready-mades generally looked pretty wrinkled and baggy after a week's wear.

Along about 4:00 P.M. the crowds in the stores began to thin out save for groups of wealthy dowagers, the carriage trade, who had no worries about how they were going to get home. Their coachmen would be answering the signals of callers in top hats at the entrance of Fields' an hour later.

Outbound shoppers presently were taxing the horsecars, clinging to their bundles and to one another, and standing on one another's feet in gay nonchalance inside, or hanging like bunches of bananas on the outside. Then as now, no matter where they lived, it was a long way to home.

It was a matter of dogma, which we got drilled into us from the time we learned to listen, that the smart shoppers went home on the railroads. Having learned this great truth in such a fashion

I have never doubted it. There were certainly lots of trains running out to the charming but distant suburbs. The Illinois Central provided virtually the only transportation to the vast sections of the South Side along the lake. The North Western and the Milwaukee railroads had made possible the settlement of such dormitories as Evanston, Lake Forest and Wheaton. There were suburban trains on the Rock Island and the Santa Fe, the Lake Shore and Michigan Southern and, for that matter, on every line that ran out of Chicago or into it.

But I learned one interesting thing about this quick and easy travel. Only about one in ten of the smart people who went home on the railroads ever landed closer than two miles from his home. The rest of the way he walked.

But walking meant nothing to the hardy pioneer. He'd been taught to walk from infancy. He never complained about it. He loved it. He walked continuously. And maybe that was because he jolly well had to.

Chapter 14

Home Carpentry

Some of the most interesting reading matter of our times is to be found in the handicraft and home-mechanics magazines—particularly among the advertisements.

"Make your own terrazzo flooring out of eggshells with the Plastico Semiautomatic Eggshell Converter, complete with extra-thickness gauge and three practice eggs, $147.00 F.O.B., Hindu Springs, Kansas."

"Do your own home repairs! Fix leaky oat bins, pipe house for gas, lay linoleum, oil hinges, shovel snow—all with the aid of our How-To-Do-It Books plus Snorkelbeiter's Power-Tooled Home Repair Unit."

"Keep a genuine Geiger counter in your basement. Nothing better to detect presence of uranium or electricity in your home."

"Murgatroyd Home Shop Unit, complete with buzz saw, planer, jointer, shaper, lathe, stamp mill, riveter, welder, trip hammer, dry dock and buttonhook."

The life of the man who used to be called "the handy man about the house" seems to be getting pretty complicated. He may retain all the genius that made him the ideal matrimonial catch in the days of, say, 1900 or thereabouts. His hands may be just as deft, but custom has staled his infinite variety.

Maybe he wasn't so quick about fixing an electric-light fixture in 1897. But that was chiefly because he had never seen an electric-light fixture. He isn't too successful today in cutting a wedge to silence a rattling window, or in tacking a calendar to the wall, or in sharpening a pencil. But that is because he generally isn't rich enough. Only the lads who support the mechanical-trade papers have enough income to spend eighty or ninety dollars on an "electric Fuller ball replacement machine" to replace a five-cent Fuller ball in a ten-cent-store faucet.

It is still possible to cut a board, when you can locate one, with a handsaw. And the painters' unions have demonstrated that you don't need a spray gun to paint a back porch. But, it appears, the amateur artisan has too much pride in his work to use outmoded tools. If he can't drive his nails with a 400-horsepower pneumatic hammer, then he's better off to leave the nails undriven.

It wasn't always that way. Household carpentry was a thriving industry in the nineties. Folks practiced it not because they were rich but because they were poor. The average head of a house, man or woman, generally got pretty deft at it out of sheer necessity.

In our home there were kitchen cabinets, bookshelves and linen closets long before you could buy such stuff at the department stores knocked down, easily assembled and ready to paint. We had a set of homemade copper pots and pans that were the envy of the neighborhood, and we had a lot of ingeniously contrived porch furniture also—a swing, geranium stands, burglar alarm and a back-yard merry-go-round. My father, who was certainly a skilled workman though definitely an amateur, made all these things with a fine professional finish. And he did it with shop equipment that couldn't have cost more than ten dollars.

In 1900, when I became interested in basement crafts because I wanted to make a toy dumpcart, he had no tools at all. They had been lost, or thrown away in moving. He started from scratch to make others—literally to make them.

He got a little help from the hardware store in the shape of three or four files, a saw and a hammer, a grindstone and a wooden screw for a vise. But after that he was definitely on his own. Out of a block of hardwood he cut the frame of a jack plane. After that he heated one of the files on the gas stove, pounded it into a blade on an old horse weight and ground it to fit the slot in the frame.

In a similar fashion he made three chisels and cut handles for them from broomsticks. There was never much more to his wood-working atelier than just that. It wasn't until long afterward that I began to realize what skill he had. Nearly everybody who had a mechanic's instincts in those days made his own tools. I had watched other men in our neighborhood do it, and it all seemed simple. I am not at all sure nowadays that it really was.

My father, thanks to a youthful apprenticeship to a tinsmith, was an exceptionally gifted sheet-metal worker. But he never had any of the bending and cutting devices that even in those remote days could be found in almost any tin shop. His metalworking apparatus consisted of a couple of mallets, a ball peen hammer, a soldering iron and some forms that he had carved out of hard-wood with his jackknife. But with such crude aids he was able to fashion seamless cooper pans with perfectly smooth, polished surfaces and turned rims. He made spice boxes and bread canisters quite like those that any talented householder can make with a dollar's worth of sheet metal and $500 worth of punches and dies today. In addition to that he was also the only man I have ever seen who could really repair a leak in a teakettle.

He undoubtedly had unusual talents, but he was by no means the only one of his kind in Chicago. It went without saying that among the things every young man ought to know were included the technique of driving a nail, fixing a faucet, replacing a window weight, putting up the screens or the storm sash, easing a sticky drawer, repairing a shade roller, putting down a carpet or tak-ing it up, upholstering a chair, installing a Welsbach gas mantle, polishing chandeliers or painting and polishing—or varnishing—woodwork. In addition to that the really adept handy man was able to lay pipe, do some elemental plumbing and keep the fires going in old-fashioned furnaces.

Carpenters, plumbers, glaziers and such had plenty of work to do in the haphazard building of Chicago. Old Man Joseph Denny, a sash-and-door expert in our block, had been laboring steadily since he was mustered out of the Union Army near Appomattox. He wasn't much hurried. The rapid rate of building construction that made a new city out of the old in the early nineties meant nothing at all to him. He made nothing but doors and windows and such things. He made good ones and he made plenty of them.

"Do a good job, my boy," he used to say to me, "and you'll never have to worry about getting work. You don't have to do all the kinds of carpentry there are. Just do a part of it better than anybody else." But it struck me, even then, that he didn't know exactly what was going on about him. Nearly every carpenter I ever saw during my childhood turned his hand to any job that needed doing. Nobody would have thought of calling in a professional electrician to hang a doorbell. Even a carpenter would have sneered at a man without sufficient skill to hang his own doors. Carpenter Denny remained in my mind as the only real specialist the period produced. The rest of the artisans were doing what they had to do, without argument or discussion. And a lot of them were making their own tools.

There were plenty of home craftsmen in those days—if you are not too meticulous about definitions. True, they didn't make things out of eggshells or plastic, and they didn't fill the world with model airplanes and radio cabinets made to look like Scotty dogs. But give them the benefit of the doubt. Maybe they were hampered by the lack of power tools—or maybe they were too busy fixing a leak in the roof or putting a new spring in the hall clock.

The man of the house was something more than a fixture in those stirring times. He earned his keep.

Chapter 15

"Games," They Called Them!

FOR quite a long time I have gone around trying to find out if anybody still plays the fascinating game called "tiddlywinks." But all the oracles are silent to the query—and you don't get much information about "jackstraws" either.

It wasn't always so. Santa Claus wore a different set of whiskers when the old century was passing out, and, with banks exploding all about him, he probably had to budget his investment in toys. Even so, no matter what your cultural background and no matter what the state of the family finances, you always knew that three presents were certain to be under the tree for you on Christmas morning: "jackstraws," "tiddlywinks" and, as we forgot to mention, "lotto."

Jackstraws and tiddlywinks, for all we have been able to learn about them, may have vanished from the ken of man. This is more remarkable when you consider the vigorous longevity of lotto. It seems to be the only game competing with baseball for choice as the national pastime—although now, as you have undoubtedly heard, they call it bingo.

Games have always held a high place in the holiday gift lists, not to mention an uncanny importance in American social life. Playing cards—actual playing cards, decorated with clubs and diamonds and aces and deuces—were still not quite respectable in some circles at the beginning of the present century. They became symbols of much functional argument. But at that time decks marked with other meaningless devices were held in almost universal esteem.

It was the custom, whenever a party seemed to be dragging, to give it a shot of adrenalin with a good, rousing game of Authors. Some of the cards bore the pictures of Dickens or Thackeray or Poe or Cooper or other literary notables. Other cards were marked with the titles of novels. You dealt and traded and paired until you had a set of authors matched with their works. The game, which was a species of Rummy deodorized for home consumption, was very popular, as it has been under other names since.

Peter Cooper's Trip to New York was another sure-fire card game. It was excellent for parties because any number of people could play without need for card tables, markers or any other such dubious equipment. And there was nothing about it to tax anybody's mind or morals.

The entire deck was dealt out, after which a sort of master of ceremonies started the proceedings by reading from a folder found at the bottom of the box. The text turned out to be a factual narrative of how Peter Cooper made a trip to New York, but the text was broken by numerous dashes. When the reader came to a dash he would nod to a player who would fill in the hiatus with whatever words appeared in his top card. Like this:

READER: "Peter Cooper went to New York carrying a——"

PLAYER: No. 1: "A bustle!"

ALL: (Laughter.)

READER: "He had lost his ticket but he offered the conductor——"

PLAYER No. 2: "His old Aunt Sarah!"

ALL: (Even more laughter.)

And so ad infinitum.

The debatable position of regular cards in decent society seems to have been due to the fact that with regular cards you could play poker or faro or black and tan, or other gambling games at which everybody lost his old homestead and his employer's egg money and never won anything. But once you eliminated the depraved figures of Kings, Queens and Jacks, the situation was completely changed. Nobody would have thought of wagering a stake on Authors, of course, unless somebody had thought to call the game Gin Rummy. Apparently nobody ever did.

The whole town sat back on its haunches to play "Pit," a card game of bids, acceptances, commitments, sight drafts et cetera, based on the procedure of the Board of Trade, which, as everybody knows, is free from any hint of gambling.

Despite excellent opportunities, nobody seems to have risked any cash on this so-called friendly game of "Pit." It was a noisy business at best—a complete riot if your host was energetic and his friends numerous and in good voice. And when it got too loud for anybody to hear anything it was too loud for anybody to post any bets.

It produced some newspaper publicity on account of fights. Such police raids as are mentioned in the records seem to have been ordered merely to suppress a nuisance.

As a game "Pit" was something like "Monopoly" of more recent memory although not quite so complicated. Aside from its lack of decorum it wasn't much different from Authors—or Rummy.

Flinch, another card game that kept Chicago's unwashed dishes in the sink for many an evening, was played with something that resembled a pinochle deck of cards except that the cards were marked with sets of figures instead of the conventional characters. And with a Flinch deck, my brethren, you could imitate any game from Old Maid to Three-Card Monte.

One could, and unfortunately very many did, lose generous

wads on variants of Flinch, in clubs, in the homes of friends, in Pullman palace cars, at church fairs and at meetings of the Ladies' Aid Society. But there seems to have been very little public resentment against this pastime—no more, perhaps, than there had been against the whittling of Tee-Totems, later popularized in a game of skill called Put and Take.

The hard-and-fast condemnation of playing cards by folks unwilling to make a compromise of any sort with evil led to some complications. Mrs. John Ellsworth, who lived next door to us, was one of these. She was always in evidence to glower darkly and disapprovingly when the neighborhood euchre club came to waste an afternoon in our front parlor. She wouldn't have one of those "devilish ducats" under her roof, she frequently observed in public. But, as it turned out, she spoke somewhat hastily. She appeared one day at our door to announce a temporary change in policy.

"My sister Frances has come to visit me," she announced excitedly. "And she tells fortunes. She really has the gift. She's much better at it than most professionals. . . . But, of course, we haven't any cards. We never keep anything like that around because nobody plays. And I wonder if you would let me borrow a deck."

So she got the deck—the one with the picture of the South Dakota Corn Palace on it. And she was very grateful.

"Come in and let Frances read your future," she burbled.

But my mother shook her head. "I don't believe in fortunetellers," she declared sternly. "I don't think one of them knows what happened yesterday, let alone what's going to happen tomorrow. And I should like to tell you that all these silly cards, like Pit and Flinch and Stock Exchange, are the same thing. . . ."

Mrs. Ellsworth flushed, but she kept the cards with the picture of the Corn Palace on them. She wasn't sure her fortunetelling sister could make sense out of the other kind.

Numbers of games with newsworthy titles came into our home —"North Pole," "Balloon Flight," "Trip to London," "Baseball" and the like. They were changing markers in games of the same principle. The players were given counters which they advanced over a marked course toward a goal. The number of squares your marker went forward or backward was determined by the number you got drawing a card, spinning a small roulette wheel or shooting dice.

All that was innocent fun, even in households where the playing of cards was strictly taboo. Our elders weren't naïve enough to think of galloping dominoes as an innocuous diversion for the kiddies. We'd have got killed if we brought a pair of dice into our homes unless they came in a box bearing the name of the Parker Game Company. That, like the changed inscriptions on the cards, made everything legal.

Chapter 16

The Vapors

THERE were generally two reasons why you couldn't be taken to the Lincoln Park Zoo on a Saturday afternoon: (1) The Clark Street cable-car system was temporarily out of order, or, as the saying goes, busted. (2) Your Aunt Minnie was suffering from a severe attack of The Vapors.

One is still at a loss to explain what was always wrong with the streetcar system. It seems the cable just had a way of snapping. As for what was wrong with Aunt Minnie, well, that is also hard to say. She had a number of things wrong with her that doctors nowadays know little or nothing about.

"The Vapors," of course, were the greatest menace to womankind in those careless days. The symptoms were dizziness, spots before the eyes and a general lassitude nearly always accompanied by fainting spells. It was, indeed, a dire ailment. It unfailingly brought a lot of off-stage thrills to theaters and gave streetcar riders a lively subject for home discussion. It was seldom fatal but frequently embarrassing, and there seemed to be no cure for it.

If you talked to your Aunt Minnie about it, you might have gathered that those whom The Vapors chose to curse were just a little proud of themselves. Not everybody in those days could get The

Vapors, just as nobody can get them, or it, now. It seems that however disconcerting it might be to flop unconscious in a puddle at Madison and State streets, the performance was always carried out with a certain social distinction. If you saw a pile of ostrich feathers and taffeta on the sidewalk in front of Hooley's Theater, you knew it was presently going to turn out to be a Woman of Distinction. It certainly wasn't going to be one of Hooley's scrub-women or Judy O'Grady, who addressed envelopes for the Quick-Fit Pants Company across the street.

The indirect cause of The Vapors seems to have been the same one assignable to most of the plagues that followed women out of the Victorian age—the unique aspiration of the sex to sit on a cushion and sew a fine seam. The direct cause of this particular malady, if you care to call it that, may be gathered from the first-aid methods most successful in treating it.

When an unfortunate sufferer gracefully folded up on the pavement everybody in Chicago who had ever read a current novel knew just what to do about it. With as much modesty as possible, one hauled out the jackknife which he carried for such relief work as well as sharpening pencils. Then, quickly kneeling by the victim's side, he took the only course possible: he cut the laces of her corset.

This operation seldom failed. The pale, stricken one came to gracefully, murmured her gratitude to her rescuer, then blushed and dropped her eyes at the thought of how her neckline had been exposed to the gaping crowd. And as for the man who owned the jacknife, his soul probably bled for her—if he'd had any upbringing at all in a well-conducted home. If he were really a gentleman aware of his obligations, he probably proposed marriage to her before escorting her to his carriage to see her safely home. At any rate that is what gentlemen—real gentlemen—did in the popular fiction of Charles Garvice and The Duchess. When blundering man became aware that a woman wore a corset, marriage seems to have been just about the least he could offer by way of recompense.

Old married women, it appears, were less troubled by The Vapors than young single ones. In the first place, with an older woman the romantic lure of a ladylike fainting spell was no longer of much use. In the second place, social usage, or maybe a lack of concern for social usage, permitted such favored persons to wear looser stays. And furthermore, the frights and torments of all the female epidemics of the era seem to have been the affliction principally of those tender young females later identified as "flappers."

It was contrary to the rule of the fine fresh aristocracy for women to work in offices, although to save herself from starvation a nice girl might be excused for clerking in a store. If a young woman had a father willing and able to support her, she frequently found herself with little to occupy her time save The Vapors or a somewhat similar phenomenon called "Going into a Decline." In The Vapors one succumbed only temporarily to the buffets of the world. When one went into a Decline, one just pined away and died.

Of the two, therefore, the Decline, which seems to have been somewhat related to tuberculosis, was the more dangerous. It was also the more popular subject for gossip over the teacups because popular information attributed it to "Love, Oh, Hopeless Love."

As recently as 1900, and for generations before that, the fair, cold beauty who bestrewed her path with broken hearts, and all that nonsense, had the admiration, if not the affection, of her sex. For such a one to go through life a spinster was excusable because the course she followed was one she had chosen for herself. For one of the lesser sisterhood to remain unmarried implied that there must be something wrong with her, a conclusion in which, unfortunately, she generally concurred with her critics.

To be "publicly jilted," which means to have failed in carrying out a widely ballyhooed engagement, was even worse. There might be some pity for a girl whose prospects were linked with a repulsive face. Lots of women had that sort of affliction, which they couldn't help. But the girl who was easy to look at but "unable to hold her man" after she had caught him got few condolences.

So one might include among the surviving maladies of the late Victorian age an entirely mental condition entitled "being disappointed in love." Its incidence was just after The Vapors and just ahead of Going into a Decline. It was seldom fatal, but it seems to have occasioned some theoretical pain among its victims and no end of trouble among the members of the victim's immediate household.

There couldn't have been much of a housing shortage in Chicago in 1898. The town seems to have been cluttered up with dank, dusty rooms whose doors were never opened. . . . "It's just as it was when she was putting on her bridal gown and they brought the news to her. . . . It was right in this room that she heard he had kissed his cousin good-by at the Union Station. . . . She shrieked in agony . . . and nobody's been in it since."

And there were countless invalids—the deeply emotional would-have-been brides who came home after waiting too long on the church steps and went to bed to die but somehow didn't.

There was one of that sort in our neighborhood, one Mary Molitor, whose record for sustained inactivity at the time when we first saw her had virtually equaled Rip Van Winkle's. Back before our time she had been clambering into the hack that had been hired to take her to the church when an A.D.T. boy arrived with a message conveying the regrets of one George Bentley, party of the second part.

Along about 1900 George Bentley's picture appeared in most of the local newspapers. Under his most recent alias as Fred Skilling he had been arrested for the murder of a woman in Seattle. That was how we came to see Miss Molitor. She decided she'd suffered enough for such a scoundrel as George was. She got out of bed, bought some new clothes and started going to parties. For one who somewhat belatedly had decided to pay no attention to "Love, Oh, Careless Love" she was quite a popular young woman.

In 1901 she married Joe Ryan, a bartender whom she had met on this new round of gaiety. The marriage turned out quite well. Joe thought Mary was a remarkable woman because she never had The Vapors and showed no sign of Going into a Decline.

Mary thought Joe was about as good as most men. And she had learned enough to take no chances.

She accompanied him to the church.

Chapter 17

Revise Your Attic

ONE of our enterprising lumber concerns is continuously advertising a plan to "convert your attic into a four-room flat."

"You may," says this announcement, "profit by the housing shortage. Pay the construction costs in a few months out of rent."

It sounds like a fine proposition save for one thought: "Where is this attic?"

Not many children of this generation in Chicago have ever seen an attic. Few know what the word means. There were such things back in the days before the town got covered with makeshift flats and multiple-apartment buildings. Every house had one, even the cottages in De Koven Street and the rambling gray tenements north of the river. They were used to store things like outmoded hats, broken furniture, trunks, telescopes, portmanteaus, bird cages, worn carpets, old newspapers, old underwear and similar moth food. Once put away, these things were never taken out of storage, save by little boys questing material for kite tails, until the original owner died and the new owner needed room for junk of his own. But nobody ever doubted the necessity for the attic until along about 1910 when the insurance companies began to talk insultingly about "fire hazards."

There just had to be a space between the ceiling of the top floor and the roof, didn't there? Very well, then. There was your attic.

I had little experience with our attic inasmuch as my practical father cleaned it out and nailed up the door that had led to it. Thereafter all the junk we collected was laid out in the hall closet. But Pete Halper, who lived next door, had a very fine attic—light, airy, roomy and accessible. And that's how I know what was done with these things before the lumber companies thought they could be made into four-room flats.

Pete's attic was an excellent spot for a rainy day, or even a sunny one if it wasn't too hot. On warm spring days I remember the "rozzum" fried out of the rafters, and the place was filled with the aroma of lofty pines and old paper. Motes of dust like diamond points danced past the two windows in square shafts of sunlight, and there wasn't any connection with the world except the rattle of somebody's lawn mower floating up from somewhere near the end of the block.

On wet, stormy nights it was pleasant to listen to the disappointed howl of the wind and the spatter of the rain on the shingles while one read about the Civil War in old copies of *Harper's Weekly* spread out under the kerosene lamp. This was our special clubroom, our retreat from a community cluttered with adults. We were very happy in it until Pete's sister, an imperfect blonde of about eighteen years, came up the stairs one day to chase us out of it.

She wanted to make a "den" out of the place, she said. A "den!" As if she didn't know that "dens" were places fixed up for your father and used by your mother to keep the sewing machine in. Dens were strictly for the men who never got a chance to light in them. What Pete Halper's sister meant when she talked about a "den" was actually a "nook." But she wouldn't listen when we tried to tell her.

"Den" or "nook," it was going to be all the same to her, and to us. Joe Wagner, her "fellah," was coming around that evening to put a padlock on the door. We moved over to my basement, which had electric light and a two-dollar printing press but was otherwise lacking in charm.

I got a look at Miss Halper's "den" one day a couple of months later. It was quite tasty, considering that a girl had rigged it up. The principal part of it was a lot of old portieres that curtained off a clearing at the front end from the exhibits of trunks and bird cages.

There was a rag rug on the floor. She'd made it out of old clothes and such scrap as hadn't previously found its way to the attic. And she'd strung some fishing net along the curtains to hold pictures of actors, statesmen, athletes, bandits and other males whom she currently admired.

The furniture consisted of a rocking chair that had always been there, a writing desk, a lamp stand, and a stool which Pete said Joe Wagner had made for her "in manual training, right out of the *Ladies' Home Journal.*" It looked very pretty to me. But Miss Halper didn't enjoy it very long.

It seems her father got a look at it and decided he'd fix up the place as a den for himself. He tore down the old portieres and put up some wooden partitions. Then he moved a Morris chair up from some place in the house along with a thing to put his feet on when he was resting. He found the place very comfortable— just what he had always wanted—until Mrs. Halper needed a place to put a sewing machine.

Meantime Miss Halper was contenting herself with something between a "den" and a "nook," a thing they called a "cozy corner," in the bay window of the back parlor. I saw quite a lot of that. It was cut off from the rest of the room by a couple of cross draperies that looked like the stuff they put into awnings. The skillful Joe Wagner had filled up the bay with a window seat which Miss Halper had covered with carpeting and a couple of dozen sofa pillows. The plan for this bit of interior decoration had come, so Pete informed me, from a newspaper picture entitled "The Sultan's Harem."

The cozy corner was fitted up with match holders and ash trays and a couple of pipe racks. Even if Miss Halper had been able to smoke she wouldn't have been able to sit down in this cheerful little retreat. Smoking or not, she might have had trouble sitting for any length of time on a bench as hard as the window seat. So Mr. Halper, with varying degrees of enthusiasm, used the "cozy corner" when he moved down from his den after it had been transformed into a sewing room.

About this time my mother began to hint that it would be nice to have the door opened into our attic. One could do a lot of sewing, it seemed, if one only had the place to do it in.

But nobody seems to have heard her. My father presently built a new sun porch and—would you believe it—it turned out to be a "den." But it was different from other "dens." It had a slanting floor like the deck of a ship, and a sewing machine wouldn't stay put on it.

I have sometimes wondered . . .

Mystery and Crime 3:

Mr. Luetgert's Wife

BETWEEN the spring of 1897 and the summer of 1902 nobody ate any sausage in Chicago.

No whim of appetite was involved in the matter. Nobody in that period knew anything about dietetics, and the fat ladies of the community were still happily ignorant of calories. The slump in the wiener market was due to some lingering doubts as to what had become of Mrs. Adolph Luetgert.

Adolph Luetgert was a sausage maker whose factory occupied a large grayish brick building just west of Commercial Street—one day to be Hermitage Avenue—on the south side of Diversey Boulevard. It is said he marketed a very tasty product. But that, so far as this observer is concerned, is pure hearsay.

The record shows that at the time Chicago quit eating sausages he was about fifty-three years old. He was German-born and respected, if not admired, in the German colony where he had lived since his boyhood. He was respected because he was the principal manufacturer of the district. He had been successful in his dealings with the banks. He seemed well on his way to complete success.

But let us not say he was popular. He definitely was not. He was morose and arrogant, and despite a gross, untidy appearance, he fancied himself as a sort of special gift to women. He was about six feet tall and his weight was something like 300 pounds.

His principal associates, proprietors of the neighborhood saloons, didn't like him very much but were civil to him because he had such an admirable capacity for beer. Louisa Luetgert, his wife, was a weary little woman who weighed ninety-eight pounds in the wrapper and hair curlers which she wore most of the time. She was seldom seen on the street except on her way to and from the grocery store.

Louisa never appeared with her husband, and put in her days working about the big house hard by the sausage works. For all the neighbors knew about her she might never have been there at all. And then, on one May day in 1897, she wasn't.

There had been a bit of spicy gossip about her before her disappearance. Early in January, Adolph had gone to see Captain Herman Schuettler at the Sheffield Avenue police station and had asked that the police do something to keep Louisa from running around with other men. Captain Schuettler said that the matter was outside his jurisdiction and mentioned that the sausage maker's own conduct was not above reproach. Adolph departed angrily and was still angry when he got home. He moved out of his house and into a cot in the factory.

A talkative policeman spread the tidings of Louisa's delinquency about the neighborhood amid general disbelief. But Luetgert himself supplied corroborative evidence. He confided to Frank Bialk, his night watchman, that he had intercepted love letters written to his wife by an unidentified admirer. So the scandal circulated while Mrs. Luetgert remained discreetly out of sight. So passed three months while the sausage business slumped and the sausage maker brooded.

The sausage mill had closed down by the first of May. But that, whatever you may have heard about it, wasn't due to thwarted

144

love. Luetgert had been planning to expand his sausage business and had been negotiating with his bank for money required to re-model the old building. Mrs. Luetgert's absence at such a crisis may be ascribed to one of those unfortunate coincidences.

The sausage maker was not entirely lonesome. Kindhearted women came to visit him from time to time in the factory office, particularly a large Palomino named Tillie. In time Mrs. Luetgert was virtually forgotten by the neighborhood and also, apparently, by her husband. . . . But perhaps not by her husband.

On Friday, April 30, Luetgert called one Frank Oderoffsky, bet-ter known as "Smokehouse Frank," and took him down to the vat room in the basement. The room contained four vats, four feet wide, four feet high and eight feet long, in which sausage meat was cooked by means of live steam. On the floor were several hundred pounds of something that looked like rock salt in large lumps. Luetgert directed Oderoffsky to break up the lumps and throw the stuff into Vat No. 1.

"And don't get it on your hands," he cautioned. "It'll give you a bad burn."

So "Smokehouse Frank" paid no attention to the warning and burned his hands. The next afternoon a deputy sheriff came to serve papers announcing that the creditors would take over the sausage mill on Monday morning, May 3. At noon Saturday all remaining workers in the plant, except Bialk the watchman, were paid off. And with that the factory was really shut down.

When Bialk reported for duty about 6:00 P.M. he was surprised to find a roaring fire in the furnaces and a good head of steam on the boilers. Luetgert was in his shirt sleeves and perspiring freely. Bialk got the idea that he had been trying to run the machinery all by himself.

At ten o'clock that night Luetgert sent Bialk to a drugstore six blocks away for a bottle of Poland water.

145

"You had a case of it," said Bialk.

"It's gone," said Luetgert. But it wasn't gone. Captain Schuettler stumbled over it six days later.

The watchman came back with the bottle of Poland water half an hour later. Luetgert sent him out for another one. Bialk, with no further argument, went out to get it. When he returned the second time he found Luetgert clamping the lid on Vat No. 1. The vat was steaming.

"Just an experiment," explained the sausage magnate as he sat down on a chair beside the vat and opened a newspaper. "I'm going to try to use these vats as part of the steam plant."

On Monday morning Luetgert went to the home of his wife's sister, Mrs. Wilhelmina Mueller, and reported that Louisa had disappeared.

"She was with me last night," he said sorrowfully. "But this morning she was gone."

"I can't believe it," protested Mrs. Mueller.

That afternoon Luetgert went to the Sheffield Avenue station and told the same story to Captain Schuettler. The captain, who had been looking into the domestic history of the Luetgerts, figured the story might well be true. But four days later he got another report. Dietrich Bickenese, a brother of Mrs. Luetgert who lived in Bowmanville, came to report that Louisa had planned to come to his home for a two-week visit on Monday.

"But she didn't come," he said. "And she didn't write. And I am afraid that something has happened to her."

The captain went over and found a neighbor who had seen Louisa alive at about ten o'clock Saturday night. He interviewed Bialk, discovered the case of Poland water and located Oderoffsky in a near-by saloon. Oderoffsky told about his burns. Captain Schuettler picked up a few specimens of the mysterious salt from the floor of the vat room and a few hours later had identified it as caustic potash.

He rode over to the old Criminal Court building and reported to State's Attorney Charles S. Deneen that he suspected murder.

"Luetgert brought four hundred pounds of caustic potash into the factory during the last week in April," he said. "And you don't use caustic potash in making sausage. I think he boiled her up in the vat and burned her bones in the furnace."

"Go ahead and see what you can find," said Deneen. And Schuettler moved the bulk of his force over to the factory. As the result of a search that had no letup for two days, they found bone fragments and corset steel in the ashes behind the factory. In the drain under Vat No. 1 they found Mrs. Luetgert's wedding ring, marked with her initials. Then they tried Luetgert for murder on the slimmest evidence of corpus delicti ever established in a Chicago court.

Attorney W. A. Vincent, for the defense, put up a good argument on the grounds that no murder had been proved, that the bone fragments could not be identified as human, that the wedding ring had fallen from Luetgert's own vest pocket as he leaned over the vat while conducting his experiment.

But the somewhat confused jury found Luetgert guilty just the same. He was given a life sentence in Joliet penitentiary, where he died a few years later.

About that time Chicagoans began to dare to eat sausage again. But for years afterward the uninformed little ones of the town continued to sing a gruesome anthem:

> He ground her up
> Into sausage meat;
> And Luetgert
> Was his name. . . .

He hadn't ground anybody up into sausage meat, of course. The plant was closed and no sausage was being made there. If he murdered Louisa, as seems most likely, he murdered her in a simple, usual fashion. He then boiled her up to get rid of the body and destroy the possibility of establishing "the evidence of the crime," the corpus delicti.

This dim-witted sausage maker almost did it. The fact that he was sent to the penitentiary for life instead of taken out and hanged indicates that the jurors probably had some doubts about something.

How Luetgert, with no experience whatever in murder and very little, for that matter, in thinking, could have worked out an almost perfect process for killing his wife is something that nobody so far has explained.

PART IV

INSTITUTIONS FOR OUR
COMFORT AND SAFETY

Chapter 18

The Galloping Fire Engine

THERE has been a movement of late to dust off a lot of old pot-stacked locomotives and roll them out for public inspection. Youngsters carve models of them out of wooden blocks, and a whole literature is devoted to the maintenance of their traditions.

Which, perhaps, is well and good—especially to people who remember when they didn't look comical or small or quaint at all. There was a time when they were rated as the most magnificent machines of a progressive age, but they weren't the only ones entitled to a green memory in this day when we seem to be remembering everything. There were other amazing steam devices that once seemed pretty close to us, entertained us no end, and, no doubt, served us well.

Where, we inquire, are all the old horse-drawn fire engines?

Life can hold few thrills like that of the old-time engine company's dash to a fire. No professional showman worked out its routine, but it presented a spectacle that was never equaled, even by Buffalo Bill's great concourse of risk and wonder.

It had basic suspense: Would the brave fire lads get there on time? It had battle noises—rattle and bang and clanging bells and a thunder of hoofs like the charge of the Light Brigade. It had the wild, headlong speed of the Deadwood Stage pursued by howling Indians—only the cast of characters was somewhat different. The pursuing horde consisted of small boys on foot and adults on bicycles. The harried-looking driver was much the same. So was his assistant who swung a long whip with noises like rifleshots.

You could hear the fire engine coming two blocks away, what with yells and bells and hoofbeats and whipcracks. You ran across lots to meet it and presently saw the kaleidoscope of brass and red that was the engine, and the billowing black cloud and the pillar of flame with which it traveled.

Three broad-chested horses, usually white, pulled this juggernaut. Cool reason now leads us to believe that they were not race horses, but we hesitate to admit it. They were fiery-looking steeds with wild eyes and a plunging gait like merry-go-round horses, only bigger. They looked faster than Bucephalus.

They came down the street abreast, with an archlike collar over the one in the middle, a copy of the hitch favored by the wolf-plagued Russian sleigh riders in the *Fifth Reader*. The driver was usually bareheaded and out of uniform except for a red flannel undershirt. He seemed to be having a tough time holding his plunging team to the course—and no doubt he had. It took muscle to stop them and they needed plenty of room.

There wasn't any modern traffic to contend with—there wasn't much of any kind of traffic—but what there was was enough. It scrambled out of the way as best it could. Looking up the street as the engine came on with an increasing clangor, you could see the buggies and wagons and pushcarts and bicycles breaking against the curbs like bow waves.

No matter how frequently pedestrians beheld this spectacle, there were few who failed to retreat past the sidewalk line, not so much to avoid the galloping fire horses as to make room for the tangle of displaced vehicles. The wiser, more experienced part of the public viewed the proceedings from front porches.

Looking back to determine why this lumbering charge should have been so much more breath-taking than, say, a circus parade or a speeding streetcar or a cavalry drill, the answer seems to lie in the look of the engine and the amazing things it did. The three white horses were magnificent, but for sheer, delirious thrill there was nothing to compare with the convulsions of the shining brass machine as it worked up a steam pressure in transit.

Out of the stack rolled dense billows of pine-scented smoke, presently sparks, and then flames that crackled and roared like a super torch. On a little platform behind the upright boiler a gnome, infrequently noticed in the performance, worked like a monkey on a stick, pouring coal into the open door of the blazing firebox. Though we didn't know much about it, he was really the most important figure in the show. It was his job to have a head of steam up by the time the engine got to the fire so it could throw water high enough to put out fires in flues and attics and other lofty places. And he never failed.

When, thanks to an engineer grandfather, we had learned a few details of the gnome's job we marveled a little at his nonchalance. On the run he never stopped to look at the gauge. He poured on the fuel and opened the drafts and turned on the blower.

A Vesuvius of sparks might menace whole blocks of frame buildings in his wake. But that was not his immediate concern. He was employed to deal with only one fire at a time. With the safety valves getting ready to pop there was always the chance that the whole contraption would blow up. But he never seemed to worry about that either. So far as I know, no engine ever did blow up—at least not on its way to a fire.

Anything from a two-eleven to a four-alarm fire in those days was bound to be a double feature. There would be, of course, a blazing flat building or a hotel or a fair-sized factory. There would be a lot of thrilling business with ladders and streams of water and the still familiar acrobatics of pipemen and rescue squads. A noble lot of death-defying acts, my brother! But in addition to that there would be from six to a dozen pumpers—the glistening engines—all shooting sparks like Roman candles, wheezing and whistling excitedly and giving the show its ultimate zest.

Around the corner in a side street would be the highly polished white horses, still nervous, still wild-eyed, pawing the earth and whinnying as if awaiting only the arrival of girls in spangled tights to start off on an equestrian ballet.

Most Chicago lads over the age of twelve today know the routine of the firehouse. They talk enough about the business of sliding down a brass pole to show that the firemen are still heroes and that their so-called enginehouse retains a portion of its old charm. Unfortunately for him, the modern boy cannot envision the spectacle that is gone because he never knew it was there.

The bell rings . . . the brave firemen leap into their boots and dive for the brass pole. But that is only the beginning. At the strike of the bell the gates of the stalls fly open. The horses come out and march to their places in front of the apparatus. The gnome sticks a light into the firebox of the engine. Down from pulleys on the ceiling flops the harness, squarely where it belongs.

Drivers, moving like a prime drill team, snap a few buckles, leap to their seats and crack the whips. The gnome, still holding the top of his pants with one hand, fans the wad of burning excelsior while, miraculously, he keeps his balance as the wheels begin to roll. The bell clangs. The white horses stick their necks into the collars. Outside the enginehouse the traffic begins to climb the curbs.

It may be a false alarm, but what of that? The excitement rises in a stunning rush. There is color, there is noise, there is movement, there is risk. All is lovely. All is confusion. And the heroes roll on to deeds of high emprise. . . .

They still have fires in Chicago—quite a lot of them, possibly. But artistically there seems to be no need for it.

Chapter 19

The Talented Waffle Man

T<small>HE</small> children of this generation come close to tears when they think of the lovely things I missed when I was young. They mention ice-cream cones, malted milks, sausages baked in a bun, Eskimo Pies, brown cows and Powerhouse candy bars. But somehow I have no regret for all this lost provender. I laugh at them and point out that not one of them tasted that most delectable of all comfits, the Penny Waffle.

Of course there were never any waffles that would compare with those that the nice man in the waffle wagon sold. They were concocted of ambrosia and other choice ingredients (including flour and water—and probably glue and plaster) according to the recipe of a famous French chef. And they retailed for one cent apiece, which put them within the reach of all—or nearly all—the children in our end of town.

There was a legend around the neighborhood that waffle men acquired great wealth and eventually retired to large brownstone houses on Lake Shore Drive. My father didn't think so. He said that most of them probably lived in pretentious establishments in somebody's alley. But everybody else of my acquaintance believed it because no other enterprise in our experience ever aroused so much enthusiasm on the part of the customers.

On the other hand, there is no published record of any individual waffle merchant who ever got a brass-band funeral out of his own mansion. It takes a hundred cents to make a dollar. Raw materials, it is alleged, cost something. A wagon represents an investment. And certainly the waffle man had to feed his horse something beside waffles. Looking back on it, I am convinced that the horse may not have liked waffles—not even his kind.

There is no way now to test the accuracy of a young gourmet's memory of the flavor of the waffle man's waffles. More than half a century of time has gone by. Taste memories are dim and distorted. And the waffle man, rich or poor, went the way of so many of Chicago's pioneer merchants. He did his bit, no doubt, toward the development of the lunch wagon, which too is passing. But lunch-wagon waffles aren't the sort he dealt out to the penny trade of the nineties. Nor is there any hint of his formula in the round, cakelike things that are called waffles on the coffee-shop menus.

The waffle man's waffles were oblong, about two inches by six inches, although they seemed to be larger at the time. They weren't brown and caky. They were generally gray or white—which color was probably due to the powdered sugar with which they were so liberally sprinkled. Once in a while you got one slightly toasted, but that seems to have been only when the manufacturer let his gasoline fire get away from him.

Normally they were white and crisp and delicious, with just a hint of tasty glue at the center. My mother said that they were never cooked—but what did any housewife ever know about penny waffles?

The waffle wagon was a flat vehicle about ten feet long. It had a permanent canopy mounted on six uprights and movable side curtains that could be lowered in case of rain. The kitchen was in front, immediately behind the horse, and the reins crossed it in iron loops suspended from the ceiling. This ingenious driving arrangement permitted the chef to continue his cooking in full flight.

The back of the wagon was the sales department, with a shelf-like counter extending around three sides of it. Receipts were stored in a tin can somewhere on the floor.

The waffle man was one of the least aggressive of the town's merchants. He had no vocal ballyhoo like the banana peddler. He made no house-to-house canvass like the milkman. He did no solicitation at all save to ring a little bell as he came into the block, or sometimes to call in a voice that could hardly be heard across the sidewalk, "Waw-awfuls, fresh Waw-awfuls."

Having completed this preliminary announcement he would pull up to a convenient corner and wait for the world to beat a path to his door—which is what the world did, as soon as it could extract a penny from its mother or a nickel from its father.

He may have been a good businessman, this lad. There are sundry evidences upsetting the theory that he ever amassed any millions. But he had some knowledge of basic psychology. He never wore out his welcome. You'd greet him today in the late afternoon and stand looking sadly after him as his white wagon rolled into the gloom around eight o'clock when the kids were being called in to go to bed. But you'd look for him in vain tomorrow or the day after tomorrow. It might be a couple of weeks before you saw him again, and then he'd be on a different corner down the street.

Sometimes he would stay away for a whole month. The uncertainty of it gave the zest of surprise to his visits and, of course, made the waffles taste all the better. You never had a chance to get tired of them, which probably was a part of the waffle man's lure. But you gave him no credit for his wise maneuvering. You didn't know for years and years that it was possible to get tired of such a delicacy.

Nobody has ever told me where the waffle men came from or where they went. They may have been common to other cities, some of them far away, but I don't know. One day such a man appeared suddenly out of the blue. I can still see him as he stopped his horse almost in front of our door. I couldn't tell what he was making, but I could smell something like burning fat and judged him to be a merchant. I brought my mother out to look at him. She gave me a penny and I ate my first waffle.

I remember, too, the last time I saw him—moving away slowly against the sunset. If I had known that this was to be our final farewell, I should probably have cried all night. Such friends, somehow, are irreplaceable—particularly the ones who sell you something delectable to eat at one cent the copy.

But the waffle man went away and he never came back. He may have gone to the Spanish-American War, he may have made a fortune in the stock market, he may have got a contract to furnish waffles to the army. But, anyway, he was gone. So too, as I discovered when I looked into the matter, were all the other waffle men in town. No solution of this mystery has ever been offered me.

The waffle business wasn't the only mobile enterprise in Chicago—nor the first. Out our way, where the unpaved streets were like isolated lanes to which horses and buggies and wagons came seldom, we had a thriving alley traffic. To uninformed youth it seemed that at least half the men in town were junk dealers.

Babies learned to talk—not well, perhaps, but loudly—listening to the call of these wandering gleaners: "Ray-uggs, ol' eye-urn. Copper an' tin."

The dealers were around every day, fine, independent traders who aroused our envy because they were able to drift lazily through life behind horses while less favored people, their customers, provided them with money. As against that, come to think about it, they, too, may have lived most of their lives in districts far removed from a mansion on the Lake Shore Drive.

They passed through our alley for ten or fifteen years that I know of, and I do not recall a single occasion when anybody ran out to sell them rags or old iron or even to say hello.

One might make a brief note also of the vegetable peddlers. They still circulate a bit out in the far suburbs, but you don't see much of them any more. They were all foreigners, as I recall them, mostly newly arrived Italians. And we liked them.

Their calls were a varied and interesting puzzle, as in the case of the watermelon merchant who was bawling to an astonished world that they were "Fine tee-mee-toes." They were also a humorous lot. They liked children and, on occasion, would give us apples.

It is significant that in those days almost nobody bought vegetables in a grocery store. Francisco or Giovanni would bring fresher ones to your door at a lower price.

We had also a horse-drawn scissors grinder who must have made his money in some other line. The bells on his front axle whanged out the same old Westminster chimes that have been announcing the arrival of scissors grinders for hundreds of years. But they brought him no business. Either nobody had any scissors or nobody wanted them sharpened. He drove through the street like a lonesome sight-seer. He was the last mounted scissors grinder I ever saw, and it occurs to me that his method of locomotion may be what turned the scissors trade against him.

When his horse died, or his wagon fell apart, the infantry scissors grinders came back once more. There was one around the house a couple of weeks ago. This foot troop must have picked up some dimes and quarters regularly during the years or they wouldn't have lived until now. But I must say that the last of the grinders toward whom I have directed this study got no more business than his horse-drawn counterpart of 1896. This one arrived at our house on the day the patent waffle dough stuck to the electric iron.

Chapter 20

Buffalo Steak and Baked Owl

THERE have been many strange restaurants in Chicago, from Kinsley's, where they advertised Buffalo Steak, to Schlogl's, where you were told that you could get Baked Owl. But, come to think about it, aside from Kuntz-Remmler's, none of them set up a fine business with the lure of incidental pearls. And at Kuntz-Rem-mler's this spread of largess, as we were being constantly informed by the newspapers, was no unusual event.

It happened every few months—oftener, if the press agent could find some city editor who hadn't as yet heard about the story. This fine old pearl dispensary and oyster shop stayed in business for many a long year and paid out an estimated $298,725.26 in free gems to blue-plate customers. But apparently this remarkable over-head made little or no difference in the net profits. Fortunately not all the patrons were interested in sea food.

Of course, as any student of marine life in Wabash Avenue res-taurants eventually discovers, the edible oyster never produces any pearls that are worth $6,273 or, for that matter, five cents. A good publicity department, however, has a worth that is far above ru-bies—although you seldom find traces of it in edible oysters either. And Mr. Kuntz or Mr. Remmler, or whoever ran this charming place, certainly realized the value of public relations.

Their restaurant is gone from us now. There came a time when city editors stayed in one town longer than a year. And when that happened nobody seemed to be interested any more in the ro-mance of the lad who forked up a fortune in a seventy-five-cent dish of oysters. But no matter: the old place still attracted the pearl divers after the press notices ran out. It seems that the food was pretty good quite aside from the romance.

Chicago had plenty of good restaurants—or at least unusual res-taurants—in those days. There was a sort of Food Fair in News-boys' Alley (east of Wells Street between Madison and Washing-ton streets) where you could get a hot dog on a bun for two cents and a cup of coffee for one cent. French fried potatoes were two cents a sack. Watermelon in season was a cent a slice, and the slices were twice the size of any restaurant portion of watermelon today.

The cooks worked in cellar doorways, protected from sun and

rain and snow by umbrellas that they furnished for themselves. No professional gourmet ever gave this area a rating in a book about where to dine. But there were no complaints.

Only a few hundred feet from Newsboys' Alley was Billy Boyle's Chop House, rendezvous for the hierarchy of the city hall, an excellent place and, as prices went at the time, generally considered expensive. A sirloin steak, for instance, might cost as much as fifty cents, and a brace of thick lamb chops were thirty-five.

Boyle's was exclusive in a nice way. Without actually throwing anybody out into the alley the management contrived to discourage unwelcome customers from coming back. Service could be delayed. Orders could be misunderstood. Things could be spilled on people's laps. And waiters could be insolent. The unpopular patron could have a tough time.

Despite this attitude toward hungry souls unliked by Boyle, the restaurant was one of the last survivors of an era where the word "service" meant something. There weren't many tables in the place. There were so many waiters that everybody got what amounted to personal attention. And the food—ah yes, the food! Boyle knew good meat. He selected it, aged it and cut it himself. He knew as much about a kitchen as any chef in his employ, and nothing came into his dining room that had not been cooked to order.

They tore down the chophouse to make way for a new hotel. To many it seemed an unfortunate choice.

Over in Randolph Street the Union Restaurant operated in an environment that seemed to have been transplanted intact from a Munich rathskeller. It offered a German cuisine the like of which would have been hard to find anywhere else in the United States.

Wiener Schnitzel Union was the specialty of the house, a veal cutlet cooked in Madeira or something. But its most spectacular presentation was Kalter Aufschnitt, the greatest collection of cold cuts that could be amassed on a tray four feet long and three feet wide. When you called for this species of delicatessen a stalwart waiter staggered in with it, preceded by a muscular bus boy carrying a large oaken stand to rest it on. It was your privilege to take as much of this offering as you wanted. The price was fixed.

You entered the Union through a bar, which was a liability because it was too popular. The reason for this was certainly not the least unusual of the restaurant's features. The building in which the Union operated was owned by a brewery whose smart lawyers had written some odd terms into the lease. One of the agreements was that the restaurant bar would serve only the brand of beer made by the lessors. The beer was pretty good, so that phase of the business made no difference. It was further stipulated, however, that the restaurant would maintain a free lunch in the bar, and that the menu of the free lunch would include all the items served inside to the paying customer.

It is a bit difficult to see how the Union made any money on that sort of basis. Beer cost a nickel, and with a glass of beer any bar customer could sit down to a luncheon that might add up to seventy-five cents. And hundreds of customers did. The restaurant ran on, however, until the end of its lease, which seems to have arrived sometime during the early days of Prohibition. It was a very noble place.

Chicago seems to have become interested in eating places along about the time of the first World's Fair, but not *too* interested. The author of the city guide for the period gave them only a passing mention.

"The city has some of the finest restaurants in the world," he observed, "and more first-class eating houses than any other city. There are 624 restaurants here, located at convenient points along the principal thoroughfares." But he gives the name of none of them. They probably had not learned how to advertise.

The eighties and nineties, if one may credit the survivors of those periods, gave the chefs their best days. The first of the town's great restaurants were hotel dining rooms and, thanks to the rivalry of hotel promoters, were exceptionally good. The Grand Pacific, under the direction of John B. Drake, was known across the country for its food as well as its rooms. And for a long time it was difficult to find a bad meal in the Palmer House, Sherman House, or the Leland, Clifton, Matteson or Windsor hotels. Maybe the elevator service lacked modern perfection in some of these places, and perhaps you had to stand in line for a turn at the bath; but there wasn't much waiting in the dining rooms, and the cooks knew how to cook.

There came a lot of memorable restaurants such as Rector's, Kinsley's, Chapin and Gore's, Quincy No. 9, De Jonghe's, Schlogl's, King's, Thompson's and the Saratoga.

The Richelieu, run by "Cardinal" Bemis in Michigan Avenue, was Chicago's most completely European dining place and nationally famous. Bemis had no liking for mass production in the food business. Everything in his place was cooked to order and carefully served. Despite this ritual you could get a dinner of twenty dishes for a dollar . . . but if you wished to give a banquet, the Richelieu could—and did—put it out on imported plates worth $100 apiece. Bemis was a bit worried about this chinaware. His wife would attend every banquet where it was used; she would wash it and put it away herself.

There were many other places, most of them forgotten now: the Tremont Hotel, the Brevoort, the Briggs House, the outlying Virginia, Del Prado, and Chicago Beach hotels. The customer in those days had the right to protest against bad cooking and improper service, a right that he exercised with great dignity and firmness. But he did not have to complain much about the cuisine and almost never about the décor of the places in which he stopped to eat. Restaurants were quiet as people knew them then. They were spacious. Waiters were numerous—and attentive—and a man who wanted to eat had room, and time, to do it in.

We have gone through some memorable vicissitudes since then. Steam tables, chain-line production, quick turnover, force-feeding, automatic stoves, blue plates and what not have made indigestion a national plague.

John R. Thompson was one of the leaders in the new movement to feed people in a hurry. He had been running a restaurant of the regular order—and a good one—when he figured that by delivering meals to twice as many patrons he could make twice as much money. So he invented the one-arm lunchroom, and that is one of the oddities of pioneering that remains with us intact.

There aren't many places left in town where one is sure of getting a good meal—virtually none in which one can bet on getting a good steak. Cooking, of the sort we used to know, is a matter of odd reminiscence. The leisurely places, except those in hotels experiencing a lull in trade, are gone where the woodbine twineth. The places where a diner can sit down without finding himself in somebody else's lap are difficult, if not impossible, to find.

If one is not too incensed by crowding and bustle and speed and noise, however, he may still find a decent luncheon or dinner. He may find it in a place that seems odd to him, for the survival of a restaurant is generally linked with the policy and preference of some one man. There have been some disconcerting periods for luncheon seekers in the war years. There was one grim time when it was possible for one to get a well-cooked, well-served meal only in some of the railroad stations, some of the hotels and one or two speak-easies.

The choice is wider now, although the railroad stations are still a pretty good average. It is still possible to get no end of vulcanized beef in no end of fancy night spots. You can still buy pepsin pills at the drugstore or eat at home.

Billy Boyle, Kinsley, Leland and Cardinal Bemis, apparently, have gone the way of their restaurants.

Chapter 21

Simply a Drugstore

A**N AD** in the window of McWhosit's drugstore, on the site where Mr. Van Nice, Ph. Reg., used to compile pills and jalap and paregoric, calls attention to a sale of "pocket tool kits," "radio sets," "books," "bathing caps" and similar drugs. It mentions also that the prewar blue-plate lunch is being furnished by the soda fountain at only a slight increase in price.

Looking at it, I recalled the wandering Greek lad whom the war had marooned behind the long bar at Shepheard's Hotel in Cairo and the strange burden of his lament:

"I want to get back to the United States, where you can buy so many things in the drugstores."

Save for the fact that this drugstore around the corner from our old house is the reincarnation of Mr. Van Nice's pioneer pharmacy, it probably wouldn't be worth mentioning. There are few items from hardware to optical goods that you can't buy in it. But what of that? What you can't buy in any drugstore in Chicago is hardly worth looking for. McWhosit's differs from the rest only because it is tonsil-deep in nostalgia—and that is not due to anything provided by the chain that operates it but to the lingering presence of Van Nice himself, dead these forty years.

Van Nice's Pharmacy was more popular with my family than

the drugstore at the Limits or the one near the Ravenswood station on the North Western Railway because it was more modern. That is to say it was lighted by gas instead of oil lamps, and in spite of its somber fixtures and wall decorations it seemed positively festive. With an open flame behind the urns filled with colored water in the window, they could be seen for a couple of blocks on dark nights. Also, which was a matter of considerably more importance, the place had a telephone. You didn't have to walk more than a mile from your house to get a connection with Joe Doakes or some other lad who had a telephone on the other side of town.

In later years the newspapers and texts on political science have had much to say about "public servants," by which they seem to mean aldermen, congressmen, senators, policemen and such. Actually the only public servant I ever knew before I was some twenty years old was Jules Van Nice, the hardy trail breaker who had built this place on the edge of a wilderness called Lake View.

Nobody ever looked on his drugstore as a mercantile establishment operated in hope of profit. To the other hardy pioneers of the community he was a sort of combination doctor and father confessor. The back of his store was a first-aid station. The front end was a sort of club where the neighborhood met while waiting for the Ashland Avenue car.

The story goes that Van Nice came to Chicago straight from a school in New York somewhere around 1888. He had $300, which was a lot of money. It was part of the estate of an uncle who had run a successful brokerage business on the principle that the customer is always wrong, otherwise he wouldn't be a customer. Van Nice invested the money in a frame building, a couple of counters and a stock of pills and opened up for business in 1889.

It was a lonely post. The Indians, it seemed, had only recently moved away. They had been replaced in this charming local scene by a lot of ex-Confederates seeking refuge from the carpetbaggers and their successors who were wandering around the South. The

Sothrons had been established in the Ravenswood district since about 1870. They were fairly close neighbors to Van Nice. But they bought their jalap and arnica and such from a man named Lee, who ran a shop up on Sulzer Road.

Van Nice's shop, as remembered by one who did not see it until several years after the opening, still smelled like what drugstores were generally supposed to smell like—carbolic acid with a faint soupçon of iodoform. Even on bright days it was a dark, forbidding place, with an over-all tint of dark brown unrelieved by the ranks of white china jars. Save for a row of little ports near the ceiling on the north wall, all the light came through the front window which, like most of the store windows of its time, was an aggregation of little panes.

A screen decorated with smoky oval mirrors and somewhat similar to a large hall tree cut off the prescription case at the end of the storeroom. Two plain, dark counters ran down the sides. In front, on the left of the door as you came in, was a showcase displaying "Good Cigars, Five Cents," "Specials, Ten Cents." Across from it was another case filled with toilet soap and such cosmetics as a woman who valued her reputation might possibly buy.

There was plenty of space in the establishment, especially during the daytime when there was seldom anybody present except Van Nice. In later years a lot of young men of the neighborhood used to meet of an evening behind the prescription case to play cards and sample the stock of spiritus frumenti. But that day was a long time in coming.

In the early days mothers bound for town on the Clark Street Dummy used to leave their babies with Van Nice. He was not only the first baby-sitter in Chicago but very likely the best. At first the owners would call for their progeny on the way home. Later, with the aid of a sort of porter known only as "Mr. Pants," he would provide home delivery at a specified time.

He got no pay for this. It was all part of his firm's policy of service.

The telephone, which he installed somewhere around 1896, caused a little trouble for Mr. Pants, who could not distribute babies and telephone messages at the same time. So Van Nice hired a new assistant to take care of this business.

Nobody else in town, apparently, had a telephone. Van Nice used to talk about the day when everybody would have one and all business would be done by a call from the home. Such an idea was too fantastic to get any attention.

The Bell Company officials during 1896 were loudly vocal about the advantages of a "conveniently located pay station in every neighborhood." Van Nice found that his drugstore had turned out to be a conveniently located pay station—convenient for somebody else.

There probably wasn't a ring on the phone during the first year of its presence in Lake View. But business got better in 1897 and 1898. Through the sleet, snow and dark of night—always after his assistants had gone home—the druggist would plod his appointed round to drag somebody to the phone to say hello to Cousin Emil on the Southwest Side. The pleased customer, out of sheer gratitude, might possibly buy a little something, such as a dime's worth of two-cent stamps. . . . Generally he didn't.

Other customers came in "just to look at the city directory. . . . Why haven't you got a later one than this? . . . That's the trouble with these outlying shops. . . . You'd think they were out in the country. . . ."

He would begin the delicate work of weighing out the ingredients of a prescription when somebody would call him on Bell's great invention—somebody who wanted to find the whereabouts of one "George Mmph. . . . You must know him. He's lived out there in Lake View or Bowmanville or Ravenswood or Evanston for a long time."

People came in to light their cigars at his free lighter or to weigh themselves on his free scales.

He put in a line of "drugstore candy"—little hard sugar squares flavored with lime, lemon, cherry, chocolate—just for the children, to whom he handed it whenever they came into the store. He got no money for the candy—only harsh words from mothers who found smears on the darlings' bibs.

He installed a soda fountain just about the time of the Spanish-American War, definitely an innovation in the drug business. Some of his customers got indignant. Drugstores were for drugs, they said. They would take their drug business to a real drug-store. . . .

But this antagonism made no impression on Van Nice.

"There's no money in the drug business," he declared, enunciating a truism that was to govern the industry long after him. "Why waste your time putting pills together when nobody gives a damn about it and the patients get well quicker when you won't give them any medicine? . . . Me, I'm going to sell ice cream and cherry phosphates. . . . And the phone's out of order unless a horse wants to call in from Washington Park."

He died pretty well off sometime around 1915. People said that his service had deteriorated terribly.

Mystery and Crime 4:

The Mysterious Mr. Dove)

THE automobile had been a part of the local scene in one form or another for several years before 1904. It had lost its novelty even with the horses that had viewed its advent with panic. In a city of violent and constant change it no longer attracted the attention of the populace, no matter what may have been the division of popular opinion regarding its worth and permanence. As a subject for conversation it had no more general interest than the steam locomotive or the trolley car. And its comings and goings were seldom given a line in the public prints until the night of November 19 and the affair of the mysterious "Mr. Dove."

You don't have to adjust yourself to envision the opening scene of this melodrama. In the fall twilight Michigan Avenue, in the vicinity of the Auditorium Hotel, looked much as it does today. There were some notable differences: the gloom of a dull night was pierced by widely spaced arc lights instead of incandescent clusters. The Art Institute and its attendant lions bulked from a shifting blackness that blotted out the lake—the smoke of the Illinois Central, whose little steam engines were still shuttling back and forth. The breakwater was unseen beyond the right of way. There was no such thing as Grant Park, no matter what the maps might say.

There were few pedestrians aside from scattering couples headed toward the Studebaker to see Mabel Taliaferro in *Mrs. Wiggs of the Cabbage Patch*. The men might have looked peculiar because ninety per cent of them wore derby hats. But nothing in their appearance would have dated the women. They wore bell-bottomed hats, fitless raglans, and skirts with what was lately known as the "new look" that dragged the ground.

For 8:30 P.M. the street was reasonably quiet save for railroad noises and the clop-clopping of high-steppers taking the town's aristocracy on its important errands. In all the stately parade of carriages there was one automobile—an open Mitchell touring car driven by a young man named William Bate from the garage of Dan Canary in Wabash Avenue. Young Bate, a college graduate and son of the president of the Mitchell Company, had come to Chicago to learn the motor-livery business. He was just about to be killed.

The car stopped in front of the Auditorium, and Bate walked into a lobby made garish by incandescent lamps badly adapted to crystal-hung gaslight chandeliers. He walked to the desk and told the clerk that he had been called by a guest named "Mr. Dove." Mr. Dove appeared while he was still talking. And because Mr. Dove was hiring an automobile and driver, he was observed by everybody within hearing distance. People who traveled anywhere by car in those days, apparently, were worth examination as curiosities.

Mr. Dove was a man of medium height, with dark hair and dark mustache. His clothing, all but a red necktie, was concealed by a long, lightweight, tan raincoat. He was carrying a canvas suitcase.

Bate and a bellboy reached simultaneously for the suitcase, but Mr. Dove said that he preferred to carry it himself. Bate led him out and installed him in the rear seat of the car, cranked the motor, got in under the wheel and drove off to the south. The clerk fixed the departure time at 9:20 P.M.

Quite a lot of people saw the Mitchell between that time and 2:30 the next morning. An automobile on a lonely road in the dead of night was a sufficiently unusual sight in those days to be given attention. But one of the strange features of the case is that nobody saw the car until it passed Nicholas Finley's saloon at Archer Avenue and Forty-eighth Street at ten minutes past ten. The police figured that at a normal rate of speed it should have reached there twenty-five minutes earlier. Ten minutes afterward, near Summit, Bate and Dove stopped at George Welbourn's saloon, had one drink apiece and inquired the best road to Joliet.

Welbourn directed them as best he could in the manner of the period: "Go straight ahead on this road till you come to the 'Y.' Then take the left fork over the bridge two miles. Turn right at the schoolhouse. . . . That'll take you to the Alton track. Turn left along the track five miles . . ." And the rest of it. The road, you may gather, was an unmarked trail with a dirt surface.

The pair, who seemed to be on excellent terms, went out. They passed through Willow Springs at forty miles an hour and were seen by Frank Coler of Banks & Coler's roadhouse. Just beyond the Sag they passed Kirk's roadhouse and were clocked at the same speed by Jim Kirk. At 11:20 they stopped at Fred Seiler's farmhouse. They had been an hour covering twelve and a half miles.

Seiler, aroused by the sound of the car, called out from an upstairs window. The passenger wanted to know: "Is this Kirk's place?"

Seiler said, "No."

The Mitchell pulled out onto the road and continued south.

Peter Freehauf, who lived some six miles farther on, heard the car go by and noted the time. It was two minutes past twelve.

Five minutes later it came to a halt at Dennis Connors' farm three miles beyond Lemont. Connors got out of bed and reached a window just in time to see the car turning around. After some backing and filling, it started north on the Chicago Road.

At 2:30 A.M. a farmer found it in a ditch near Freehauf's farm. "Mr. Dove" was gone. Young William Bate was sitting behind the wheel and slumped over it. He was dead. He had been shot through the head.

The police did what they could do about the matter, which wasn't much. There were a few unexplained bloodstains on the cushions of the back seat. The stains could have been made only by Dove or by some other passenger who had traveled unseen by the numerous witnesses. There was also a scrap of paper on which was a scribbled exercise in short division—23,400 divided by three.

A man in a red tie and tan overcoat walked into Julia Hauser's boardinghouse in Joliet on the afternoon of November 20 and rented a room. But by the time Mrs. Hauser had heard of the murder he had disappeared. And that is just about as close as the law ever came to picking up the trail of the lost Dove.

The senselessness of the killing, even more than the fact that it had been done in an automobile—that it was probably the first automobile murder in the world's history—aroused Chicago as few crimes have ever done. The suggestion that the chauffeur had been shot in an effort to collect his fare seemed preposterous. Physical evidence tended to show that the car had been stopped or slowed down until it was barely moving at the time of the murder. If "Mr. Dove" had wanted to avoid paying his fare, he could have got out and walked away—as indeed he did anyway. Young Bate had answered a routine call to meet a man he had never seen or heard of before. The murderer's motive, whatever it was, had developed between 9:20 P.M. and 12:15 A.M.

Detectives thought for a time that the problem in division might indicate a three-way split of loot totaling $23,400—an intriguing theory but, like everything else in the case, incapable of proof. Nobody, so far as the police could learn, had lost $23,400. Nobody had appeared in the cast of characters to claim a third of it.

Who was "Mr. Dove"?

Why did he want to go to Joliet? Or did he?

Why did he carry a suitcase in an automobile as far as Connors' farm?

Why did he murder a stranger?

Most people who figured in the mystery are dead, including, most likely, the mysterious "Mr. Dove." But the current crop of policeman don't like very much to be haunted by ghosts out of the improbable 1900s. They'd like to be told the answers, even after forty-eight years.

PART V

THE THEATER
AND ALLIED
ENTERTAINMENT

Chapter 22

Punch Versus Judy

O_NE_ of my small nephews looked up from his comic book the other day to commiserate with me about the sad lack of interesting things in the days of my childhood.

Somebody had told him that in those dark ages there weren't any comic books—which is not quite the truth—and that, furthermore, there weren't any such things as radio, automobiles, airplanes, speedboats, ice-cream cones, moving pictures or television. All of which inventory is correct except that we were just beginning to get the first short, flickery movie.

From the point of view of the lad born around 1940 it must appear that we were only a step away from the sod-shanty period of pioneering and that aside from fighting Indians we must have had a pretty dull time of it. All I can say in answer to that is that it didn't seem so. After the Indian battles, when we had cleaned up the old squirrel rifle and curried the mustang and baked our simple prairie meal of corn pone on a flat rock over a fire of twisted hay, we found time and opportunity for quite a lot of amusement.

One of the advantages that we had over the modern child was the exchange rate on small wampum. Every now and then you could contrive to get a penny, and, believe it or not, there were things you could actually buy with pennies—any number of things.

We didn't have ice-cream cones. We didn't see much of ice cream until late in the nineties. But we could buy red pop for three cents a bottle at the grocery store. Sometimes we could get the large economy size for two cents. We could get penny waffles—on most days. We could get sugar buns at the bakery, a different kind every day. And the amount of molasses candy you could buy for a penny was amazing—or maybe our hands were smaller in those days.

Candy, of course, is no novelty to my small nephew. But he will never be able to lay in a supply for the price we paid for ours. He will never have the thrill of buying a waffle made to order in a wagon pulled by a real horse. He'll probably never make molasses taffy in his own kitchen and pull it till it gets to be black or white, depending on the color of his hands. He'll probably never even learn how to make fudge.

We didn't have a radio. But eventually we had phonographs and four or five records which we could play whenever we liked and over and over again until they, or our mother's patience, wore out.

We didn't have five-reel movies. But we had "Real Life Dray-ma" at the Howard Theater that was every bit as exciting and twice as natural. We had periodical "magic shows" whose programs in later years included a few movie subjects. The "Real Life Dray-ma" was as long as such shows usually are. The magic business lasted only about an hour and fifteen minutes, the length of time one could sit comfortably in a hard-bottomed undertaker's chair. Anyway it was long enough. Perhaps, as time went on, we might have had a three-feature magic show. But, unfortunately, such a thing had been given no thought when a change in juvenile thought laid the magicians away with the old phonograph records and the penny waffles.

We didn't have automobiles when we were babies. But we got

around, and it was always easy to hitch a ride on the milkman's bobsled in winter.

Maybe we didn't have television, I might tell my small nephew, but we did have itinerant Punch-and-Judy shows off and on the whole year round. And did this critical young man ever see a Punch-and-Judy show? Did he ever weep for the harried heroine or gasp his appreciation for the magnificent drama of the piece? He did not.

The Punch-and-Judy operators would wander about in the open during the summer. They would canvass the neighborhood for contribution before they set up their pitches. Presumably they did fairly well at it, for they came back as continually as the non-monkey organ grinders. The with-monkey organ grinders moved in a wider orbit. You seldom saw one of them oftener than a couple of times a year.

Punch and Judy, and all their gaudy associates, as my nephew would probably have to be told, were wooden puppets worked by a single operator behind a screen. Punch was what you might call the hero of the drama, if it had any. He was also the husband of Judy.

The plot was fairly simple but quite direct. Inasmuch as all members of the cast talked like parrots—thanks to a reed in the operator's mouth—it was a little difficult to follow their conversation. But the words, as a matter of fact, didn't make any difference at all. Judy was nagging her stalwart husband, and everybody else who took part in the action was trying to do him in.

So, with wild applause from the gentle children in the audience, he murdered Judy and all sorts of other strange beings until overtaken by Death in the end. It was probably a highly moral presentation, if anybody had stopped to think about that. Nearly everybody of my acquaintance went to see the Punch-and-Judy exhibit as often as it came around. It was a sort of social event.

In wintertime the Judy shows were seldom independent. They

were part of magic shows, generally presented in some hall near the school and always indoors.

I do not know why, but such halls—rambling, drafty assembly rooms—were always to be found near schools. These magnificent places probably had been built for lodge use—or maybe by the producers of magic shows. Anyway, they were always available and the magicians, who were usually husband and wife and a helper named Malvolio, would rent them.

A day in advance of the performance these wonder workers would visit the schoolyard at morning recess time and work their greatest wonder. They would make several hundred kids aware of miracles to be shown after tomorrow's classes for a mere pittance. They would distribute cards: "This card and ten cents will admit bearer to The Greater Peccadillo Magic and Cinematographic Company's Stupendous Carnival of Mystery. . . . Caribou Hall. . . . 3:45 Thursday afternoon."

So that evening you would work some preliminary magic on your parents and get the required dime. Next afternoon when school let out you would run all the way to Caribou Hall in order to get a seat up in front. The hall was generally cold enough to make an overcoat fairly comfortable. The seats were always undertaker's portables. But the show was certainly entertaining and educational, and certainly worth a dime.

The he-magician would open the program with a repertoire of card tricks. The she-magician would then strap herself into a sort of shoulder brace that held a harmonica in front of her face. After that she would play the harmonica and an accordion at the same time. For an encore she would reach greater heights of performance by whanging a drum with her foot. Joe Cook later tried this trick, but he required the assistance of "Four High-Wy-Ans."

Then the he-magician took a lot of things out of a plug hat which he furnished for himself after nobody in the audience seemed to have one. He did a lot of amazing things with a set of

182

steel rings. He poured ink, milk and water out of the same bottle. And he made the she-magician disappear out of a locked
trunk.

After this there was an intermission while the assistant named
Malvolio went around selling the regular Four Dollar Greater
Peccadillo Magic Packet for five cents. I always bought one of
these mysterious packages and always got a collection of cardboard
nickels and other stage money and several sheets of instructions
on how to make it disappear.

At the end of the intermission the he-magician put on the movies. He did the best he could to darken the hall by pulling down
the curtains, but it was still pretty light when a brilliant white
square appeared on the screen and began to wander around trying
to locate itself.

It would seem impossible to project moving pictures—any kind
of moving pictures—on such a screen under such conditions today.
Maybe the projection light was brighter; maybe the film was thinner. Maybe our eyes were better.

Anyway, these movies were excellent. The finest magic in the
whole show. We were seeing a new magic being born and knew
it was magic. My nephew takes it for granted, really nothing in
itself.

The white square would fiddle about the screen. The magician
would continue to try to get the place dark. Then eventually, just
about the time the kids began to whistle and stamp their feet, the
bright light was switched off. A sort of gray blur took its place
and then, so help me, there were the movies. They glow in the
memory as if I saw them for the first time yesterday.

"I count them over ev'ry one apart. . . ."

There was a blacksmith in his Sunday clothes, including a satin-
backed vest, going through the motions of shoeing a horse. The
he-magician explained this costume. The blacksmith hadn't understood what the photographer wanted, he said. The photog-

rapher said that he wanted to take a moving picture of the smith and smithy to show how a horse is shod. The blacksmith understood only that somebody was going to take a picture, and he remembered that for picture-taking the subject ought to look his best. All of that made no difference to us.

The ornate blacksmith put some iron on his forge, heated it up, gave it a considerable beating on the anvil and then attached it to the horse's hoof. This business didn't seem at all prosaic to us. The pictures were moving, weren't they? Most of us were looking at the cinema for the first time in our lives and we didn't care a hoot about what happened to the people pictured there. It was the movement that interested us—only the movement.

When the horseshoeing was finished the he-magician announced another remarkable cinematographic triumph. We sat through a thrilling race between two high-wheeled bicycles. Here was more movement—wild movement. Some of us had seen races between high-wheeled bicycles and knew how they generally finished. Perhaps we were waiting for the certain spill and the rush of the doctors and the arrival of the ambulance. But even when this contest ended with no accident whatever we were satisfied. Even had both riders been thrown and killed they would still have been minor attractions. The picture was the thing. The movement of the picture was beyond description.

There were other things like that before the end of the show. We had about thirty feet of a good horse fair and maybe fifty feet of new-looking buggies on some drive in New York. We had another twenty-five feet of a bathing beach. And then the climax: a railway train—an express train—came rushing at us head on. I didn't get my breath for three minutes.

Well, maybe you can see why we weren't so severely bothered by the absence of radio, television, ice-cream cones and the rest. We didn't miss the plot in these pictures brought to us by the magic show. There had been no shootings, kidnapings, social prob-

184

lems, love interest or other falderal. But we had had an experience such as my blasé nephew doesn't get in any moving-picture theater today. We had had a Thrill.

We hadn't believed that a moving picture could really move and we had seen that it could. We had seen a great miracle. Our world had changed because a blacksmith in a shiny vest had stiffly swung his hammer.

The trouble with my nephew is that almost since the time when he first opened his eyes he saw everything—movies, planes, automobiles, television. Up to now he has never seen the beginning of anything.

With us it was different. We had been skeptical about moving pictures—and there, all at once, we had seen them move.

The other magic of the magic show may have been pretty remarkable, and some of it undoubtedly was. But in comparison it didn't amount to anything.

Chapter 23

To Die a Thousand Deaths

ALONG with so many other viewers-with-alarm I am saddened at times by the thought of what so-called progress has done to the opportunities which the nineties spread so lavishly at the feet of eager youth.

Admittedly the kids nowadays have plenty to occupy their time, what with movies, baseball, basketball, hockey, playgrounds, swimming pools, skating rinks, juke boxes, lotteries and television in saloons. But to me, and I shall confess to a certain bias in the matter, their loss seems greater than their gain. Never will one of them know the thrill of pushing the Midnight Express at a theoretical sixty miles an hour across the stage at Howard's Theater— or the Criterion or the Alhambra—or the surge of emotion at turning the cardboard buzz saw on which the beautiful heroine is about to be cut up into neat lengths of two-by-four.

In the spring of the year in my day, few of the eighth-grade boys ever got home from school until just before dinnertime. If anybody had asked us the reason for the delay we should have said we were watching a man make things. This was truth—and all truth—so far as it went, but it lacked enough detail to make it a complete explanation.

186

As a matter of fact, we were simple moths lured by the glamorous brilliance of the *theater* as evolved by Lincoln J. Carter. Just as surely as our little girl classmates who wanted to play Dorothy in *The Wizard of Oz,* we were stage-struck—although not quite in the same way.

The scenery port of Howard's Theater, where first I became acquainted with the inside of drama, gave onto Lincoln Avenue, a couple of hundred feet south of Belmont Avenue. On the balmy afternoons of days when there was no matinee it was quite likely to be standing open.

From the threshold you could look straight across the dimly lighted stage, a mysterious bourn whose bright fringe emphasized the blackness of the empty auditorium. On the stage the scene makers and stage carpenters plied their fascinating trade.

There are circumstances, of course, in which a small boy might have looked in on this unusual business without feeling the urge to become an actor—if, when first discovered, the stage carpenter had been contriving a floral arch, for instance, or screens of that tinsel claptrap so essential to musical comedy.

First impressions are what determine careers. But in my case I got something more than a first impression. Rather, I should call it a revelation. The man was making a life-sized locomotive. Hardly knowing what I did, I walked in and asked him if he needed any help.

"Sure," he said. "You can hold this damned headlight and give it to me when I ask you for it." It was as simple as all that.

Your present-day eighth-grader, surfeited with sensational newsreels and superduper spectacles in technicolor, cannot possibly know what sort of thing was this Ten-Twent-Thirt melodrama in that brilliant period just before its crash. Probably he wouldn't like it anyway. But we were children who took our art where we found it and looked upon it with yearning, not to say love.

By then we knew the movies. They had come a long way since

the little magic-show reels. And there were four or five store-front theaters in the neighborhood, complete with undertakers' chairs and piano, where you could see the latest two-reel dramas and help to sing the illustrated song besides.

But we were too blasé, or not quite blasé enough. We looked upon these upstart exhibitions as something greatly inferior to such active and noisy productions as Willie Live in *Across the Pacific,* or such heart-satisfying works as *Nellie the Beautiful Cloak Model.*

These melodramas talked. They moved. They were alive. Also they were cluttered up with train wrecks, Gatling-gun battles, sinking ships, storms at sea and catastrophic affairs that were tangible and right where you could get a look at them.

If you are old enough you may remember "the real *Fifteen Horsepower* automobile" that crashed into a conservatory to save the girl in *Black Jim's Revenge.*

Thousands of people are still alive who cheered the horse race— "With Actual Horses"—at the great climax of *In Old Kentucky* at McVicker's Theater, and fainted when the heroine swung herself across a chasm two feet deep on a conveniently suspended rope.

There was a falling elevator in *Nellie the Beautiful Cloak Model,* a slack-wire escape from a burning building in *Broadway After Dark,* a race between an automobile and a train in *The King and Queen of Gamblers.*

Raymond Raymond, as Willie Live in *Across the Pacific,* anticipated Violin-Case Hunt a couple of decades by carrying around a Gatling gun in a suitcase.

Besides the much favored buzz saw, many other implements of violent death tended to make the heroines of melodrama a poor insurance risk. There was the neat process of pulling a lady apart with papier-mâché elephants in *Maid of India,* collapsing walls and exploding mines in *Convict No. 1109,* a disintegrating river steamer in *Ace Diamond of the Mississippi.*

The snowstorm in *East Lynne* led through suitable meteorological changes to a hurricane in *Pirates' Treasure* and a roaring flood in *Old Ohio Home,* all of which were rendered negligible by a five-eleven forest fire in *Girl of the Timberlands.*

An auto leaped the gap of an open drawbridge in *No Mother to Guide Her.* A somewhat eccentric rescuer rode a horse along the track of an elevated railroad hotly pursued by a couple of cars in *All for Love.*

Some competent critics held that the high point in scenic illusion was reached when the battleship *Maine* was blown up—not in Havana harbor, as you may have supposed, but on the Criterion stage. This local explosion was to make a Roman holiday for customers who had come to view *With the Roughriders in Cuba.* But I doubt the justice of the award.

There was still the midnight express train in *The Midnight Express.* And I have always considered that as the motive power of the engine on this terrifying train I achieved my greatest dramatic success. The deafening applause of an audience lifted from its seats still rings in my ears. Phooey on your bursting battleships!

My opportunity came quickly after I had been commissioned to hold the headlight by the stage carpenter of Howard's Theater.

"Look," he said when I had completed my technical task. "Maybe I got a good job for you . . . pays fifty cents. Can you push this thing fast?" He pointed to the beautiful locomotive and I gave him a satisfactory demonstration.

"Fine," was his encouraging comment. "I'll show you what you got to do. We're shorthanded. Be here tonight—seven o'clock."

I don't remember what the play was about. I don't know that I ever saw it. The harrowing life of the heroine, her numerous escapes and the unshaking malignity of the villain were all preliminary to the great dash of the Midnight Express. I waited, thinking of nothing save this great climax as I stood by the fine

189

engine in the wings. My hands were sweaty, my head reeling.

Suddenly I heard as from a long, long distance the beating of the drums. In slowly increasing volume they heralded the approach of the express from some mountains that I judged to be about two blocks west of Ashland Avenue.

With magnificent calm I took my place inside the locomotive in front of what was called "the pushing bar." My moment was at hand. It was a matter of seconds now. The train was rapidly approaching. It was here. I hardly heard the snapped command of some property man and I was on my way. I pushed ... and the audience responded ... there was an ear-stunning burst of cheers.

The rest of the train, which had been folded up like an accordion to save space, began to unravel behind me to be refolded as we reached the opposite side.

I emerged beaming as the curtain came down, received my fifty cents and looked at the clock. I could hardly believe my eyes. I stepped out through the scene port into Lincoln Avenue and ran, and ran, and ran. With no locomotive to push I was able to run considerably faster.

It was eleven o'clock when I burst into the front hallway of our home and my parents asked me where I had been.

Somewhat breathless, I told them. "I have been running the Midnight Express," I said truthfully. Then I felt the sudden touch of my mother's hand on my forehead. She was trying to find out if I had a fever.

What happened then is a vague memory.

Chapter 24

The Good Show

Fʀᴏᴍ its earliest days as a city, Chicago seems to have been a good theater town. Rice's Opera House was opened in 1847. It wasn't such a remarkable place, but it was the best in the neighborhood. Junius Brutus Booth, father of the lad who was one day to assassinate Lincoln, played Richard III in it in 1848.

Mooney's Museum was running in 1849. And a gladsome place that was. It got some glorious acts. Adelina Patti, then aged seven years, sang in it in 1850.

Uranus Crosby completed a new opera house and was presenting philharmonic programs in it in 1850. It is said that quite a few of his audience knew what the music was about. McVicker's started business in 1862, during which year John Wilkes Booth was the principal attraction.

In 1891, John Flinn, local historian, wrote:

It is said by those who have made a study of the matter that there are more places of amusement open daily and nightly in Chicago than in any other city on the globe.

Chicago in recent years has become a dramatic center of the first rank. Many new plays are produced here every season for the first time. The stamp of Chicago approval assures the success

191

of a drama throughout the whole country. Architecturally, the amusement houses in Chicago are the best in the United States.

The Auditorium, opened in 1889 by Madame Patti, who had grown a bit older no doubt, was the grandest of show places. Thanks to the engineering genius of Louis Sullivan, who built it, it still is one of the most perfect theaters acoustically in the country. Looking over the press reports of its opening, one is struck by a modesty—almost a reticence—about the things that made it important. But it must be remembered that this was really the age of good theaters. In the late seventies and early eighties not a single pre-Fire playhouse was left in Chicago. Modern ideas, and one must say good ones, had gone into the rebuilding of those the Fire had wiped out.

Hooley's (later Powers'), in Randolph Street between La Salle and Clark streets, had tried to set a new standard in entertainment. "The Parlor Home of Comedy," they called it in those days. And in a procession of plays by Bronson Howard, William Gillette, William Clyde Fitch, Charles Hoyt, Augustus Thomas and James A. Herne it justified the boast during the nineties and well into the new century.

To this theater came Maude Adams in *The Little Minister* and *Peter Pan,* Mrs. Leslie Carter in *The Heart of Maryland,* Blanche Bates in *Naughty Anthony,* Julia Marlowe in *The Countess Valeska,* John Drew in *The Squire of Dames,* Ethel Barrymore in *Trelawney of the Wells.*

Many a time when I was considering the condition of the latter-day stage as a hired reviewer I found it easy to recall every one of them. Not that the plays at the turn of the century were great and lasting drama. You run upon most of them now only in obscure collections. But there is no doubt that great actors presented them. And, in the case of the Hooley-Powers programs, theater-wise managers booked them.

Changes were coming into the drama. Over on the North Side at the Criterion Theater, Lincoln J. Carter was beginning to produce the melodramas that were to the theater of the day what the comic strip is to current literature. Since the success of the widely advertised *Black Crook,* which, by the way, was the opening attraction at "Hooley's Parlor Home of Comedy," great scenic extravaganzas had replaced the old-time musical comedy. They were amazingly impressive.

I recall that I wept when, at the age of seven, I was taken to see *Robinson Crusoe.* My childish heart probably was awed at the stupendous beauty of it all, and likewise I was incensed because somebody had fumbled his attempt to blow up a man-size property parrot with a firecracker. During my adolescent years I saw *In Old Kentucky* at McVickers every Christmas week. I cannot now explain why, except that it is possible to make a habit out of almost anything.

The Windsor Theater, at Clark and Division streets, was one of the better new playhouses. I was first taken there at the age of eight to contemplate an offering entitled *The New Woman.* I liked the theater all right; they sold candy in the lobby. But the drama bored me to literal grief.

This time I cried with purpose until my sympathetic aunt, who didn't like *The New Woman* either, took me over to Kohl and Middleton's museum to look at the assorted wonders.

Central Music Hall, northeast corner of Randolph and State streets, was offering concert programs. The Grand Opera House, after several reincarnations at its present site, was producing a pleasant brand of modern comedy.

There were several variety theaters: The People's, on State near Congress; The Park, in the same block; Lyceum, on Des Plaines Street between Madison and Washington streets; Litt's Standard, Halsted at Madison Street; Jacobs' Clark Street Theater, Clark Street near the bridge; and the Waverly, Madison at Throop

Street. The vaudeville of the period, despite all this opportunity given it for display, was not very good.

Havelin's, on Wabash Avenue between Eighteenth and Twentieth streets, was a good spot where you could see less sophisticated offerings than those usually on display at Hooley's. I seem to recall such things as *Rip Van Winkle* and some version of Sherlock Holmes. The theater was a success, despite its odd location.

The Chicago Opera House, at the southwest corner of Clark and Washington streets, never had a bad season from the day it opened until the day they tore it down. It is linked in my mind with two productions, Hanlon's *Superba,* the greatest of all pantomimes, and *Captain Careless,* which I, apparently unsupported by anybody else in town, judged to be the funniest musical ever written.

Superba, with a cast of acrobats and a couple of carloads of scenery, brought effects to the stage that had never before been considered possible. Its climax came when a life-size locomotive tore through the backdrop, came charging toward the audience and eventually hung suspended over the heads of the terrified patrons. I still see it in my sleep.

The Chicago Opera House was playing vaudeville in 1902. As I mentioned to my mother when I got home, the bill was amazing; but looking back on it I don't seem to remember much except that May de Sousa, "Operatic *Cantatrice,* late of *The Chaperon"* and famed introducer of Bathhouse John's "Dear Midnight of Love," was one of the widely advertised performers. She sang a couple of little numbers like "After the Ball" and "Go Fly a Kite" and "Ireland Is the Spot That I Call Heaven." The words escape me and also the tunes. But I can assure you that they had none of the charm and verve of the Bathhouse John composition. I was really disappointed in May de Sousa, but that was probably because I had expected so much of her. I knew her great capabilities.

194

The end of the bill was "The Kinedrome—Greatest of All Moving Picture Machines," and I am still conscious of the effort I made to be kept there by my grandfather for the second show so that I could see it again. It was exhibiting a little number called *The Great Train Robbery,* which I think was the most thrilling exhibit I had ever looked at. Grandpa was firm, however. He said he had looked at enough train robbery. So he went home.

I am aware, now, that I was looking at the real beginning of the Motion Pictures in America. Until somewhere around 1900 the movies were merely detached studies of blowing flowers, blacksmiths shoeing horses, passing trains or buggies or wagons, people waving greetings to one another and that sort of stuff.

The Great Train Robbery was different; it had a plot. It had scenes and actors and dramatic suspense. In the end the villain was defeated and right stood up in triumph and everybody cheered. All of this lasted fifteen minutes or thereabouts, but it was a very laudable and stimulating presentation. In recollection I feel no wonder that I forgot the words of May de Sousa's songs.

The Masonic Temple Theater was putting out a dozen acts of vaudeville in 1900. The management, under J. J. Murdock, was obviously attempting to make every ticket buyer comfortable, happy and contented. "Umbrellas loaned free to our patrons," read an advertising note at the top of the program. "Deposit fifty cents and return umbrella within one week in same condition and your fifty cents will be refunded at box office."

"Bargain Matinee, twenty-five cents," read another intriguing notice. And then, just before the list of performers, this little gem from the Chicago *Evening Post:* "Ladies—the prettiest, wisest, and most charming women take their hats off in the theater."

The bill then mentioned two musical numbers by Martin's Temple Orchestra, and there was another warning. It was a bit tougher: "Notice—Ladies will please be kind enough to remove their hats during the performance so as to comply with an ordinance passed by the city council. Those failing to comply will be requested to do so by an usher."

There was also a bit announcing that children in arms would not be permitted in the theater during afternoon or evening performances. When they could get in was not specified, but as I recall the programs it made no difference anyway.

Floradora, I remember, played at McVickers in January 1903. It probably wasn't the greatest cast ever seen locally in *Floradora.* I don't recall any of the actors who appeared in it, but it was a wonderful thing of sunshine and music. I remember going out of the theater into the cold and the snow. And I'm not likely to forget the trip home on a Clark Street cable car. But it also comes back to me that I brought home a bit of sheet music that was played around our house for quite a long time.

My mother wasn't so interested in it. "What did you buy this for?" she inquired a bit acidly.

"Because it is very beautiful and I liked it," I answered her. And she looked at me curiously.

"I don't see why," she said.

And in retrospect I don't know exactly why either.

The piece of music was entitled "Oh, Tell Me, Pretty Maiden." Come to think of it, it doesn't seem so exceptional.

Superba, with a whole collection of Hanlons tumbling about the stage, came to the Great Northern Theater that same year. I went to see it, of course. I never missed a chance to see *Superba* or *Fantasma* whenever they lifted a curtain in town. Neither of these great pantomimes ever changed, but there was never any lack of novelty in them. I suppose that in a way they were the predecessors of the silent moving pictures. Nobody said anything in them. But everybody moved, and continued to move, from the first moment of them to the last bow. I used to get up from my seat completely dizzy and almost unable to tell where I wanted to go.

196

That same year brought another brand of nonsense called "Weber and Field's delightful musical travesty *Fiddle Dee Dee,* a potpourri of dramatic falderal in two scenes." I must say that I was not too bright about this one. I had sat through about an hour and a half of it before I discovered that Weber and Fields were not in the active cast. Their parts in this dramatic falderal had been taken by C. William Kolb and Matt M. Dill, later known to the trade as Kolb and Dill. I guess they were pretty good—but, of course, they weren't Weber and Fields.

One thing that impressed me as I sat in some confusion trying to decide whether or not I ought to start out for home was that it took a lot of people to make a potpourri of dramatic falderal in two scenes. There were at least half a brigade of girls in all sorts of costumes, most of them sedate. There was an orchestra of some sixty pieces in the pit. There were strings of dancing boys, singing boys, tumbling boys, and boys just posing to make scenery; but anyway, probably a couple of hundred people and perhaps a carload of scenery had been landed in Chicago and carted to the Great Northern just for this exhibition. You'll probably never see its like around here again. Maybe now nobody cares.

I suppose childhood was just about finished for me when *The Wizard of Oz* came around to the Grand Opera House in 1906. I thought it was lovely and, for that matter, still do. Everybody in the performance seemed much more beautiful, much more real, much grander than the odd collection I had been following from time to time for some ten years. Mona Desmond was Dorothy, David Montgomery was a Tin Woodman, and Fred Stone was a Scarecrow. I should presently have to be going back to school—to school in Kansas, where Dorothy was picked up by the cyclone—and I felt somehow that I would never see such beauty again. Somehow, I felt, Chicago would probably be gone away when I came back . . . and, in a way, I was right.

The advertising in some of the old programs is increasingly in-

197

teresting. In 1902 the Louis Weber Company, of 113 East Harrison Street, was picturing a couple of well-dressed men in tight pants, wearing hats that looked as if they were about to take wing. You could buy these neat outfits and pay for them "while wearing the clothes at $1 a week." I wonder if anybody ever did. Ladies' skirts were being advertised for five dollars by the Ladies' Custom Skirt Company, 183 East Madison Street. The lady in the line drawing was hanging onto her hat and an umbrella and looked quite impermanent.

The Hub, a department store that is still extant, presented a full-page picture of a brawny-looking gent in loose fitting pants, a somewhat small derby hat and a coat that looked something like a smoking jacket. This ensemble, one was told, could be dragged away for thirty-five dollars—the whole business. The Washington Shirt Company was sounding the drums for its dollar shirt, a nifty bargain with detached collar and cuffs.

There was one fine spread for the "Saratoga Restaurant and Oyster House at 155 Dearborn Street, opposite National Bank." The attraction of this fine eating place was "sixteen supper-room boxes, opera-box style." It was mentioned that there was a carriage entrance at the rear.

Gold mines were freely advertised in these programs of amusements, probably for contrast. The Mount Shasta Gold Mines Company stocks were going to make everybody rich day after tomorrow. "A hundred dollars invested in Calumet and Hecla stock," read this half-page of information, "realized $154,600." And nobody would say that such a yield had not been pretty good. Right across from the Mount Shasta call to fortune was the drawing of an iron maiden in suitable pose. But this was a more familiar bit of news. A corset company was offering a straight front, bias-gored girdle for $2.75, and who would be without one. . . . It had no brass eyelets.

Well, that gives you an idea of what sort of a world I was leav-

198

ing when I went out of Chicago in 1906. It was the sort of place where you could go to see Hanlon's *Superba* once in awhile, or buy some stock like Calumet and Hecla for a dollar and stand to make a couple of hundred thousand dollars. You could buy Berry's caramels for eighteen cents a pound. You could telephone by relays to almost anywhere. You could ride to the West Coast "on the Overland Limited which gets into California on the fourth morning."

You could also get a ticket at a theater by asking for it at the box office an hour before the performance.

A paradise, my brothers, a paradise.

Chapter 25

Old Jokes Never Die

I<small>T IS SAID</small> glibly that television is going to revive vaudeville and, glory be, this may be true!

Certainly no connoisseur is going to deny that this most modern of miracles has revived some of vaudeville's most popular jokes.

Television, we hear, is going to bring "new and undreamed-of possibilities for entertainment in the home"—possibilities for entertainment which, one supposes, will not be confined to the broad scenic panorama of wrestling matches and amateur performers on bagpipes and mouth organs.

It is going to bring the great outdoors—the mountains, the plains and the roaring oceans (along with the neighbors' children)—right into the living room. And your old armchair traveler will be able to wander in a few seconds from the Taj Mahal to the Sitka Fish Cannery without getting off his cushion. It is going to be a very interesting world, thanks to television. But then, one remembers, thanks to one thing or another, it was always going to be that.

There were quite a lot of intellectual diversions in Chicago in the days when I was first able to notice such things—drama circuses, pageants, pantomimes, tableaux, cycloramas, dime museums,

200

penny arcades and such—diversions well within the tolerance of your Aunt Fanny and just as interesting as any you might find in the whole country.

Vaudeville had reached its finest development and you could look at it in half a dozen theaters for ten, twenty or thirty cents, depending on what kind of seat you wanted. These theaters, known for obvious reasons as "Ten-Twent-Thirts," gave you as part of the regular program such moving pictures as so far had been loosed on the world. Whether you identified them as Kinetobiophusanimatographs or the Motiographs or merely the "Flickers," they didn't seem like much of a menace or much of an entertainment. Children are the supreme realists. When they had spent years of their lives watching trains moving and horses running and neighborhood comedians making silly faces, they weren't much overjoyed to see the same things on a moving-picture screen—after they grew accustomed to pictures moving at all.

It wasn't until "legitimate" theaters all over town began to close their doors that anybody began to remember what the seers had said about the cinema. The movies were bringing into the outlying residence districts, if not into the living room, "unlimited possibilities for entertainment," while they were giving the kiss of death to some of the things that television is going to revive.

We were pretty skeptical in 1908 about a plan to pipe music into the home over the telephone wires. In the first place, this treat came over the Automatic Telephone system—presently to be absorbed by the Bell Company—and nobody in our end of town had an automatic phone.

In the second place, such a broadcast put out an end result worse than that of the current phonographs, which was pretty bad. We laughed at the unintelligible squawks of the device as applied to a paging system in a downtown hotel. And it was going to be quite a long time before we would hear of a man called Lee De Forest. At the moment, Lee De Forest was cooped up in a West

Side rooming house experimenting with what he called a three-element vacuum tube.

So after a while radio came along to bring what they called entertainment into the living room; and after that the moving pictures learned to talk; and somebody began to unveil theaters in Chicago that had been dark for thirty years.

It has always been the idea among purveyors of so-called amusement that change brings improvement. The notion is not indigenous with them. It seems to have originated with people who found that you could improve bad merchandise with good advertising. Such were the salesmen who weaned the American market away from the Jersey sweet potato and made us eat yams. They made a more durable watermelon by breeding out the sweetening element. They strengthened our teeth by boiling the cheese so it would keep in hot weather. They cultivated our taste for skim milk in ice cream, corn sirup in preserves and paraffin in chocolate. And some of the blessings brought to us by the cinema, wireless and video (to date) are probably appreciated by the folks who like durable watermelon.

It comes to me that the movies, which were supposed to outstrip all competition in displaying the spectacular, haven't lived up to their promises. They worked with heroic energy for years and years to make themselves insufferably dull.

Color did something for them after fifty years of waiting—but not too much. Not even color has given them the eye appeal or the gusto—the life—of an old-fashioned extravaganza.

It is not merely a homesick memory that prompts this observation. We had occasion the other day to look through some old magazines illustrated with some rather bad half tones of yesterday's theatrical offerings. They'd be a fine thing for some latter-day producer.

What has become of the production with "Twenty Carloads of

Scenery—TWENTY CARLOADS," "a Sixty-Piece Orchestra," and "a Chorus of 150 Beautiful Girls?"

Where is the old Comic Opera so lavishly filled with tenors and people in fancy dress, and astonishing volumes of sound, and mechanical scenic gadgets no end, and the alluring atmosphere of comfort and affluence?

Musical comedy is still with us, here and there. But old-timers will remember that musical comedy was a makeshift invented for little theaters like the old La Salle, where the actors had to dress in the basement and climb a ladder to get up to the stage. Many of these things have been amazingly successful. The La Salle comedies established a vogue in Chicago that lasted for years. But a musical comedy, to be successful, must be more than ordinarily good. It must have an outstanding cast, catchy music, funny lyrics and top direction. Even so, it will be light, frothy, forgettable. It is amusing. It stirs nobody. And generally it lacks quite a lot in its sound effects.

Looking backward, we shall not ask for any repetitions of such things as *The Miracle,* which required about four trainloads of equipment and couldn't be produced in an ordinary theater without about six months of reconstruction.

But we recall that every couple of months Chicago could look with unending wonder on such things as *The Black Crook, Babes in Toyland, Aladdin and His Wonderful Lamp, Robinson Crusoe, Top of the World, King Dodo, The Prince of Pilsen, Old Heidelberg, The Sultan of Sulu, The Sleeping Beauty, The Wizard of Oz, The Red Mill, Cinderella* and *Chu-Chin-Chow.* Such things were called extravaganzas and made no attempt to be anything else.

In addition there were operettas like *The Chimes of Normandy, Erminie* and *Robin Hood; opéra bouffe* like *The Grand Cham of Tartary;* comic operas like the Gilbert and Sullivan revivals; light opera such as *Fra Diavolo* and *The Bohemian Girl.*

No matter what their classification, these musical affairs were filled with verve and joyousness as they were filled with people, and most of them were incredibly beautiful. They could be thrilling. Nobody is likely to forget the kidnaping scene in *The Bohemian Girl* when a troop of horsemen galloped onto the stage and up a mountain trail into the upper flies. Nor is anybody who saw it going to forget the exploding dragon that turned into a battalion of dancing girls in *Ali Baba,* nor the fairies who flew over the heads of the spectators in *Mr. Bluebeard.*

There was sheer wizardry in what the critics used to call the "stage effects" of these shows, something that photography, active or static, has never captured. The movies, with all their amazing techniques, have never produced an illusion like the floating castles in *Little Nemo,* or the dissolving wilderness that surrounded *The Sleeping Beauty.* Nor have they ever made the cold chills run under your spine as they did in *Neptune's Daughter* when rank after rank of mermaids marched down a stairway into a pool of water—and never came up.

One looks with a jaundiced eye on the announcement of the new electronic arts concerning the amusements that we are about to enjoy without leaving our chairs. We aren't likely to see any soul-stirring ensembles in the moving pictures because cinema spectacles have little appeal to people who know all about trick photography. We aren't likely to see them on the stage because (a) they cost too much, and (b) when there is so little chance of getting into a theater without six months' notice, the customers will look at anything. And as for television—well, it takes a lot of doing to compress 150 chorus girls into a frame twenty inches by twelve.

Chicago has certainly progressed a lot in the last sixty years. Buildings and the price of butter are both several stories higher. Seats in streetcars are now finely upholstered and comfortable—if you can find one. Typhoid, celluloid collars, bustles and the theater have virtually gone from us. But be of good cheer. An old voice

204

remains in the background to tell us everything is going to be all right. The "new and undreamed-of possibilities for entertainment" are pouring in on us as they always did. The movies were a miracle, radio was a miracle, talkies were a miracle and television is a double miracle. And when we look at a miracle we do not ask what it produces.

Chapter 26

The Gramophone Miracle

Do you remember when you first heard the phonograph perform? Life is capable of few greater miracles.

Your modern child looks on jet airplanes as his grandfather looked on birds in flight—things too commonplace to provoke thought. With similar nonchalance, today's tot accepts the fact that he can see a lot of characters endlessly boxing or wrestling on a television screen. His living-room contact with this great miracle of science gives him no sense of magic, for in his experience miracles have always been a dime a dozen.

But it wasn't that way when I was six years old and I talked my Uncle Bob into an expedition that finished in a minor-league wonderland in Clark Street.

Later I was to identify this hall of enchantment as a penny arcade. But labels, however accurate, fail to tell of its fascination. I have never known a more marvelous day.

In memory the place is still vivid enough to convince me that the general appearance of penny arcades hasn't changed much in fifty years. For that matter, neither have the attractions. There were the customary walls of red and gold, paneled with mirrors, ceilings studded with lights in bottles that were unlike anything ever seen before. Back in the end was a shooting gallery worth only passing attention because I had seen shooting galleries almost every place I had ever been. Along the sides of the room were rows of dull silver boxes on pedestals—the bioscopes, or the kine-tographs, or whatever you choose to call them.

You can still find such things around town—probably the same machines showing the same deadly pictures of girls in New Look nightshirts throwing pillows at one another or pouring water on amorous guitar players from upstairs windows. So far as these pictorial exhibits were concerned, I was probably as blasé as a child of 1952 would be in contemplation of an atomic bomb.

I hadn't exactly seen any real moving pictures—that is to say, I had never seen any moving pictures projected on a screen by a thing like a magic lantern. But somebody had given me a thick little book which consisted of pictures of a couple of men named Sullivan and Corbett. It was much the same as the shows of this interesting pavilion. You held the book up in front of your eyes and fanned the pages with your thumb. The gentlemen named Mr. Sullivan and Mr. Corbett then proceeded to whang the day-lights out of each other.

The action of the bioscopes wasn't much different. The feature of this arcade that made one remember it when other models had come along fifteen or twenty years later was a row of smaller boxes standing on pedestals near the door. These devices were called, as nearly as I can remember my uncle's translation of the label, Phonogramatoscopes. They had glass covers through which you could see some wheels and a black cylinder. Each was draped with lengths of rubber hose branching out at one end of the device to earpieces.

Uncle Bob stepped in front of one of these intriguing devices. He handed me the stethoscope thing, told me to put the black rub-ber ends in my ears. When I had done all this he put a penny into a slot.

The wheels began to move. Presently I was aware that the cylin-der had begun to rotate. But my interest in this commonplace procedure was suddenly interrupted by a thin, high-pitched,

nasal voice squawking something about Ed-ee-son Reck-kords.

Uncle Bob was standing there laughing, and I supposed he was playing some sort of trick. I walked around the machine, as far as the hose would permit, trying to catch a glimpse of the vocalist who now had begun to sing. But the little man who wasn't there continued to be somewhere else.

I stood absorbed as the words began to make sense—words which, to this day, remain stored in a memory that probably should have been put to better uses:

> "Oh, Mister Captain, stop the ship,
>   I want to get off and walk.
> I feel so flippity, flippity flop
>   Oh, take me back to New Yawk."

I was much too confused about the whole affair to ask any questions. But Uncle Bob explained.

"It's the little engine that makes the sounds," he told me. "This is what they call the phonograph. Sounds make dents on the black cylinder and when you reverse it the dents make sounds—see?"

"No," I said. "Where is the little man who sings?"

"There isn't any," replied Uncle Bob patiently. "It's all done by machinery." That was the first time I had ever found reason to mistrust his judgment. I must confess that I wronged him for many a year.

The Spanish War was well under way before I got another chance to listen to a phonograph. This treat came to me through the courtesy of one of my grandmother's neighbors who in retrospect seems to have been a smart opportunist. He was preparing to go west and give what he called "Gramophone Concerts" in the culture-starved towns of the frontier.

To me his phonograph was something of a disappointment. It played on disks instead of black cylinders, and from my experience at the penny arcade I was able to guess that this was a basic defect.

Despite this handicap, the music was pretty good.

There was a highly amusing bit called "Cohen on the Telephone." We didn't know much about telephones, but we all knew that Cohen was having a lot of trouble with it.

And there were drums and fifes and martial tunes and the stirring beat of marching feet:

"Good-by, Dolly, I must leave you,
    Though it breaks my heart to go. . . ."

"One lies down at Chickamauga
    Many miles away. . . ."

"One ate the meat that old Alger sent
    Just as the sun went down. . . ."

I have wondered many times since then how our host fared in bringing culture to the Indian country. The records, by now, ought to be worn out sufficiently to be played in juke boxes.

Chapter 27

The Good Old Circus

O<small>UR</small> nephew Donny, aged three years, went to the circus the other day, a five-ring affair with a square division of clowns, a tank corps of elephants, scores of mechanical gags such as collapsing automobiles and a couple of large cannon that shot pifformers into nets. Somebody asked Donny what he thought of this pleasing exhibit.

"I liked the ride on the bus," he said. "The elephants were big."

All of which, so far as we are concerned, comes under the head of a fair commentary.

The kids in our neighborhood may have had some odd ideas about tent shows. Each July for a decade or more the circus came regularly to the vacant lot in Ashland Avenue north of Cornelia Street where years of impromptu gardening had left a couple of permanent, grassy rings.

We were always out to give it an early-morning welcome, to do the little jobs that theoretically would get us free admission, perhaps to wear a bandsman's coat and carry a sign in the parade. Nothing much came of this endeavor. City mains and convenient fireplugs had ended the necessity for carrying tubs of water to the elephants—and none of the other jobs about the tent seemed to merit a pass. But no matter. We could always hope, and our parents were pretty sure to take us in on the night of the performance, anyway.

We got to know this particular show almost as well as if we had traveled with it. We took a certain pride in it, a sort of proprietary interest. We argued its merits in public. We applauded it without stint. But to tell the truth, we didn't like it any too well, not after we had seen it unload and put up the tents. It was called "Gentry Brothers' Dog and Pony Show." And what a horse or a dog could do in a circus ring had ceased to surprise us.

Size didn't make much difference in a circus in those days—not to critics of our years. Primarily we wanted action of the sort the wild West shows furnished. And if wild West shows ran to grandeur, that was purely incidental.

I recall that when I first saw Buffalo Bill's Great Concourse of Heroes of the Great Plains I was terribly disappointed. I didn't care much for the heroes. And the show didn't have any clowns. Some of the substitute offerings seemed boresome and a waste of time. I was ten or eleven years old before I realized that the targets in Annie Oakley's sharpshooting were actually glass balls and not self-exploding Roman-candle bubbles.

I went into ecstasies over the Indian attack on the Deadwood stagecoach, and was even more cheered by the same act when they relabeled it "The Charge up San Juan Hill." Sioux Indians, doubling in brass as Spanish infantry, looked natural enough to suit anybody, and there will never be anything in the drama of America to equal the sudden opening of fire with a Gatling gun.

You listened spellbound to the *rat-tat-tat-tat,* and you looked at the brave hey-rubes in blue uniforms falling heroically all over the sawdust, and you saw the flag go up over the canvas blockhouse which swayed just a little bit under the strain. But it was the realest spectacle you had ever looked at, the realest you were ever going to see, including the no-fooling battle for St.-Lô. And you went home positively numb.

The horse-opera movies are largely responsible for the vanishing of the old wild West shows. But there were other causes. Personalities, real or synthetic, had a lot to do with the success of these pageants—Buffalo Bill, Sitting Bull, Pawnee Bill, Calamity Jane, Annie Oakley and the rest. Some of them stayed for a long time, possibly because they had been part of a regime that was recent enough to be interesting. And when they died there were no new characters to take their places. Hundred and One Ranch was a huge success for a time. It put on an exhibition of trick riding already popular in Cheyenne as the "Roundup," and soon to astound a new generation of dudes as the "Rodeo." But trick riding is one thing and the circus is another.

Pawnee Bill's Great Wild West Show and Exhibition of Wonders came to our lot one year when the Gentry Brothers were preparing to quit the road. Nobody in the vicinity had ever heard of Pawnee Bill. Some of us aren't sure about his identity even yet. But he wasn't taking any chances on a dim personality in a business where personalities meant so much. Listed as part owner and manager of the Exhibition of Wonders was one Frank James. Our mothers heard about it and went around to make sure that all the windows were locked. James, it seems, was still well and unfavorably known.

He took no active part in the performance. There were rumors that the management feared trouble if he appeared, that the authorities—federal? state? county? local?—had threatened to close the show if he did. It was suggested that Frank was getting old and that he had never liked to ride a horse anyway, which seems to make a little more sense. At any rate, his part in the proceedings was to stand near the ticket taker where everybody entering the tent could get a good look at him.

He was a tall, rather square man, as I remember him—sad-faced, slouchily dressed, and a great disappointment to me. I don't know what I had expected to see, but I have since come to realize

212

that the only way he would have looked natural would have been on horseback, fleeing the posse in a shower of bullets.

Nearly twenty-five years had gone by since the shooting of Jesse James in St. Joseph, Missouri. Frank, on that historic morning in April 1882, had been thirty-eight years old. So he must have been close to sixty-two when he gave the charm of his uplifting presence to Pawnee Bill's instructive pageant, and as an old man he seemed to be out of character. None of my little companions had ever heard of an old bank robber; bank robbers never lived long enough to get that way.

There isn't much else that I can recall about Frank James except the interview conducted by little Freddy Simmons, a neighborhood pet who wasn't considered very bright. An older boy, subsidized by Freddy's parents, was leading him into the tent when he suddenly stopped in front of James.

"Are you Frank James?" he inquired in a loud, shrill voice.

The great man sourly admitted his identity.

"Oh, gee!" mourned Freddy. "I thought you were going to be Jesse James."

Frank James was startled enough to blurt out a reply. "Jesse James is dead," he said.

"I know that," replied Freddy. Maybe he didn't mean it.

Mystery and Crime 5:

Bad-News Tillie

THEY were plowing up the last celery patch in Lake View to make room for Weiblinger's saloon when Bad-News Tillie moved into Ashland Avenue near Cornelia Street. Her advent was considerably more spectacular than the unloading of Gentry Brothers' Circus half a block down the street, and was reviewed with unmasked interest by all the kids of the neighborhood and most of the adults.

Tillie didn't bring any moving van filled with the customary oddments of furniture generally revealed on such occasions. She was more practical. She appeared on the scene seated by the side of the driver of a steam roller behind which, on four stonemason's trucks, was hitched a long, narrow, two-story house. Tillie's possessions, whatever they were, remained where they had always been—inside the house. And nobody got a look at them until long years afterward.

A moving crew got the house onto its waiting foundations before the day was out. In this work they were greatly encouraged by Tillie, who cursed at them with a spectacular vocabulary in English, Polish and German. When they had finished she chased away the observing children and retired through her somewhat inaccessible front door via a stepladder. The spectators then moved on to the circus which, after Tillie's show, seemed to be lacking in savor.

Next day it became obvious that Tillie had come to stay. By the time the mannerly little children had gathered around she had a nondescript washing hung on a line in what was to be her back yard, and bricklayers were filling up holes in the underpinning of her house. Moreover, as determined by test, the ladder had been attached to the house with wooden cleats. Public interest waned rapidly.

The house, when it was permanently emplaced, looked like what it was—a large square box, badly in need of the coat of paint it was never going to get. But Tillie had some eye for improvement. Maybe she found it inconvenient to get in and out of the place on a ladder. Anyway, at the end of the week a brewery truck arrived at her address carrying a spiral staircase of rusted iron.

Afterward came workmen who argued for a long time with Tillie about what they were going to do with the staircase. It was too long to serve the front door, the foreman mentioned in two languages. It couldn't be cut off with a hacksaw because it was the wrong curve. It was going to look pretty ghastly no matter what was done with it. And he suggested that maybe she might throw the thing away and get somebody to make her some stairs and a porch out of wood.

Tillie solved the problem with the directness that the neighborhood was presently to recognize as her most charming characteristic.

"Run it up to the second floor and make a door out of the upstairs front window on the east," she directed in German. "Then you can nail up the front door downstairs. I won't be needing it." The foreman translated this order to his workmen and thereby let the neighborhood know what to expect.

"She's certainly going to have a fine-looking place," he men-

215

tioned to give the message a personal touch. And he was right about that.

The result was something that people came from miles around to see. The little children would linger for hours just to observe Tillie making her exits and entrances. Unfortunately they were never around when she emerged at night swinging a lantern in front of her 200 pounds of bulk. John Spetti and Mike Mullen, conductors on the Ashland Avenue car line, who were frequent witnesses to this odd procedure, christened her place "The Ashland Avenue Lighthouse." And the name stuck.

In time, from one source or another, we learned the name of our new neighbor. She was Mrs. Herman Gratzburg. She had come from Bowmanville. And she had a wispy little husband whose apparent object in life was to keep out of her way.

"He's fine man," Tillie told Mrs. Volk in the grocery store across the street. "He's good to me. Never sticks around the house. Never bothers me. Just fine man."

That was her last observation on the subject, but a few of the neighbors began to draw conclusions from what they could see for themselves.

Mr. Gratzburg sometimes got up enough initiative to get drunk at Schulze's saloon no great distance away. But he never was sufficiently ingenious to enlarge on the program. He would come home, find himself unable to negotiate the winding stairs and sit all night on the bottom step. Next morning he would appear on the street with a black eye or a bandaged head. He worked somewhere as a freight-elevator operator, but nobody ever found out much about that.

Before coming to Ashland Avenue the Gratzburgs had lived near some carbarns in Clark Street and, whether because of this proximity or not, Tillie had developed a definite allergy toward streetcars.

There was a story that some conductor had once given her a misdated transfer—or maybe had refused to accept a misdated transfer from her. There was a further report that in retaliation she had assaulted the motorman and broken some windows. These allegations were never proved. But it is true that she had been known to the trade in the old neighborhood as "Bad-News Tillie" for a considerable time.

She was some fifteen years in the Ashland Avenue Lighthouse and had an eventful life. Every now and then the police came from Town Hall station to arrest her for throwing rocks at passing streetcars—or for one thing or another. But nothing came of it.

Tillie acquired a dog that seemed to have been trained to detest blue uniforms. But inasmuch as few trolley-car crewmen ever went by her house except in streetcars, the dog had a lonesome time of it. After a year or so in a mistaken moment he bit a policeman and died. The hazard of riding through the 3500 block in Ashland Avenue decreased from that day forward.

So, with little change in routine, the years went by until one night Herman Gratzburg made friends with a streetcar conductor named William Gavin in Schulze's bar. When Herman decided it was time to go home Gavin escorted him not only to the foot of the iron stairs but all the way up to the second-floor door. A bucket of water barely missed him on his way down.

The next day, July 15, 1905, was to be memorable in the neighborhood. Tillie appeared in Volk's grocery store and bought a bar of soap.

"He's no good," she told Mr. Fred Volk, the proprietor.

"Who?" inquired Volk.

"Herman, my old man," explained Tillie patiently. "All the time with streetcar conductors he runs around. So now I guess I kill him."

"So?" inquired Volk. "And how are you going to do it?"

"With this," said Tillie. And she held up the cake of soap.

Volk repeated the conversation with considerable amusement to

217

everybody he saw that day, including the policeman on the beat.

But the next day he would have had difficulty reconstructing a smile. Toward evening of that day Mrs. Gratzburg was back in the store, looking fairly happy.

"Well, I do it," she said. "The old man. Now he's dead. No more streetcar conductors for him."

Volk took a second look at her and called Town Hall station.

The police came. They found Herman in a bathtub with the back of his head caved in. It seemed likely that he had slipped on a cake of soap which they found underwater at the bottom of the tub. A detective asked Tillie about it.

"Sure," she said in German. "I guess maybe he slips on that. I try hard to fix him up again. But he don't pay no attention to me. He just lies there."

"And when was this?" inquired the detective.

"Three days ago," said Tillie.

"Well," snapped the policeman, "where's that cake of soap you bought day before yesterday from Volk?"

"Oh, that," said Tillie. "That's right here." And she produced the cake of soap from the kitchen sink.

So they buried Gratzburg. Then they took Tillie in for mental tests. And they turned her loose again.

At last reports she was living on a little truck farm near Bensenville.

"I like it here," she reported to one of her old German friends. "It's a nice place. No policemen, no streetcars, no streetcar conductors. And there's no way you can get drowned in the bathtub because there isn't any bathtub. There's just some water that squirts in from a thing up near the ceiling. And I wonder what those policemen wanted with me when Herman died."

"I don't know," said the friend. And, for that matter, neither does anybody else.

PART **VI**

CULTURE AND
THE ARTS

Chapter 28

Lo! The Poor Wooden Indian

Among my best friends when the old nineteenth century breathed its last was a very fine sculptor who carved wooden Indians for cigar stores. His name, as I remember it, was Walter Campbell, and he maintained an atelier in the basement of one of those seagoing boardinghouses just north of the old Rush Street bridge.

He was so old that he had to wear a jeweler's glass eye for his fine work—which didn't seem to me to be very fine—but in spite of that and other infirmities a lot of people, including me, rated him as the top wooden Indian carver of North America. I found out about him because his shop was next door to a magazine distribution center where I could get dime novels for a nickel and nickel novels at two for five. This will show you something of the depths to which his art had fallen. I had to discover it by accident, for the Chicago schools at the time seem to have discounted hand-carved Pocahontases and sturdy Hiawathas as examples of our native culture.

Art appreciation was cultivated in the lower grades by means of the Perry Pictures, a gallery of black-and-white half tones that sold for a penny apiece. They purported to be true copies of paintings by a lot of outlanders named Murillo, Botticelli, Velásquez and Rembrandt. Old Walter Campbell was not in the catalogue.

I remember that I was annoyed about that. I had a long colloquy about it with my teacher in third grade. At the end of it she said, rather stuffily, "But if Indians are such important art, why didn't the great artists paint Indians?"

And I recall an answer which I have since thought covered the subject.

"Because," I said, "the great artists never saw an Indian."

Very likely I was led to the magazine shop that brought me into contact with Walter Campbell by Dion O'Banion, my little friend and fellow newspaper merchant. He certainly seemed to know all the oddities in town and certainly demonstrated his interest in the near North Side some years later by getting himself shot in the middle of it. At any rate, I was received readily by Mr. Campbell, who appreciated my interest in his wares. Thereafter I was one of his most frequent visitors and definitely his enthusiastic proponent in local art circles.

Nowadays, unless you are a frequenter of museums, you won't see many specimens of the work of Sculptor Campbell or the thousands of other unknown chiselers who went before him. But in the nineties there were more wooden Indians within a mile of the site of Old Fort Dearborn than there had been live Potawatomi at the time of the massacre.

In this raw town with no pride of ancestry there were people of historic background and splendid tradition. Some of them could have traced their forebears back to the year 1700 when the first of their wooden tribe displayed his bundle of nonsmokable cigars to the citizens of Boston. No tobacconist for the next 200 years would have thought of trying to do business without them any more than he would have thought of dispensing with materials for ignition, such as flint and steel and tinder, or a little charcoal brazier, or sputtering sulphur matches, or a grass gas torch swinging on a rubber base.

In Chicago the wooden Indians seemed like the only institution likely to remain unchanged tomorrow and the next day, until the end of time. All of which goes to indicate that you never know.

It may be that their elimination was due not to any fault of their own, nor any lack of public appreciation, but to subtle changes that crept into the tobacco business almost unnoticed. As recently as 1900 nobody would have thought of going to a tobacco shop to bet on a horse or to buy neckties, soda water, whisky, fountain pens, lip rouge, stockings, candy or hundreds of other things for which an Indian could claim no responsibility. You could buy any of a dozen brands of chewing plug, an endless variety of five-cent cigars or pipe mixtures compounded to your own formula.

You couldn't buy cigarettes, not in the better-class places, because cigarettes were looked on as the vice of the lowest form of animal life. And you never saw a woman in one of these shops because there was nothing in any of them that a woman might want to buy. The wooden Indian stood outside the door whatever the weather. It seemed impossible to do any business without him.

Inasmuch as Walter Campbell was an active part of what amounted to the country's most flourishing advertising business, it is not remarkable that he was quick to notice a restlessness in the trade he served. He would speak of it bitterly and for hours on end.

"When you are dealing in a specialized product, you can sell only to a specialized market" was the burden of his song. "And frills and furbelows in the tobacco business don't do a wooden Indian no good. I been at this sculpturing for maybe fifty years, man and boy, and I know what I'm a-talking about.

"I started out to be an innovator. Up in Canada I got the idea of making totems for the French fur shops. They wasn't Indians. They was what they called *'couriers du bois,'* which means 'wooden couriers.'

"Them wooden couriers was the first trappers. So I made some. They didn't sell at all. Not a-tall. An' that certainly showed me there was no place for novelty in business.

"But you can't tell these tobacco men that. I seen it coming, this nonsense. Once you could put out an Indian with one feather in his bonnet an' dress him up in leather pants. But seems like styles change. So pretty soon I'm workin' on full-size war-bonnet head-dresses, an' the lowest priced chief you can turn out has to wear beaded war moccasins.

"That ain't all—you got to show every vein in the feathers and carve out every bead. You got to make the hair look like it's just come out of a wig shop. An' you've got to carve fingernails—good ones—an' give the Indian lines on his hands that a fortune-teller could read.

"These newfangled see-gars are comin' in with paper bands on 'em. An' the wooden-Indian buyers insist that you put bands in bas-relief on every doggoned smoke in the Indian's bundle.

"If you do an honest job on an Indian nowadays, it takes you twice as much time as it did when I was starting out. Prices ain't improved much. An' besides that you got the cutthroat competition of crooks who make the delicate parts out of plaster an' paste 'em on."

Despite such difficulties, Old Walter did fairly well for several years before the last retreat of the cigar-store redskins really began.

Between 1900 and 1903 he turned out some of his great master-pieces, notably a gay figure that stood on the northeast corner of Chicago Avenue and Clark Street—a sort of mezzotint Pocahontas with a headdress that, apparently, had been designed for her by the Empress Eugénie.

Another work that came of his final magnificent effort was an eight-foot Powhatan, "all hand carved out of solid maple," well

224

displayed in front of Joe Geddy's place at Twenty-second Street
and Wabash Avenue. Despite his stature, Powhatan, in the main,
looked like most of his distinguished line. The classic expression
of the ordinary wooden Indian was one of bland aloofness. Powhatan was even blander and more aloof than his prototypes.

The chief wore a standardized costume from war bonnet to
beaded moccasins. And he stood with his right foot forward as
wooden Indians had been standing for uncounted dozens of years.
But he wasn't entirely the same as the earlier exhibits from Walter
Campbell's wooden wigwam. In this design the great sculptor had

225

taken an opportunity to express his irritation over modern trends. Powhatan came into the world with a large hand-carved watch attached to his belt by a hand-carved chain complete with a large, wooden, hand-carved Masonic charm.

In place of his customary tomahawk he carried a pistol. In his right hand, along with his cigars, he displayed an obvious corncob pipe. In his open left palm he held a collection of small change or, as it was known to his people, wooden wampum.

Powhatan is conceded by critics to have been Walter Campbell's finest work. At any rate, he was the last wooden Indian the old master ever chose to carve. The lowering of tobacconists' standards had been bad enough. But there were other signs of disintegration in the trade and these Mr. Campbell could not fail to interpret.

In 1900 a finicky City Council passed an ordinance forbidding shopkeepers to clutter up the sidewalks with picturesque emblems of their business. The ruling affected not only wooden Indians but isolated barber's poles, the fascinating exterior showcases of pawnbrokers, whistling peanut roasters, the stuffed bears of the furriers and other similar menaces to traffic. It was, indeed, a sad day.

"Well," said Old Walter in his farewell to the Indians, "I've been getting ready for this. I made my mistake in the beginning when I thought this kind of art would go on lasting just because it's lasted a couple of hundred years. It ain't too late to correct the mistake. I'm going to do something permanent.

"Mark my words. In ten years all the cigar-store Indians in this town are going to be made out of plaster. But not by me.

"When that happens I'll be sitting right here carving out wooden horses for harness shops. Horses ain't goin' to change. An' we're always goin' to have thousands of them . . . thousands of them and thousands more as the city grows. . . ."

So the wooden Indian became a museum exhibit and Old Walter didn't do much better.

226

I didn't get down to see him for something like four months that winter. The weather was pretty bad and I stayed wrapped up most of the time. When I got into Rush Street again Campbell's studio was closed.

I don't know what had happened to the magnificent old artist.

"Campbell?" queried the man who ran the magazine shop. "I dunno exactly what did happen to him. Went out of here all of a sudden. Beats all. Heard somebody say he was goin' to California. . . ."

He may have found out something that changed his mind about the permanency of horses.

Chapter 29

Art *with a Capital* A

MANY odd things happened in 1897, as perhaps you may remember. Queen Victoria had a diamond jubilee in London, somebody in New Jersey grew, so we have been told, a strawberry one foot in circumference, Hinky Dink went to New York to help Tammany elect a mayor, and a platoon of infantry, armed and under full pack, started wheeling from Montana to Missouri to test the bicycle as an implement of war.

But even more spectacular was the amazing reception that Chicago gave to something called "passe partout."

The arts of the nineties, hereabouts, were many and varied. Virtually every home where there was any respect for culture had a couple of hand-painted oil paintings—the work, generally, of the eldest daughter of the house—which depicted cows in the meadow or "The Mount of the Holy Cross."

Home decoration of china had reached a peak of popularity that it was never going to surpass. Pyrography, which is to say the burning of geometrical designs and pictures on wood, was just coming into vogue. And then, on top of it all, came passe partout. It is difficult to explain to one unacquainted with such cultural techniques just what passe partout was and how it got that way.

228

It is considerably more difficult to touch the reason why it virtually hexed the whole community. One can only try.

Passe partout is the French for *master key,* which is another clew that means nothing. Its basis was a roll of gummed paper ribbon, somewhat like modern adhesive tape except that it came in variety of colors—a wide variety. Whatever it may have been designed for is something nobody in my ken ever knew. Its American use was to frame pictures. Picture framing, up to the time of its arrival in North America, had been singularly complicated. Then, as now, you had to have a frame, a pane of glass and a mat. The principal trouble was that the frame had to fit the glass.

If you set out to make your own frame, or you tried to get the corners square, or you had to cut the glass crooked or stretch the picture sideways several yards, maybe you couldn't do it. Such operations were considerably beyond the scope of the average home mechanic—especially in 1897.

As a result the city was fairly well supplied with shops where framing was done professionally—at a small charge. Every department store had a magnificent stock of ready-framed pictures of the sort you may still see hanging in hotel rooms: "The Duchess of Devonshire," still-life portraits of grapes, oranges, apples and bottles, "The Midnight Eruption of Vesuvius" or "Moonlight on Niagara Falls." "Wilhelmina, Girl Queen" and "The Poppy Girls" had still to attain popularity.

The amateur interior decorators of the eighties apparently had made some effort to free themselves from professional interference in the no doubt important presentation of art. Much of their art was still extant until the beginning of the present century, but one must admit that it was little more than a compromise.

The housewives who later turned to the depicting of strange flora in teacup bottoms, chocolate pots and shaving mugs put in a lot of time developing what is, or was, called "The Red-Hot Resin Technique."

You took a ready-made frame, new or old, and covered it over with trickles of melted resin which produced an effect something like Greek Coconut Candy. Then, when the resin was hard, you daubed it generously with gilt paint.

This process, aside from its decorative results, brought little progress to the art of picture framing. Always you had to have a frame, and somebody—generally outside your own household— had to make it. Passe partout changed all that.

To prepare a picture for hanging according to the passe-partout system, you first got a picture—a photograph, a half tone or home-talent water color, or some sketch out of a magazine. You stuck it on a piece of cardboard trimmed to give a margin of about a half inch all around and cut a "mask" for it out of a sheet of paper the same size as the cardboard. Finally you got a sheet of glass of similar dimensions.

With all these spare parts assembled, you wet the passe partout with your tongue. (The gum was generally flavored with sassafras.) You pasted the tape along the edge of the glass, folded it back on the mounting board and trimmed the corners, or at least I hope you did.

That is all there was to it except to find some way to hang it on the wall, and generally this was done by pasting a ring or a loop of string to the back with another bit of passe partout. All in all it was not what you'd call a complicated business, and it changed the looks of walls in Chicago's living rooms and bedrooms virtually overnight.

The city's glaziers were in for a period of prosperity. The old-time picture-frame makers were virtually out of business.

A lot can be said for passe partout aside from the fact that it kept no end of female art enthusiasts from covering more canvas with "The Mount of the Holy Cross." It also ended the vogue for draped easels six feet high, as they used to stand in our front par-

230

lors, and it also put a stop to your "Uncle Oscar in Full Beard." You couldn't get "Uncle Oscar in Full Beard" in anything near the measurements of a passe-partout picture.

The art displays in Chicago homes during this exciting era probably did not get any better. But they certainly got smaller. And you certainly could not very well exhibit a four by five-inch portrait on a three by six-foot easel.

One thing, of course, led to another. The yen for the decorative struck the housewives of the village like a fever. And so, as the saying goes, they were suckers for pyrography. So, for that matter, were all the living souls in the community—the old, the young, the lame and the halt—everybody who had a couple of hands and a foot.

Look around your attic or your basement storerooms and you are sure to find specimens produced by this odd mania. Flowered taborets and wooden plaques embossed and burned with tulips and the unrecognizable profile of Queen Wilhelmina are still extant all over town—bits of flotsam that mark the high tide of an art just as the gravel reefs of northern Illinois outline the farthest advance of the great glacier.

One will admit, of course, that the glacier was larger and that it probably had a more lasting effect.

It may be hard for a youthful critic to believe that anybody ever produced any of this stuff on purpose. But, take our word for it, nearly everybody did.

Pyrography was not only a cultural movement but a great natural industry.

It sprang, so its promoters said, from the whimsey of sixteenth-century topers in England, who used to make doodles on the walls with red-hot pokers. It was brought within the reach of the Chicago multitude at the end of the nineteenth century through the invention of a better tool. The hot poker was replaced by a hollow platinum point with a couple of air holes in it and a handle that gave it something of the appearance of an electric soldering iron except that it was about the size of a fountain pen.

From the other end of the handle a rubber hose led to an atomizer filled with benzene. The whole business was explosive—but who worried about that? You heated the point over an alcohol lamp and then pumped the atomizer to keep it hot.

The fire department loved this gadget just as it loved lighted paraffin candles on Christmas trees.

With the hot point you could make scorched lines on almost any sort of wood. And, if you were a good draftsman, you probably got an orange crate and figured out your own designs. For less gifted artisans the stores provided plaques, boxes and pieces of small furniture made with basswood on which suitable flora and fauna, arabesques and who knows what were printed in outline. You worked over these until the atomizer blew up and the house took fire.

One remembers this period with poignant nostalgia, although the tears of memory are not so numerous as those produced by the fumes of burning wood under your artful hand. You could smoke a ham in any parlor in Chicago during that period of artistic fervor, even though you might have had some trouble reading a newspaper. It was a generous sort of movement because none of the half-million practitioners engaged in it ever made any burned whatnots for himself. All this lovely handicraft was produced as gifts for somebody else.

In the end it made no difference because you generally got back as much as you gave. That was probably what ended the craze: the day came when everybody had a couple of cords of burned wood on hand and could find no place to put it.

Passe Partout, Pyrography, Painted China! There were no worries about Christmas presents in that gladsome era. Everybody knew in advance what he was going to get. And he always got it. As for the city's art appreciation, it was virtually unanimous.

It is logical, I suppose, that one generation should accept with an abiding calm such advantages as it may have inherited from another. Modern children see no miracle in airplanes any more than in pigeons. They are likely to find a horse more worthy of serious contemplation than a new automobile.

What stenographer can envision the day when there wasn't any typewriter? Moving pictures talk, and why shouldn't they? DDT, of course, is pretty well known as something that somebody invented for use in the war . . . but who realizes that the fly swatter was not always with us like food and clothing and cold and heat— and flies.

Chicago's standard of living in the 1900s—what with pyrography, passe partout and other cultural influences—was about as high as that of other big cities in the world—perhaps a little higher. But the denizens of a recently built glass flat might not be able to give it proper appraisal.

At the time of the first World's Fair there were numerous elegant mausoleums in Monroe Street, Adams Street, Prairie Avenue and Lake Shore Drive—the dwelling places of the well to do and the socially elect. They evidenced more than anything else the progress of Chicago's thought for better things. Most of them were massive, gloomy piles of rock. Some of them had impressive brownstone fronts and nonimpressive brick backs. All of them had bathrooms—at least one to a house—for this was an age of lavishness when the better hotels were advertising the convenience of a bathroom on every floor. All had indoor plumbing, gas lights and delicately contrived spitoons. You didn't care if the plumbing happened to be noisy—as it so generally was. The noise advertised the fact that you had it.

You made your cuspidors things of beauty by covering them with embroidered silken skirts similar to the pants on lamb chops —but larger. Justly proud of your expensive illumination you displayed it in expensive brass-and-crystal chandeliers. When these ponderous affairs tore loose from the ceiling, as they had a way of doing, and fractured somebody's skull you were never entirely inconsolable. The newspaper accounts of the affair were sure to attest your opulence.

Quite a number of those mansions had central heating, generally in the form of a hot-air furnace that served at least the first floor. A few of the later ones were heated by these newfangled steam radiators that seemed to be doing pretty well in large office buildings. Such innovations, however, were still looked upon by the majority of Chicagoans as impractical and dangerous.

Gas grates made to look remotely like log fires were in considerable favor and gave out about as much warmth as gas grates do today. But despite all these indications of a new and more comfortable day in home design, coal-fired heating stoves—the good old base-burners from Quincy, Illinois, or Piqua, Ohio—still had many vigorous proponents, even in the dwelling places of the rich. Everybody burned anthracite which cost about three dollars a ton.

Every home worthy of the name had a front parlor with a bay window in it, a back parlor with no window in it, and a dining room equipped with a plate rail. The back parlor was the family gathering place.

In the middle of this back parlor was a "library table" with a red shaded lamp on it and spread with copies of Will Carleton's poems, the latest opus of E. P. Roe, *Chatter-Box* for 1887 and similar Christmas presents. Near by was a worn Morris chair, the throne of the head of the house when he was reading his evening paper. The lamp may have been a kerosene burner, a holdover from a day less generously blessed by inventors, but it was more likely a gas-consuming affair, fed by a rubber hose from an overhead jet. In its most advanced stage before the widespread use of electricity, it was equipped with a Welsbach burner, which produced light by burning a little fish net called a "mantle" to a stiff white ash and heating it to incandescence with the gas flame. The lamp shade frequently took fire, which added zest to a long winter evening. This hazard continued until electric light became common and the lamp was replaced by an angular and ugly contrivance of sheet metal and stained glass in what was known as the "Mission Style."

On one side of the room was a bookcase generally seven feet high and four feet wide, containing *Chambers's Encyclopedia, The Home Medical Library,* the complete works of Charles Dickens and William Makepeace Thackeray, *The Prisoner of Zenda, Trilby, Gulliver's Travels, Jane Eyre, Beside the Bonnie Briar Bush* and a large assortment of "subscription books" such as *Great Men and Famous Women, Footprints of History* and *Great Disasters Illustrated.* These latter were all in sets of several volumes which the lady of the house had painstakingly acquired by purchasing a section at a time for fifty cents a section.

Maybe there was a writing desk in the room. It was likely to contain two post-office pens and an empty inkwell, and an array of pigeonholes filled with bills, dress patterns, recipes and unanswered letters—the same then as now.

In a majority of the kitchens the two-burner gas plate with a portable tin oven was more or less common. But the bulk of the city's cooking was still being done on coal-burning ranges. Among the rich and in a large percentage of the homes of the unrich the kitchen was usually established in the basement, where it would be close to the fuel supply. The dining room was a sort of desert space behind the back parlor. It accommodated a large round table quite likely to be made of golden oak, and a sideboard of imposing dimensions whose usefulness was sometimes difficult to detect. Around the room, about seven feet above the floor, ran the plate rail displaying dishes hand-painted by home talent or won at card parties. They made an elegant decoration.

The front parlor, separated from the back parlor by sliding doors that were always closed, was seldom in use save for the entertainment of Important People, funerals and practicing on the melodeon. Few people of the household were likely to know exactly what was in it.

Generally it was a mysterious bourn kept in perpetual shadow by drawn shades. No matter what the status of the householder, its furnishing followed a respected and unvaried pattern.

On one side was "the mantel" with a fireplace, real or imitation, topped by a beveled plate-glass mirror.

On the mantelpiece one had the choice of wax flowers under a bell glass or a generally silent bronze clock beset by the figure of an angry lancer on a horse.

A little brass table with an onyx top stood in the bay window, supporting a large lamp with a tasseled shade.

In a conspicuous corner would be an easel upholding the massive gold-framed portrait of somebody with a beard. Most likely this exhibit would be draped with a long silk scarf.

The furniture was usually an ensemble of straight-backed chairs which had little similarity except in the fact that they were all uncomfortable. Against the wall opposite the mantel stretched the sofa, covered with horsehair or velour and manufactured, no doubt, by the inventor of the Iron Maiden.

Somewhere in this jungle you would find the Parlor Organ or the upright piano or a large and fancy harp. Whichever you found would be under a velvet runner or a Spanish shawl. It would resemble all other musical instruments kept in front parlors in that it would be continuously out of tune.

The front parlor through the years remained virtually unchanged save that the mantel was eventually replaced by the console—a tall, broad mirror flanked by wooden Corinthian pillars. The console resembled the mantel in one respect. It, too, was totally useless.

The mystery of this fine old closed chamber seems to have gone on because nearly everybody forgot about it. Some architect, whose name now is unfortunately forgotten, pushed back the sliding doors about the time of the First World War and stood amazed at what he saw.

"What on earth would anybody want with a room like this?" was his fair query. And nobody seemed to know.

The homes of the wealthy never knew the ministrations of professional interior decorators, so they weren't so ghastly as one might believe. They were furnished largely in somewhat heavy imitations of English baronial halls or chateaux of the First Empire. There was nothing very bright and gay about them, but they had good hardwood paneling and Adam ceilings that were beautiful if bogus. And with the advent of electricity some of them had features of striking novelty.

One recalls the sumptuous residence of Charles T. Yerkes, the streetcar promoter—a large stone castle over on the West Side. On the newel post of the grand staircase stood a marble statue of Venus with electric lights in her eyes. No matter what you may say about modern developments in the art of adorning the home, nobody has ever invented anything more tasteful than that.

Chapter 30

The Music of the Corn

If it is true, as so many experts have declared, that you can judge a community by its songs, some future historian is going to take an odd view of Chicago as it got along in the years of its adolescence. The gay, lusty young city of the nineties will show up in the textbooks as a place of great suffering and continuous weeping—a vast desolation populated mostly by undertakers and orphan children. For the best-selling sheet music of the period was probably the most lugubrious expression of the art since the discovery of middle C.

A frequent visitor at our home, which, by and large, was about on a par culturally with other homes of the neighborhood, was a pretty young contralto named Miss Jewel Greer. She had a jolly disposition and her voice seemed to be all right. But she was a girl of her times, and her repertoire showed it. She lingers in my memory as the town's most able interpreter of the obituary.

Cheerily she would take her place beside the coffinlike square piano. With a smile of sweet sympathy she would charge through the weirdest songs of tragic corn ever gathered together outside of a two-corpse wake. Little Boy Blue's sad passing was almost a

238

comic episode compared to the real heartbreakers that she rendered in sobbing tremolo. Her finest performance was "Hello,
Central, Give Me Heaven," a pathetic bit about a poor little tot
who wanted to talk to her departed mamma over the telephone.
The *modus operandi* required some explanation because telephones at that time were not in general use. That she managed
to convey the general idea to her audience gives you a fair idea of
her genius.

The children mentioned in the dirges of the nineties were all
pretty innocent—as well as hungry, homeless and bereft. I recall
one in particular who wanted somebody to paint her a picture of
Mamma, who had died suddenly, presumably a victim of The Vapors. There were far too many other flaxen-haired babies in a continuous stew because their fathers were a lot of drunken louts who
spent all their pay at the corner pub and then reeled home to beat
up the family.

A few of the mournful infants, it is true, had loving fathers, but
all those rare specimens were dead. The songwriters' epidemic,
apparently, spared neither age, virtue nor sex.

Probably nobody had much to cheer about after the World's
Fair. There had been a panic—the oldsters were convinced that
the fair had caused it. There had been sizable labor troubles. And,
as I recall it, the streets at night were crawling with "sandbaggers"
ready to hit you on the head with a sockful of sand and make off
with what few cents you happened to have left in your pocket.
Of course we weren't bothered by sandbaggers out our way. It
took too long to reach the neighborhood and there would be nobody on the streets after you got there. But that didn't prevent the
sad songs from being continuously popular.

Considering songs as an expression of popular temperament, it
seems as if there might have been some excuse for the laments if
the troubadours had stuck to economic themes in their weeping.

But there were no songs about how "Papa Got Fired from the Deering Plant," or "The Corner Grocery Won't Let Us Charge Things Anymore." To all the high-minded minstrels the principal trouble with the world seemed to be Love—Love with its accompaniment of sudden death.

My attitude toward this theory was a little skeptical. I thought maybe you might get along without Love if you had enough money. But money apparently was so unfamiliar to most people that it didn't seem to bother anybody. So the home concerts just went on sobbing the familiar themes: "She's O-only a Birrud in a Gill-u-did Cage," "Take Back Your Gold—Wi-huth Go-hold You Cannot Buy Me," "She Lives in a Ma-han-sion of A-hay-king Hearts," "She Was Happy Till She Met You" (you with your waxed mustache and a trunkful of jewelry).

It seemed to me then that these laments were the property of the female keeners such as Miss Greer. But, come to think about it, the males weren't very chipper either. They sang loudly about many brave hearts asleep in the deep, and asked people to toll the bell for darling Nell, and ran a blood pressure about an unidentified soldier who lay dying on the battlefield.

The Spanish-American War produced a lot of lyrics such as "The Blue and the Gray," "Break the News to Mother" and "Just As the Sun Went Down." "A Hot Time in the Old Town To-night" was the loudest if not the most beautiful hit of the period. A lot of the keeners were displeased with it, however, because it seemed to mark the end of the depression.

Delicate sentiment continued to meet considerable favor for quite a long time. Bathhouse John Coughlin, whose "Dear Midnight of Love" was easily the finest composition turned out by any alderman in the world in 1898, was an earnest worker in this promotion. You may have a copy of his lovely ballad on your music rack right at this moment. Maybe you haven't. But here is the gist of it:

When silence reigns supreme,
　　And midnight love fortells;
If heart's love could be seen,
　　There kindest thoughts do dwell.
In darkness fancies gleam,
　　True loving hearts do swell;
So far beyond a dream,
　　True friendship never sell.

REFRAIN

Dear Midnight of Love,
　　Why did we meet?
Dear Midnight of Love
　　Your face is so sweet.
Pure as the angels above,
　　Surely again we shall speak,
Loving only as doves,
　　Dear Midnight of Love.

There was more to it, but this will give you the general idea of what the piece was like.

Mme. Emma Calvé, the great operatic soprano, was simply overcome with emotion when the alderman invited her to introduce his song to a "nonpartisan audience" at the Chicago Opera House. She declined because, she said, she did not know the English language well enough to do it justice.

So little May de Sousa, later to become a star in musical comedy, took over the job with the assistance of a fifty-voice chorus and a brass band. It was quite a remarkable performance.

Despite some technical difficulties the Chicago *Journal's* critic was able to mention that the piece was written in "dactyllic tetrameter and hypercataleptic meter," and that little May had done as well with it as could have been done by anybody on earth. And pretty soon all Chicago—well, quite a section of Chicago—was echoing the chorus.

Alderman Coughlin wrote some other attractive lyrics, although none of them seems to have reached the high mark set by "Dear Midnight of Love." In one of them he showed some feeling for the older forms of the dirge:

In her lonely grave she sleeps tonight
   By the side of the drainage canal.
Where the whip-poor-will calls at the midnight hour,
   They've buried my darling Sal.

A mile this side of Willow Springs,
   Not far from the Alton track,
They've planted my Sal, my dear old pal,
   And these tears won't bring her back.

That the "Lonely Grave" did not have the vogue given "Dear Midnight" was due, probably, to a demand for the more romantic style in song—a style which Coughlin himself had helped to create. It had its day in vaudeville and went away.

It must not be supposed that vocal laments, the predecessors of "blues" and "torch songs," were ever completely eliminated from the repertoires of Chicago singers. The vogue was too well established. Such songs were increasingly popular when the moving picture got under way, and "illustrated ballads" became a part of every program. It was customary, then as now, for a sad-faced soprano to render these things in slow tempo while scenes of love and trouble were flashed on the screen.

Bathhouse John Coughlin hung up his harp about 1900 and never twanged it again. He probably felt that he had done enough.

After all, there is not much difference between songs and poems —especially some of those produced locally. So when Harriet Monroe produced *Poetry* magazine in the nineteen hundreds this new tribute to Chicago's culture was enthusiastically received.

The intelligentsia of the Fifty-seventh Street Studio Belt began to discuss Vachel Lindsay and Ezra Pound and a newcomer named Carl Sandburg—which was all well and good except that it seemed to indicate a suspiciously tardy appreciation of art. It might be mentioned that some of Chicago's sweet singers had risen to national fame without any noticeable applause from the literary experts. As has been mentioned, those minstrels and harp players who didn't get recognition outside the city limits had no cause for complaint. Their productions were well received by a populace still unaware of its critical gifts.

Ballads had succeeded in the beginning because they dealt with familiar and poignant subjects. Bathhouse John had received instant acclaim because he had instinctively added the touch of romance and poetry. So it occasioned no surprise when somebody who chose to remain anonymous stirred all Chicago with a homely neighborhood chronicle:

> Oh, times are changed around Morgan Street:
>   The bums don't holler no more.
> And Sairy Presho don't get drunk
>   And throw them out of the door.
> For she has changed her residence.
>   She's going to move away.
> "To 'ell with her and the likes of her,"
>   The other bums all say.

As nearly as your research department can discover, the heroine of this song was somebody who lived in Morgan Street along about 1885. That she was a character unique among a collection of characters is the opinion of Michael Sullivan, a retired policeman who in that period was walking a beat along Lake Street.

"I remember the song," he says. "The neighbors used to object to this woman. She sold beer and homemade yacky-dock in her parlor without a license. It was a sort of beer parlor, you might say. And she was about fifty years ahead of her time. The lady didn't sing the song herself. The neighbors, they sang it at her."

Another ballad by a native song contriver whose name escapes me had a long roaring success. It seems to me that I heard it at least once a week between 1895 and 1905. It was done in what a contemporary critic called the "culinary method" and was naturally a sensation with the folks who didn't eat too regularly during the depression that followed the World's Fair. Try it on your piano:

> She's my chicken pie, she's my oyster pie,
> She's my sweetness and she's tasty.
> She's my candy heart, she's my apple tart,
> And she fills my every dream.
> She's my Sally Lun, she's my currant bun,
> She's my steak and kidney pie.
> She's my lollipop, she's my chocolate drop,
> She's strawberries and cream.

And before you leave the subject you might recall a few lines from that thing they were singing in 1928 about "You're the Cream in My Coffee." When Chicago lyricists innovated a style it stayed innovated.

Toward the end of the nineties the composers had a lot of competition from the cakewalk school of lyrics. In 1898 the woods were crowded with patriots grinding out songs in praise of Dewey (the admiral, not the gifted governor) and Schley and the Rough-riders—and the *Maine*.

But the "Shake a Leg Mah Honey" output died quickly of mass production, and the "Dewy Were the Regent's Eyes" arias lasted only as long as the Spanish-American War, which wasn't very long. In the end the good old folk ballad proved its permanence.

In the nineteen hundreds candy pulls, Halloween parties and other home festivals still were being enlivened by the saga of "The Rock Island Express":

244

> Eternal is the greed for gold
> While life is short and fickle.
> They blew the safe in the baggage car
> And they killed poor Kellogg Nichol.

And one continued to hear resonant echoes of the once popular piece about the Cronin murder:

> Pat Cronin was a doctor and a patriot as well.
> And how the traitors murdered him I now propose to tell.

You can't really say that these things lacked historical significance. They began, most of them, in the news of the day, and they wound up in vocal tradition.

There was an old boy who lived across lots from us in Lake View who had an undoubted gift for this sort of composition. His name was George Fife, which may or may not mean something to you if you are a connoisseur of balladry.

By trade he was a clerk in Doberman's Lincoln Avenue Saloon, but in his private life he was a frustrated minstrel. Most of his spare time he spent appearing on the programs of neighborhood benefits where he sang his own songs, accompanying himself on a portable reed organ for free. His peak performance, as I remember it, was a sort of hymn he dashed off to commemorate the Iroquois fire:

> The theater was crowded
> With a gay and happy throng
> Of people who had come to see
> The play and hear the song.
> When what is this that strikes the ear
> In accents rising higher?
> The crowd sits back with horror thrilled
> As someone hollers "Fire!"

CHORUS

Oh, the terrible Iroquois fire,
The terrible Iroquois fire!
There's many a broken heart tonight
On account of the Iroquois fire.

This ballad, naturally, was a tremendous hit. But Fife didn't make any money on it. Lots of really fine pieces had a similar fate. It is difficult to figure why, unless something was wrong with the copyright law and there wasn't any association of authors, composers and publishers. In this group was one of the hardiest perennials ever produced. It was sung all over the Middle West for a couple of generations without benefit of royalties.

One refers, of course, to that terrifically stirring song called "The Ballad of the *Lady Elgin*." It was one of those exceptional things produced under tremendous emotional stress. The composer heard the shocking news of the *Lady Elgin* and, the next day, had finished his song:

Up from the poor man's cottage,
    Forth from the mansion door,
Sweeping across the water,
    And echoing 'long the shore,
Caught by the morning breezes,
    Borne on the evening gale,
Cometh a voice of mourning,
    A sad and solemn wail.

CHORUS

Lost on the *Lady Elgin*
    Sleeping to wake no more
Numbered in that three hundred
    Who failed to reach the shore.

Some critics of the present generation fail to see any charm in this ballad. I can still hear the verdict of one of them who said it must have been produced by a deaf-mute illiterate recently graduated from a saloon. But you never can tell. The author of "The Ballad of the *Lady Elgin*" was Henry Work. And about one of his other ballads there has been no complaint. The name of that one was "Marching Through Georgia."

Chapter 31

A Touch of the Comics

THE comic strip, about which we are still hearing no end of debate, is said to have received its start in the form of little bears and tigers produced by Jimmy Swinnerton in San Francisco in 1892. But the youth of Chicago was ignorant of this important trend in art until William Randolph Hearst established the *Chicago American* in 1900.

By that time Swinnerton's little animals had become minor characters in an extensive pageant. R. F. Outcault was producing a single-picture comic called "Hogan's Alley" in which the central figure was a small buck-toothed lad dressed in a yellow garment like a nightshirt. It took no great imagination to identify him as the "Yellow Kid."

Hogan's Alley was a sort of plaza surrounded by tenements whose occupants were shown each week in a variety of activities— chasing cats, feeding canary birds with syringes, fighting, singing, riding bicycles on parapets, climbing ropes, playing musical instruments or dropping flowerpots on one another from the numerous windows. If you craved action in art, here it was—and plenty of it.

But that was only the beginning of the colored comic supple-
248

ment. There was going to be a lot more of it and a lot more talk about it.

Cartooning genius had run wild during the five or six years before Mr. Hearst came to Chicago. The strips had taken on something of the character they have now. Taking inspiration from the kinetoscope or the cinematograph or whatever they called the early movies, they contrived to tell a story in a series of pictures. And thus the palpitant world acquired Foxy Grandpa, the Katzenjammer Kids, Happy Hooligan, Maud the Mule, and Mutt and Jeff.

Plots were simple in that early day, and there were no serials. Always in the last picture of every strip came a definite climax. That it was generally the same climax apparently did not make the comic less humorous. Maud the Mule kicked somebody, the Katzenjammers dumped something onto the head of Uncle Louie or tripped up the Captain, Happy Hooligan found himself in his customary peck of trouble. And next week they started all over again to attain the same ends.

One thing about the early comics is that they made some attempt to be comical. They didn't go in very heavily for human interest. They didn't have much to do with nice little boys. And they never presented precocious little girls taking their elders by the hand and leading them over precarious roads to great riches. There weren't any hard-boiled detectives chasing maniacal crooks through miles of color engraving and endless years. The hillbilless with nothing to wear but a chemise was under cover in her mountaintop boudoir. And, one recalls, there weren't any brave aviators engaged in secret missions to rescue bad-eyed females or save the naughty world.

The characters of the comic-strip parade in the 1900s were clowns who behaved like clowns. Their humor was broad but it was basic. And we shall skip the argument over whether the artists were right or wrong in making it that way. The world was still simple enough to chuckle when somebody got a kick in the pants and to roar at the sight of a fat man slipping on a banana peel.

Happy Hooligan and his associates were generally accepted as very real and pleasing figures by the newspaper customers. They were also very real and satisfactory—if not so comic—to the lads who compile the figures for circulation.

It is interesting to note that despite the highly moral tone of these celebrities in the strips, and their great popularity, there were still a few people in the country who refused to recognize them socially. My mother, for instance, took a very dim view of them—and not because she had to read me the caption lines and the balloon conversations. She thought they were vulgar or, what was even worse, undignified.

Other parents in our block complained that such little hellions as the Katzenjammers put wrong ideas into the heads of children and undermined their respect for their elders. I take it that these critics were always in fear of being blown up with dynamite or having the house pulled down over their heads by means of cables attached to steam rollers. I know very little about other people's reaction to the comics, but my own was quite simple. Hans and Fritz Katzenjammer were little boys quite like myself, but they lived in a different world. In their world it was quite all right to break up the dishes with a hammer or throw hand grenades at one's relatives. Such antics, of course, were nice to contemplate. But they weren't the vogue in the world I lived in. I had been taught that along with other things.

As it turned out, the loudest critics came to admit that they had entertained a lot of needless worries. In the course of the years nothing had happened to them. If their houses fell down, it was due not to bombs but to age. And all of us, the sweet little children of the area, had been kind and thoughtful in dealing with our

250

elders—or anyway just as kind and thoughtful as we'd been before there were any Katzenjammers.

Perhaps some of us lost our respect for dignity as represented by plug hats and boiled shirts. But we never thought of wearing a Hooligan tin can for a hat or adorning ourselves in one of the Yellow Kid's nightgowns. We admired Hans and Fritz for their amazing courage and inventiveness. In a way, I guess, we envied their success against adult supervision. But no matter how intoxicated we may have been by the thought of their grand achievements, we never sawed the props out from under the front porch or assaulted the neighbors with field artillery.

We realized quickly what one of the differences was between the world we lived in and that occupied by the Katzenjammers: they had all the equipment they needed and we didn't. They could do strange tricks because they had cannons and trucks and explosives and ladders and tools and flying machines. Without such apparatus we were as inept as simple savages. Whether or not we wanted to give our relatives the fits, we couldn't. So far as our neighborhood was concerned, the comic strips never led us into any crime more terrible than ringing doorbells.

Not all the strips that brightened our lives in those tender years were pure slapstick. The meticulous Winsor McKay, one of the most imaginative artists of his generation, joined the procession with "Little Nemo," the adventures of a small boy in the land of dreams.

The cast of characters, out of deference to the current vogue, contained one very fine hoodlum equal in all specifications to Happy Hooligan, or Circus Solly, or the as yet unborn Moon Mullins. This stalwart, who was always contriving to gum things up, even in Dreamland, was a little man called Flip. He wore minstrel-show clothes, had a blue face that he might have borrowed from a baboon and was always shown smoking a huge cigar.

Children loved him, however much they may have disliked his face.

The story of Little Nemo was a pictured fairy tale. The dreaming lad was constantly moving past glorious backgrounds—cloudy castles, lacy spires, brilliant gardens, floating mountains—and if the action led to the inevitable kick in the pants, well, what of that?

The beautiful princesses and air-borne horsemen and other nice people were never involved in such matters. They were the assignment of Flip, who had been created just to take the kicks or, on occasion, to give them to other characters quite like himself. And a belly laugh is a belly laugh, even in Hogan's Alley.

All in all I liked the comics, and I am quite sure I was no exception in our neighborhood. Whatever the baneful influence of this form of art, I fail to recollect that any of us bothered the policemen much. We went to school regularly, like the good little tots we were. And we always remembered when Sunday was at hand—the day of church and quiet and peace and rest. In such an environment Maud the Mule and the Yellow Kid occupied a position of high priority.

Chapter 32

The Oratorical Business

$\mathbf{T}$HE moving pictures and the radio and television have been responsible for quite a lot of annoyances—see your daily newspaper for details. But whatever their faults, they have contributed something ineffably fine to the remnants of civilization that we enjoy at the moment. By getting people out of the house of an evening or by imposing long periods of domestic silence, they have brought the good old living room back to its original status as a place to sit in and relax. Gone is the somewhat boring neighborhood prodigy who could always get to your house despite rain or sleet or snow to show a few card tricks. And also gone is the nineteenth century's crowning menace, the female elocutionist—gone with the wind that she furnished herself.

I wonder if in our so-called halls of learning they still teach little girls—and boys—to speak pieces. The last few graduation exercises we have attended were singularly free from dramatic readings of "The Wreck of the Hesperus" and "Paul Revere's Ride." But you never can tell. In some of our school basements troops of talented young womanhood may be training to overwhelm the world with a mass recital of "The House That's Never Been Lived In," with "gestures that originate at a point over the heart." And

253

old fugitives from the parlor dramatics of the nineties must never relax their vigilance.

The unfortunate part of the elocution business was that it always popped up unheralded. If you were as old as six years, you knew it was going to happen. That was certain. But there was never any preliminary warning—no invitation, no advance notice. All of a sudden there it was, a menace almost impossible to miss.

Here is one of those Sunday-evening gatherings that nobody was ever able to see or provide for. The Gilligans, who "just happened to be driving by in our new rig," came in "for only a minute," all four of them, and stayed to accept a cup of tea and a slice of cold roast beef. Then Ella and Minnie Miller, or their reasonable equivalents, would drop in to show off a couple of new hats. The Andrews boys—Harry, John and Richard—would ring the doorbell about six-thirty on an alleged canvass of the neighborhood. They were peddling tickets to the Old Settlers' Picnic or working their way through Barber College by making the world safe for crayon enlargements. Five minutes later the Lange sisters, who lived a few doors down the block, would show up because they had noted the interesting appearance of Harry, John and Richard. And there would be others on the front porch before the evening was over. Among them was certain to be Miss Whosis—any Miss Whosis—who, whatever her lack of other charms, certainly had the gift of free-running recitation.

The evening would be getting on pretty well as such evenings went. Old Man Gilligan would be sounding off to the man of the house about some unthinkable plot to elect a Republican alderman in the First Ward. The Andrews boys—Harry, John and Richard—and the Lange sisters—Gracie, Maisie and Julia—and the Miller sisters—Ella and Minnie—would be holding a caucus on some new show at McVicker's that none of them had ever seen. Sundry females would be cutting up some old acquaintances. . . . And the hostess? Well, you never had to doubt what she'd be doing. She would be listening with rapt attention to Miss Whosis telling about her recent trip to Paw-Paw Lake.

There would presently be a rising tide of babble from the front parlor with murmuring echoes throughout the house. And then it would happen. Halting a dozen conversations, the lady of the house would rise with her inevitable announcement.

"Folks, I have just made the most pleasant discovery! Miss Whosis is a professional elocutionist and has given dramatic readings at Orpheum Hall in Philadelphia and at Hyde Park Athenaeum in Chicago, and at the Tip Top Moving Picture Theater and—well, just about every place. . . ."

Here it was customary to pause while the audience murmured suitable phrases of surprise, pleasure and anticipation. The audience had no trouble doing this, whatever might be the majority opinion of dramatic readings. It was well trained in parlor courtesies, and to sneer at talent, boring or otherwise, would have been considered wretchedly impolite.

"And," the lady of the house would proceed unnecessarily, "I am sure Miss Whosis could be persuaded to speak a piece for us."

The guess was always right. Could Miss Whosis be persuaded to parade her art? You bet she could.

She was always on her feet before the dull echoes of the crowd's urging had died away: "Oh, do!" . . . "Yes, indeed, please do, Miss Whosis!" . . . "Give us that beautiful one about the dying gladiator. . . ."

The lips of everyone from Old Man Gilligan to the smallest Lange sister moved with gracious phrase, even though a lot of faces in the gathering may have been just a little unenthusiastic. Everybody went through the ritual despite the fact, or maybe because of it, that every other male and female in the place was also a parlor elocutionist. Without ever having heard Miss Whosis they didn't think much of her. But she had contrived to beat the field to the center of attention, and it was only sporting to applaud.

255

So Miss Whosis stepped forward to the spot in the bay window most favored by declamationists. She took a dramatic pose alongside the curly-legged brass table with the onyx top. She smiled the shy smile that she had acquired with the first $2.50 lesson in Miss Julia Arthington's Elocution School. She fluttered a filmy handkerchief in a languid hand, and she recited. Boy, how she recited!

"I shall give you first," she would begin (showing that, as usual, there would be plenty of wonderful parts to her performance). "I shall give you first Will Carleton's touching poem, 'Over the Hill to the Poorhouse.' "

The Delsarte system, guaranteed to make all women charming through a routine of body movements and trained facial expressions, was just slipping out of favor with the intelligentsia when Miss Whosis started to make a lifework of elocution. But its influence was still abroad. She told of the lonesome trip to the poorhouse with gestures each of which started with a drooping curve from the vicinity of her heart. The hand then moved in a series of shorter arcs to suit the words of the piece: quick circles to denote a galloping horse or an oncoming tempest or a tidal wave; an upward hoist to interpret lofty ambition, spiritual aspiration or the ascent of the Matterhorn. A succession of lesser loops depicted a more gentle rise or the awakening of the spirit or the bursting of a small firecracker or the dawn of hope. With these simple, stylized signals Miss Whosis made the poor mother's trip to the poorhouse something no one was likely to forget. With the speaker's well-trained voice sobbing in the background you could almost see the bereft old girl—anyway, you could hear her.

The only trouble was you got so used to hearing about such heartless treatment of Mother every time some female got up to recite that you no longer appreciated the tragedy of it all. You always reacted properly to the finish, though. Mother got rescued from the poorhouse and, fortunately, that brought the piece to an end.

Miss Whosis went on, of course—and on and on. She stood on the bridge with the brave Horatius and rode the plains with Laska. She helped the moronic youth in "Excelsior" to carry his inappropriate banner up to the mountaintop. It was expected of her. And a traditional, if not entirely entertaining, evening was had by all.

The lady is gone now—and what a pity! Changes in modern life, one might say a regrettable apathy toward parlor culture, have driven her into distant memory. That is why so few old-timers ever find a word to say against the movies, or the stage, or the radio. It is always easy to walk out of a theater or turn a switch.

It is difficult now to remember that in the 1900s little boys, too, learned to speak pieces. They jolly well had to. They ruined afternoons and evenings just as their sisters did and as purveyors of entertainment were considerably worse. No matter! Nobody cared, They had social status—the sort of social status that only the stumbling recital of a splendid lyric can give one.

When you were able to memorize "The Monk Felix" or "The Charge of the Light Brigade" you were not only permitted to show off in front of adults, you were requested to. You stood there with your hands in your pockets and your eyes fixed hypnotically on the ceiling and bravely mumbled your lines. One line at a time you ticked the piece off and came to the end with great surprise. You got all sorts of heartening applause—which should have been even more surprising: "He never took a lesson in his life." . . . "He knows longer poems, but he's a little bashful about reciting them." . . . "And he's only eleven years old—just think of that!" . . . "Some day he's going to be a regular actor—his heart's set on it." . . . "And he'll do fine at that—he's got the knack of it!"

Sometimes the performances paid off in more tangible benefits. Strangers in the house were generally good for a nickel or a dime, although close friends of the family might get a little calloused toward the difficulties of the Monk Felix or King Robert or Roderick Dhu. And there were always neighborhood socials, bigger, better and more numerous than we have seen since the coming of the automobile and movies. These splendid binges were alike in a couple of essentials: they had avalanches of ice cream and the chairman of the program committee was always distracted. The scheduled entertainers, who were probably crashing the gate at some other party, seldom showed up. So a little boy with a one-piece repertoire could always achieve popularity and a liberal award of dessert just by being on hand.

Your reporter knows this to be a fact, inasmuch as for several years he was a sort of emergency attraction at celebrations given by neighborhood schools, kindergartens, churches and civic societies and marching clubs. He mentions this merely as a fact and with no spirit of boastfulness. However smugly satisfied with himself he may have been at the time and whatever the size of his reward in ice cream, pop or candy, he lacked the sense of timing that makes the great actor or the successful chiseler.

Like all the rest of the little lads of his day, he learned one piece. It was called "The Night before Christmas" and received tumultuous applause when ladled out to tired audiences for Christmas, Easter, Ground-Hog Day or the Fourth of July. It was noticeable, however, that the returns for this rendition were better at Christmas, though hardly good enough to justify the learning of another piece.

Elocution teachers working with classes in the schools made their appearance in the late nineties. They were ambitious girls, not too talented, who wanted to remake the world into a place where everybody would one day be reciting "The Wreck of the Hesperus" at everybody else. They didn't last because they failed

258

to realize that for every dramatic reader you ought to have at least one dramatic listener. But they lasted long enough to confuse the status of poetry in the community for nearly a generation.

Longfellow met the popular demand with "The Hesperus" and "The Ride of Paul Revere." Whittier and the old lady who gave Stonewall Jackson his comeuppance at Frederick Town, Maryland, were high in professional esteem. But this Shakespeare that you used to be hearing about—well, in an era of smart young elocution teachers he just lacked the zip, even if the sixth-grade Marlowes and Mantells had been able to figure out what he was talking about.

So the highwayman "came riding, riding, riding, *riding,* up to the old inn door . . ." and brave Horatius held the bridge, and the boy stood on the burning deck, and the Elizabethan dramatists were pretty well forgotten. . . .

Those were the days!

"Young Lochinvar is come out of the West. . . ." And he's up to no good, you can bet on that. Lochinvar was determined to snatch a bride out of Netherby Hall. And you can still hear little John Beubler, aged twelve, shouting about the whole sad business.

And there was "Laska"! One forgets her purpose in life and most of the other things about her except that she was always riding over the plains at somebody's side.

And there was another character who got into trouble—as people in dramatic readings were so likely to do—by going A.W.O.L. in the Civil War. "Deserter? Yes, Captain, the word's about right. . . . Though it's uncommon queer I should run from a fight. . . . I who fought all my life for the rights of my ranchy with the wily Apache and the cruel Comanche. . . ." Despite the fact that his difficulties were howled from every stage and in every front parlor in Chicago for years and years, nobody nowadays can remember what became of him. . . . Gone, all are gone, the old familiar Indians.

The gallant six hundred were hardy perennials at graduation exercises and such things. King Robert of Sicily, appareled in magnificent attire, seemed likely never to die. The parlor walls echoed each night to his memory. And the Count de Lorge, almost daily and with varying effect, continued to throw "the glove, but not with love, full in the lady's face." (You may remember that she had sent him after it into a den of lions.)

But these familiar heroes were by no means the only ones of that heroic era. Miss Elsie Goodale, the teacher of elocution and Delsarte who worked our neighborhood, knew quite a lot that were just as noteworthy. I still shudder to think of "The Little Circus Boy" and how I struggled to memorize the details of his career.

The story is opened by a commentator on his way to what he calls "the churchyard on the hill, the village of the dead," and there with fine dramatic timing he discovers a headstone bearing an epitaph: "Here lies the little circus boy, who did the best he could." Then, of course, he tells what happened.

The little circus boy apparently was a noble lad, but he couldn't ride a horse for sour apples. The manager, revealed as a three-ring dastard, failed to see that the little boy wasn't trying to clown. So one night when the little boy lit in the sawdust on his face things came to a climax. To wit:

> "The manager picked up the boy
>   Whose limbs were strained and sore.
> 'You fell off purposely,' he cried.
>   And angrily he swore."

He was still swearing when the little boy made his ringing protest: "I did the best I could." With that he died and everybody was sad. It was a great misunderstanding all around.

And then there was Gaudentis, the very greatest of Miss Goodale's paladins. He was an architect in ancient Rome, and he went like this:

> Beside Vespasian's regal throne,
> Skillful Gaudentis stood.
> "Build me," the haughty monarch cried,
> "A theater for blood!
> A citizen of Roman rights,
> Silver and gold in store,
> These shall be thine, let Christian blood
> But stain the marble floor...."

The offer was not good enough. Gaudentis didn't want any citizen of Roman rights, even as an imperial award. So somebody else built the arena and the opening show consisted of Gaudentis and two lions. I can still remember the long silence that greeted me when I told the judges of a declamation contest about it in 1901.

Hardly a man is now alive who remembers Vespasian's regal throne, or "The Little Circus Boy" who did the best he could, or "Old Ironsides," or "How They Brought the Good News from Ghent to Aix."... And perhaps it is just as well.

Chapter 33

The Whitechapel Club

Police Inspector John L. Revere took a couple of us to look at the headquarters of the Whitechapel Club before it moved out of Newsboys' Alley to make room for the LaSalle Hotel. He wasn't exactly a member, but he had a permanent entree to the place as a purveyor of bloody shirts and hangman's rope.

The Whitechapel Club, in case you don't know about it, was that kind of club.

My little companion and I were suitably impressed. The room was close-fitting and somewhat morose. Even in the glare of four gas flames it was dark. The ceiling, which slanted like an attic roof, seemed to be bearing down like the top of a letter press.

All of that seemed right and proper to us, for the place was filled with wondrous things. There were human skulls tastefully hung to the chandeliers and doorframes. Swords, dirks, rifles, shotguns, hatpins and derringers decorated the walls with no hint of a woman's hand save for a lace-edged handkerchief above the piano.

"Addie Meeker's handkerchief," the inspector explained. "She put chloroform on it to kill her husband . . . not enough chloroform. He woke up and killed her instead. Very sad affair."

"What happened to him?" we wanted to know.

"Oh, him? Why, that's his skull over there near the window—the one with the gold tooth."

And so it went from one delectable subject to another until mid-afternoon when a few of the members strolled in and wanted to use their clubroom. The inspector gave us a fast ride home in his police buggy, and we filed away a hope that one day we might prove worthy of membership in so interesting an organization.

We never did. By the time we were old enough, the Whitechapel Club had passed out of Chicago into local folklore. Just about that time we came to realize that, after all, it had not been a police society or a den of murderous conspirators. It had been something of a literary society, no less—an organization interested in mental uplift and as devoted to cultural pursuits as, say, the Cliff Dwellers' Club. One draws erroneous conclusions from exhibits of hemp nooses and assassins' knives.

The Whitechapel Club came into being in 1886 because it seemed like a good idea to such exuberant spirits as Finley Peter Dunne (Mr. Dooley); Brand Whitlock, later mayor of Toledo and United States minister to Belgium; George Ade; T. E. Powers, cartoonist; Horace Taylor, cartoonist; W. W. Denslow, illustrator; Charlie Holloway, afterward a leading mural painter; William E. Mason, afterward United States Senator; Dr. G. Frank Lydston; Dr. Frank W. Reilly; Opie Read, novelist; Ben King, poet; John C. Eastman, not yet publisher of the Chicago *Daily Journal;* Alfred Henry Lewis, author of *Wolfville;* Hobart Chatfield Chatfield-Taylor; Frederic Upham; "Grizzly" Adams; and Tomo (Tombstone) Thompson.

In one way or another the founders of the club, and such worthies as they later admitted to associate with them, were tangled up with the arts.

Some of them wrote. Some painted. Some played on harps.

263

All of them enjoyed conversation, chairs with soft cushions, cheerful song and a bottle standing ready at a convenient table. The club made no effort to provide more than these simple necessities. It never had any money in its treasury. It never really had a treasury. But it always had plenty of members.

Very likely Dr. S. Spray, for many years in charge of the Elgin mental hospital, was responsible for the macabre motif of the Whitechapel's decorations. He had a collection of skulls which Charlie Holloway and Tombstone Thompson converted to globes for the gas jets by sawing off the tops and boring holes for mounting in the bottom. Presently other donors came around with similar trinkets.

The center table in the club's social room was a coffin resting on a sawhorse. Under glass in the middle of it reposed the skull of a female police character celebrated in life as Waterford Jack, the Queen of the Sands.

The Sands, a district of tough resorts north of the river and adjoining what is now the Gold Coast, had been put out of business by Long John Wentworth. But the Queen, undaunted, changed her address and continued her business. As a gracious gesture in leaving the world, she bequeathed her skull to the Whitechapel Club, or, at any rate, that is how the story went.

The adornments of the Common Room, which was also the only room the club happened to have, were other things, of course, beyond the weapons of killers and the relics of Jack Ketch. In the course of the years the most celebrated artists in the country had dropped into the hole in the wall off Newsboys' Alley for an evening of wassail and palaver. In token of which, they all left signed sketches of one thing and another, all in all a collection that might well have brought good prices in the art mart. But it didn't happen that way. Completely out of funds and about to lose its beautiful home, the organization eventually was absorbed by the Press Club, which, by some processes never lucidly explained, had become wealthy. A lot of the Whitechapel Club's cherished possessions got lost in transit from Newsboy's Alley to the new quarters.

The membership made one notable but deficient effort to refinance in 1891 when the city seems to have worked itself into a drool over a mayoralty election. Out of their theoretical cloister came the club politicians with their own ticket.

"Tombstone" Thompson and "Grizzly" Adams were selected as a nominating committee. They promptly named Hobart Chatfield Chatfield-Taylor as the Whitechapel party's choice for mayor on the ground that he would get some sort of double billing on the ballot.

They were thoroughly polite about it. They visited their nominee and told him that, while it was their wish to use his name in full panoply, they might be content to use any part of it in a pinch. Mr. Hobart Chatfield Chatfield-Taylor bowed to destiny and urged them on.

So the club held another meeting. This time the entire membership was assigned to serve on a finance committee, or, as they called it, "the touch committee." Once they had been sworn in they wandered into the city to solicit funds. They did quite well, too.

When the returns came in on election day it was discovered that Chatfield-Taylor lacked a little of being the people's choice.

He had mustered a thousand votes, but the total was much less than he needed. He wasn't downcast, however, and neither was the club membership. The important feature of the election came with the report of the touch committee. It was shown that thanks to the eager work of the committeemen, $900 in campaign funds now rested in the club treasury.

This phenomenon is said to have inspired Ben King's most favored poem, "If I Should Die To-night!" . . . Well, maybe it did.

"If I should die to-night
And you should come to my cold corpse and say,
Weeping and heartsick o'er my lifeless clay—
    If I should die to-night
And you should come in deepest grief and woe
And say, 'Here's that ten dollars that I owe'—
    I might arise in my large white cravat
    And say, 'What's that?'

"If I should die to-night
And you should come to my cold corpse and kneel,
Clasping my bier to show the grief you feel—
    I say, if I should die to-night
And you should come to me and there and then
Just even hint of paying me that ten,
    I might arise the while;
    But I'd drop dead again."

Mystery and Crime 6:

The Phantom Bridegroom

THEY buried Dr. Alleyne Hensley, wealthy physician and scion of the Hensley family of Norfolk, Virginia, far from the family lot in Ardmere Cemetery. The impressive last rites were in charge of the Hobos Union of America, local 337.

The body was on view in Chicago as it had been previously displayed in Atlanta, Georgia. Literally thousands came to look for the last time upon the face of Dr. Hensley at the Western Casket Company's morgue on North Michigan Avenue—which was somewhat surprising inasmuch as he had not been very well known here.

He was tastefully dressed in a $200 tweed suit, which was pretty expensive for a period in which Ten Dollar Tom Murray was willing to provide twenty suits that looked quite similar for the same price. His rugged face seemed a bit sad in death. But there was nothing ethereal about him. You would have picked him for anything on earth but a phantom bridegroom, and your judgment would have been utterly wrong.

The tragedy of Dr. Alleyne Hensley belongs to Chicago only because his mysterious journey ended here. More properly it had to do with Atlanta, because that is where Miss Anna Waite Carvon

267

lived. It was from Atlanta, shortly before the First World War, that she set out so gaily and so eagerly to marry him.

Anna Waite Carvon was the daughter of the Reverend John George Carvon, pastor of an Episcopalian church. A lonely child who made friends with great difficulty, she had grown up amid all the advantages of a cultured, comfortable home. She had an excellent education, played the piano well and when she could conquer her shyness was a good conversationalist and a pleasant companion. As she grew older she came at last to take a part in numerous church activities and made many friends—all of them women.

The women of the parish liked her. They invited her to their parties and she in turn invited them to the rectory. But until the coming of Dr. Alleyne Hensley there were no men in her life. When she was a child, boys terrified her. As a young woman, correct and cold, she stood aloof from all the young men of her circle. They, apparently, were quite content to have it that way.

Miss Carvon was never a beautiful girl, but she wasn't ugly by any means. She had nice manners and grace and considerable charm. But that made no difference. She entered her early thirties without a suitor and with no prospects. It was a difficult thing for her friends to understand, the more so in that when she was thirty a grandmother died and left her a small fortune.

Mrs. Mary James, who was closer to her, perhaps, than anyone else outside the family, spoke to her about it.

"I suppose it's because you don't want to get married," she said. "Certainly you ought to be able to get a dozen beaux if you cared about having them."

Anna smiled. "But I do want to get married," she said—and Mrs. James remembered the speech verbatim for years afterward. "I do want to get married. Every normal woman wants to get married. . . . But she has to make careful choice. Someday I'll

268

tell you about the handsome physician I met last year when I was visiting my Aunt Gracie-May in Norfolk. . . ."

Not long after that Miss Carvon's friends heard that she was receiving packets of mail from Virginia. To close confidantes at the time she would read excerpts from them—poetic declarations of love. Beautiful presents came, too—cut-glass vases, ormolu ware, tooled leather and the like—all expensive but in the best of taste. Every day this fervent suitor asked her to marry him.

Presently all the town was buzzing about Anna Waite Carvon's tempestuous admirer. The newspapers constantly demanded photographs of him and learned his name. Miss Carvon's friends accused her of jealous selfishness in concealing him. She greeted all this interest with a Mona Lisa smile. Presently, when a few skeptics were beginning to doubt the existence of Dr. Alleyne Hensley, she invited some of the town's best gossips to an afternoon tea. She announced that she was leaving the next day for New York to be married.

She would be back with her husband in a month, she said. Perhaps she could persuade Alleyne to buy a local practice. But anyway, she would be the happiest woman in the world—no doubt of it.

The next day she went away, radiantly happy—almost beautiful. Most of the friends she had made during her childhood were at the station to see her off. Few things of similar note had happened to her since the Civil War.

She was gone only three days when the home town received the tragic news: Dr. Alleyne Hensley was dead. He had been struck down by a streetcar as he stepped from a carriage at the entrance of the church where he was to be married to Miss Anna Waite Carvon.

The newspapers printed that much of the story, embellished with miscellaneous data concerning the would-have-been bride and her family. But there was no additional information until the distraught woman arrived with the body five days later—and not much then.

"I have brought him home to Atlanta with me," she explained, "because he had no family and I was almost his wife. . . . I feel that I have the right. . . ." She laid a spray of tiny yellow roses on the coffin and went to her old room.

Sentimental Atlanta was shaken by the magnitude of this tragedy. But not the Reverend John George Carvon. He knew his daughter too well. When Anna Waite came downstairs in the evening to resume her place at the head of the coffin he was gentle but firm.

"I've been talking to the coroner's office in New York," he said. "And nobody named Alleyne Hensley came to a violent death there last week or during the past ten months. I have also consulted the American Medical Association in Norfolk. There is no doctor named Alleyne Hensley on the Norfolk register. Also, this man obviously has been dead longer than five days. Now who is he?"

"I don't really know," replied Miss Anna, drying her eyes. "He was found dead on the railroad tracks in a switchyard outside of Chicago. They had him in an undertaking place. I claimed the body and bought him a decent suit of clothes and a coffin.

"I didn't think it meant much to him, whoever he was. And it meant a lot to me. It's a lot less distressing to be a figure in a great tragedy than to go through life as the woman nobody wanted. . . ."

So Dr. Alleyne Hensley came back to Chicago and again was laid out in the back room of the Western Casket Company. Throngs passed his bier—but none of the thousands had ever seen him before.

After a week of this, Manager W. J. Duffy once more released the body, this time to Jeff Davis, president of the Hobos Union, who said that a needle and thread found in the suit the man had been wearing when picked up identified him as a member.

Dr. Alleyne Hensley had a fine funeral. The Episcopal burial service was conducted by the Reverend Irwin St. John Tucker at the old Cathedral of Saints Peter and Paul on West Washington Boulevard. Dr. Tucker also preached a funeral sermon, and at the end played a recessional on the organ as some 200 hobos moved to such conveyances as happened to be assembled outside.

There was only one sign to indicate that the uniquely honored tramp in the expensive coffin had once been a wealthy physician and the scion of a prominent old family of Norfolk, Virginia: some woman had insisted on leaving a badly wilted spray of small yellow roses on the box lid.

PART VII

THEIR VIRTUES BOLD

Chapter 34

Marine Disaster

THEY tore the end off a cottage on Irving Park Road near the American Hospital about twelve years ago to make space for a nurses' home. And that, of course, is hardly worth mentioning in the public prints except for the fact that a few old-timers in the vicinity were wondering what had become of the front door.

The door, so local folklore experts had maintained for about seventy-seven years, had come from the wreck of the *Lady Elgin.* If so, it was probably the last memento of one of the world's greatest marine disasters—one of the largest in the history of steam navigation and definitely Chicago's own.

For an inland city Chicago has produced considerably more than its share of great sea stories—ghastly tragedies like the sinking of the *Lady Elgin,* the overturning of the *Eastland* at her dock, heartbreaking epics like the wreck of the "Christmas ship," the *Rouse Simmons,* incredible sagas like that of the lumberyard clerk who bought the 4,000-ton *City of Paris* for $900. And it has furnished the locale for at least one mystery as great as any that ever came out of blue water.

During the First World War the front pages of the country's newspapers were filled with speculation about the U.S.S. *Cyclops,* a naval collier that had disappeared somewhere on a journey from the Pacific coast to the Atlantic. The puzzle of what happened to it on a rough voyage of several thousand miles is still unsolved and remains a subject of interest and argument wherever seafaring men are gathered together. But to Chicagoans old enough to remember, it should have seemed like the familiar counterpart of the more eerie story of the S.S. *Chicora*. The *Chicora*, a ship of Chicago registry, sailed out of Milwaukee on the ninety-mile run to St. Joseph, Michigan, on January 21, 1895, and left no trace. No relic of the vessel's existence was ever seen again. Small boys on both sides of the lake scoured the beaches diligently for a number of years, your correspondent among them. But when the *Chicora* went, apparently, she went to stay.

Marine disasters on the lakes generally survived in a manner out of all proportions to their importance. That was probably because the water was normally tranquil and storms and wrecks and sudden death seemed hardly possible.

There was still plenty of conversation about the *Lady Elgin* in the late nineties. She went down on September 8, 1860, before Fort Sumter was fired on, before Abraham Lincoln's first election. But, despite the horrendous happenings of the Civil War and the lesser calamities of a cholera plague and the Great Fire, the memory of her ghastly finish was still vivid in all the lake ports.

The oldsters, many of whom could not possibly have seen her, still discussed the wreck with bated breath and an air of personal concern. Most of the lads of my generation went through boyhood under the impression that the ship had been sunk only yesterday or the day before.

It is natural enough that the *Lady Elgin* should not have been forgotten. Lake Michigan had a more important place in the imagination and concern of the city than it has had since the development of the railroads.

The lake was an important road out to the east. For most of

every year it provided transportation for the wheat that this area produced and a return of materials and tools that the growing community needed. Even aside from that, the smashing of the ship—northbound from Chicago to Milwaukee—may have been the greatest marine tragedy since the invention of steam power. It was certainly the cause of the greatest loss of life recorded to that date on inland waters.

Three hundred persons were drowned somewhere north of Lake Bluff. Less than a hundred were saved. Remains of the victims were still being found along Lake Michigan's shore between Evanston and Highland Park as recently as 1923.

The *Lady Elgin* was a remarkable ship. When she sailed out of a Canadian port in 1851 she was not only the largest steam vessel on the Great Lakes but very likely the largest afloat in all the world. She was a paddle ship 300 feet long and rated at a thousand tons. She was bigger than the *Natchez,* twice as big as the *Cirius* and seventy feet longer than the *Great Western*—which three were the undisputed queens of the Atlantic. Even so, the comparison is unfair to her inasmuch as the Atlantic ships were propelled by sails as well as steam. The *Lady Elgin* was not concerned with sails.

This ship was built to carry the mails but lost the contract when the Grand Trunk Railroad was built into Chicago in 1858. Gurdon S. Hubbard then bought her, refitted her as a gaudy excursion steamship and started regular service between Chicago and Milwaukee.

In August 1860 there was much bitter debate on the subject of the Fugitive Slave Law. The state of Wisconsin, as a result, came close to the point of secession. State officials, in open defiance of the government, declared they would not enforce the law. There were angry mass meetings and threatened riots, and the adjutant general made a quick canvass to find out how much reliance he could put on his militia.

Three companies of Irish-Americans, most of whom lived in Milwaukee, announced that they would stand by the government, whereupon they were disarmed and disbanded. In the hope that they might get help from their compatriots in Illinois they chartered the *Lady Elgin* and moved in force to Chicago.

They were well received, particularly on the west side of town by other Irish. They were wined and dined and given contributions toward their cause. Along about midnight they rolled back onto the big steamship, cheered by their success and shouting prophecies for a new day in Wisconsin. Most of them were asleep at two o'clock the next morning—September 8—when the schooner *Augusta,* loaded with lumber, suddenly came southward out of a roaring storm squarely in the *Lady Elgin's* course.

There was some argument afterward about whether or not the *Augusta* had been displaying riding lights. At any rate, nobody saw the schooner until she rammed into the excursion ship just aft of the port wheel. It was a fatal crash, for the *Lady Elgin* was breached below her water line.

Captain Malott of the *Augusta* seems to have been a little confused about what had happened. He knew that he had hit something, for he called out into the dark, "Do you need any help?"

Having shown this courtesy and received no answer, he apparently thought that he had performed his full duty. He sailed on through the night into Chicago. Thirty minutes after the collision the *Lady Elgin's* engines fell out through her bottom.

One lifeboat was successfully launched—a yawl commanded by steward Fred Rice, who tried vainly to patch up the hole in the *Lady Elgin's* side. But he was able to haul only a few passengers aboard. From 5:00 A.M., when daylight came, until two o'clock in the afternoon, he testified afterward, he had nothing to do except sit there and "watch people swimming in the water and drowning." Most of those who survived saved themselves by clinging to wreckage and drifting ashore before the gale.

278

Edward A. Spencer led a group of students of the Garrett Biblical Institute, now a part of Northwestern University, in repeated rescue attempts. Spencer himself swam out seventeen times to bring half-drowned victims ashore. A plaque recalling his heroism was installed in Patten gymnasium in 1921.

Milwaukee, with 350 orphans in a single city ward, went into mourning. Business came to a complete standstill in Chicago as crowds surged into the railroad stations to board trains for the north shore.

Captain Malott was arrested and, through some fault in the maritime laws, released. He died in another maritime wreck a few years later.

For decades music-hall ballad singers throughout the Middle West always included in their repertoires a popular piece called "Lost on the Lady Elgin." A copy of it stood on the rack of every melodeon in Chicago. There were records of it in Swiss music boxes. Illustrated replicas of its chorus hung in black frames, particularly in the Irish colony along "Archie Road." Brass bands blatted it dolefully as a dirge at the funerals of politicians. The towns about the lower end of Lake Michigan had little chance to forget the *Lady Elgin,* even if they had wanted to.

Sixty survivors of the wreck were still alive when a memorial convention was held in Chicago in 1910. Few of them were quite clear about what had happened. For the most part they had gone to sleep in beds. They had awakened to find themselves struggling in water. Somehow they had reached the shore alive.

Admittedly the tragedy had come to seem a little less near and poignant in 1910. There had been other disasters. There had been other dramatic news events with great loss of life and few survivors. There had been fires and epidemics and merciless tricks by the water. And the people who escaped with their lives from these scourges were not too much concerned with one that had happened before the beginning of the Civil War.

I heard about it from Grandpa Wilson, who had been in Chicago when it happened and who knew a lot of the local Irish who had had relatives aboard. His descriptions were much more vivid than those of the aged sixty who came to the survivors' convention in 1910. His account of the wreck may not have been entirely accurate, but it was certainly dramatic. It was filled with noise and fire and freezing water and deeds of high emprise—and it was different, somehow, from any of the other accounts of what happened out there on the night of September 8, 1860.

I was a little surprised in later years to discover that quite a few of the *Lady Elgin's* passenger list were still alive and well. I had gathered from Grandpa's account that the loss of life was 100 per cent. But I never asked him for further elucidation.

After all, there didn't seem to be much doubt that the *Lady Elgin* had actually been rammed and sunk in a Lake Michigan storm. Any youthful investigator in moments of grave doubt could always journey to Irving Park Road near Broadway and take a look at the cabin door that some cottage builder had salvaged. It was a bit narrow and possibly a bit thin, but it was certainly a long time in service.

At the time of the sinking of the *Lady Elgin,* and for many years afterward, steamships got very minor attention in Chicago's harbor. They were gaudy enough and novel enough, and they undoubtedly could carry freight and passengers quickly about the lakes. But there weren't enough of them. Sailing vessels, large, cumbersome, slow and built of wood, jammed the river for miles.

The river was deepened for them, although their draught wasn't very great. Turn bridges, which became one of the city's most noticeable characteristics, allowed their passage at every block. Bridges had a way of getting stuck, and so did ships. Almost from the beginning of the settlement, water transport and its vagaries made a fascinating spectacle.

280

The location of Chicago on the site it has occupied all these years was due to its offering of a link between the Great Lakes and the Mississippi Valley, or, in other words, to the short portage through swampy land between the Chicago River and the Des Plaines River. The cutting of the Illinois-Michigan Canal through this portage made it possible to run a barge line to Joliet and thence by way of the Illinois River to St. Louis. The Drainage Canal, which came long afterward, provides a practical waterway for much bigger ships. Twelve-hundred-and-fifty-ton submarines made the passage from the lakes to New Orleans in World War II.

Lake ships, from spring until fall, transport the iron of the Mesabi Range down through the lakes to mills in South Chicago and Gary. Ocean carriers from Sweden conduct a regular trade between their home ports and this end of Lake Michigan. Canadian paper comes by ship to Chicago newspapers with the regularity of a streetcar line. Excursion ships canvass the lakes on journeys long or short throughout the summer. And no end of odd cargoes pass southward to the canal while the weather is favorable.

So Chicago, the bulk of whose citizens will never have to set foot on a boat or travel a yard by water in all their lives, looks with friendliness at the lake, remembers the legends that began with the *Lady Elgin* and feels a relationship for the seamen who brought populations to the Atlantic coast. Chicagoans talk of the prosperity that Lake Michigan has brought to them, and they half believe the odd lore that their fathers and uncles and grandmothers heard every time the high wind was blowing over the water.

One of the most interesting people in our old neighborhood at the beginning of the century was a man who was building a tugboat in his back yard. There was a considerable division of opinion among the younger set concerning his mental status. For the back yard was on the west side of Ashland Avenue, the tugboat was twenty-five or thirty feet long and eight or ten feet wide, and the lake was nearly two miles away. But when I asked him how he was going to solve this difficulty I got a simple answer.

"You've seen houses moved, haven't you?" he inquired. "Well, then . . ."

That was the beginning of a beautiful friendship. In time I came to learn that his name was Oscar Nelson and that he was the son of another Oscar Nelson who, he said, had been a fireman aboard the *Chicora,* the ship that disappeared.

He looked the part. He was a tall, dark, dead-looking man who peered at you through heavy-lidded eyes and seldom smiled. At work on his boat he wore black overalls. On the street he always appeared in a black suit, white shirt and black necktie. Whether or not he was still grief-stricken five or six years after the loss of his father nobody had any way of telling. But the vanishing of the *Chicora,* as nearly as I could make out from his conversation, was quite the most important thing in his life. Since 1895 it had motivated all his actions and eventually had launched him on his career as a back-yard boat builder—an amazing denouement.

The *Chicora,* if we have failed to mention it, was a combination freight-and-passenger ship running out of Chicago. On the night of January 21, 1895, she picked up at Milwaukee an unexpected load of freight consigned to St. Joseph, Michigan, and canceled plans for going home. There doesn't seem to have been much regularity about the business of little ships in those days. The *Chicora* transferred half a dozen Chicago passengers to some other carrier, booked another five who wanted to go to St. Joseph and eventually set out on a run to the east. The night was calm and fairly warm for that season of the year. But a rousing gale came up sometime before morning and that was the end of the *Chicora.* The death list was set down as twenty-four crewmen and five passengers, none of whom was ever seen again.

For days thereafter tugs and coast guard cutters moved slowly back and forth along the established lane between Milwaukee and

St. Joseph. The lookouts saw nothing—not an overturned lifeboat, nor a cork ring, nor a belt, nor a drifting plank or a scrap of debris. How this could happen is one of the things that has always puzzled lake sailormen. That sudden storms of deadly violence develop in these waters is no secret. Some twenty ships, including a big car ferry, were wrecked by a gale off northern Michigan in a single night in 1913. But never, either before or since the *Chicora* headed out of Milwaukee on her last trip, has any ship on the lakes vanished so completely.

"And I'm going to find her," Oscar Nelson declared. "I'll never rest until I do. That's why I'm building this tug. I'm putting glass-covered ports in the bottom. When I get her launched she'll be like those glass-decked boats they've got around Catalina Island. I'll be able to look through the deadeyes and see down into the water to the bottom. And I'll find the *Chicora*, wherever she is."

I certainly had great hopes for him. His quest was just the sort that any ten-year-old child would have longed to join, and those of us who passed most of that summer in the Nelson back yard made serious efforts to be taken on as part of the crew. But Nelson would have none of us.

We rallied round one day to see him depart with his tug aboard a low-slung stone wagon that he had rented from some monument maker near Graceland Cemetery. He seemed just on the verge of success that morning. But he didn't find the *Chicora*. Or, if he did, he never told anybody about it.

He had a successful launching and sailed off into the blue without delay. Five days later a squall capsized the boat a few miles from St. Joseph. It was found, easily enough, by a Coast Guard vessel. But there was no sign of Nelson, then or ever.

Save for surviving residents of the old neighborhood, few people in Chicago remember Nelson or his tugboat. The short press reports of the boat's sinking seemed quite casual about it all. They made no mention of what he was looking for, which, I have always felt, would have been well worth their comment.

Chapter 35

The Urge to Better Things

E<small>VEN</small> as seen through the pink haze with which memory covers all things, there doesn't seem to have been much in the neighborhood of Lincoln and Belmont avenues in 1902 to rank it with Menlo Park, Kittyhawk or Oak Ridge as a center of scientific research. But you'd be surprised. We had with us in those days Messrs. Joseph Thompson, William Adams and Frederick Frueter, just to mention a few local geniuses. And there were plenty of others, indeed.

Willie Adams was probably the most noticeable of all this striking group. He had invented a five-wheeled automobile—probably the only five-wheeled automobile, the only five-wheeled vehicle of any sort—the world had ever seen. Adams, to do him justice, was a quiet, patient man whose modesty was obvious to his hundreds of admirers. But there was nothing modest about the gadget he had devised in his back-yard laboratory somewhere in the hinterlands of Roscoe Street. The whole North Side was conscious of it.

Few of us who observed his spectacular progress knew anything at all about automobiles. We had seen a few of them on memorable occasions. We had listened to jokes about them in circuses. We had seen models of them displayed in downtown shops and

284

less frequently along Lincoln Avenue. But looking back with the advantage of a little more experience one judges that the basis of the Adams working model was a two-cylinder, chain-driven Something-or-Other with the motor under the driver's seat. The great inventor's fifth wheel was on an axle in the middle of the frame where, in a modern car, you would find a transmission and drive shaft. You didn't have to look twice at the fifth wheel to see it. It was six feet in diameter and a foot wide—a hollow drum of steel—and it was connected to the engine by a drive belt. The four other wheels apparently were just there.

This charming equipage cranked on the side and was steered by a handwheel instead of a lever. The driver's seat was just an unupholstered wooden bench. The rest of the car was just an open framework. We thought that feature of it was highly commendable. It was a fine idea in any automobile to have all parts of it readily accessible.

There weren't so many paved streets in the area, even in 1902, but Marshfield Avenue had four or five blocks with a fine surface of uneven red brick which made it very suitable for the testing of five-wheeled automobiles. It was, moreover, a quiet stretch of road—a region of modest, well-kept homes and trim lawns—just the thing for an inventor who wanted privacy.

So every now and then Adams would trundle his car out of an alley near Roscoe Street and start north.

We, the large public who gathered to watch the spectacle that summer, were a little too young to decide whether or not noise ought to be a principal feature in a motorcar. The Adams exhibit had plenty of noise—noise of a sort that none of Chicago's horseless carriages had ever had before or would have again. And we loved it.

Whatever the driver may have wished, his journey toward Addison Street was one of roaring triumph. The street might be completely empty as the machine swung out of the alley. There wouldn't be a kid in sight except for babies in perambulators on front lawns—and they were all asleep. There wouldn't be an adult on three blocks of sidewalks. And the quietude would be so deep that you could hear the singing of birds, the humming of insects, the whisper of a gentle wind in the drooping trees.

Then the hollow drum of the fifth wheel would hit the brick pavement with a crash that could be heard halfway to the South Side. From kitchens and basements and back yards for half a mile would come housewives and kids and dogs on the run. The air would fill with ecstatic, reverberant cheers. Never did an inventor have a more enthusiastic claque.

The housewives might sometimes look pained—particularly those who had sleeping babies or suffered from migraine. But the kids would howl and the dogs would bark continuously, and with never a loss of volume. As the howling spectators reached the curbs of Marshfield Avenue the din would be loud enough to drown the racket of the fifth wheel. No wonder the patient Adams was encouraged to keep on trying.

As the log of his experimental drives is set forth here, it may seem that the trip was just a joyous romp, three blocks or four north, a magnificent turn around and three or four blocks of outsize howling on the way home again. But one remembers it wasn't as simple as that—not at all.

Mr. Adams seems to have equipped himself with machinery less suited to his needs than to the width of his purse. Aside from the bedlam of the fifth wheel the most noticeable thing about his vehicle was engine trouble—lots of engine trouble—engine trouble four and five and six times to the block.

As he dealt with it he showed signs of a touching sadness. His lips would move as if in prayer, but, thanks to the roars of the little spectators, one could never be certain just what he was saying. He would fiddle with something on the dashboard in front of him,

286

alight with a large monkey wrench and give his attention to the silent motor under the seat. In the beginning it took him a long time to get the thing moving again. Sometimes he was so long at it that the kids and dogs and visiting housewives went away to other interests and left him alone in the peaceful streets.

But he knew few days like that. As time went on he grew more expert, or maybe he learned more about the things that can happen to a two-cycle engine. At the end of his first week he was sufficiently agile to hold the vigorous attention of his claque. He never lost me, anyhow. I lived on Marshfield Avenue and I didn't have any place else to go.

During the summer there were changes in the fifth wheel. First it was equipped with new sorts of sprocket wheels. Then it was made a little taller, then a little shorter, then taller again. It was given more width, then taken out and replaced by a counterpart, this time aluminum or some such stuff instead of steel.

We used to exchange remarks about these changes. So far as we could see they didn't affect the operation of the machine a bit. They didn't give any more speed. They didn't make the engine any more willing to work. The breakdowns apparently were just as frequent as they had ever been. The noise—whether the wheel was tall or short or wide or narrow—made of steel or some less hardy metal, was still the most immeasurable Ragnarok in the world's history.

Looking back on all this across a somewhat varied memory, I am convinced that Mr. Adams and his five-wheeled automobile were the chief attractions of 1902 and that 1902 was one of the most exciting of my childhood years. Adams kept tooling up and down Marshfield Avenue for several months. Occasionally he was accompanied by other men whom he permitted to ride in the front seat with him. Once in a while he would stop, not because the engine had quit but because he wanted to. He would explain things to these poker-faced strangers leaning over the side. That went on until the snow flew and he went away. We never saw him again.

Frederick Frueter was another engaging character of that period. Like Mr. Adams he was a mechanic of sorts. But he was a different kind of technician. He was a diamond maker. At that time your observer was in the newspaper business—which is to say that he peddled newspapers in a sort of loose partnership with one Dion O'Banion, a manly little fellow who was one day to acquire some note in another field. One of the customers on the route turned out to be Mr. Frueter.

Frueter was a dark, short, stocky, scowling man who wore a black slouch hat that would have made him look mysterious even if he hadn't been a diamond maker. He performed his wonders in a sort of woodshed behind the flat building in Otto Street where he lived with his wife and a couple of small children. The wife contributed to his scientific research by taking in washing.

There was no secret about the nature of his work. It had been widely discussed in the neighborhood almost since its inception, and there was a general feeling that it might turn out all right.

A high-school physics teacher who took his evening beer at a local pub explained that diamonds are crystallized carbon while coal is uncrystallized carbon. So all Mr. Frueter had to do was crystallize a lump of coal. It was a fascinating prospect.

O'Banion and I used to pay frequent visits to the shed and look at it earnestly. But we never saw the inside of it. Mr. Frueter was just as forbidding as he looked, and he made no effort to conceal his distaste for little boys who wanted to find out about the wonders of nature. But we forgave him. It was obvious that a diamond maker must have a lot on his mind.

It occurred to me early in our relationship, when I saw Mrs. Frueter struggling up the back stairs with a large basket of some-

288

body else's wash, that he might have financial embarrassments. So, just to help in the cause of human enlightenment, I decided to give this worthy technician his evening paper without cost.

Three months went on—lovely summer months with weather that permitted an almost daily search for knotholes in the walls of the shed that was the diamond factory. But there came one evil day when Frueter was waiting for me as I arrived with the *Evening Post.*

"What do you mean by letting this bill pile up?" he roared. "If you'd collected every week it would never have come to $2.36 by now. You are fired."

I was deeply hurt. I didn't get a chance to tell him what I had been doing. He turned about and went up the stairs in what looked like a towering rage. He took the *Evening Post* with him.

I don't suppose that the Frueter experiment added many diamonds to the world's supply. At any rate, the technician never gathered up enough money to offer me my $2.36. But I feel that both he and I deserve some commendation for trying.

I found ready solace in following the career of Joseph Thompson, a third inventor. Mr. Thompson was constructing an airship.

He was a thin, tall, affable man whose hangar was in a vacant store on Lincoln Avenue near Cornelia Street. His calling was advertised by a painted cloth sign over the door: "This Is the Home of the LAKE VIEW AIRSHIP." Thompson and his wife occupied rooms at the rear of the store. Mrs. Thompson also took in washing.

We—Dion O'Banion and I—got acquainted with Mr. Thompson one day by walking into his shop and announcing that we would like to look at the airship.

"It isn't done yet," explained Mr. Thompson. "I'm working on it. But it takes a long time to finish an airship. I expect to have this one finished in time to beat Santos-Dumont in the airship race at the St. Louis exposition and win the fifty-thousand-dollar prize. Here's the drawing of it. It will look just like the drawing."

He displayed a sketch of a large cigar with a basket hanging from its middle.

"It's not like other airships," he explained. "It's got a sort of tunnel running through the gas bag. The propeller works in the tunnel. It sucks the air from out in front and reduces pressure up there. Then it blows the stream out in back to drive the ship."

You might possibly call this the first hint of jet propulsion. But, no matter. We didn't know anything about that.

"I'm going to build it out of six-ply goldbeater's skin," the inventor went on. He paused for a reply while we wondered why a goldbeater should have a more suitable skin than anybody else.

"It will be a good tough airship," he said. "And I'm getting all ready for the day I get it done so's there won't be any delay about getting it down to St. Louis in time for the big race.

"Right here is the hydrogen generator. It used to be a whisky barrel, but I fitted it up with these valves and things. It's got a mixture of zinc and hydrochloric acid in it. That makes hydrogen. So you see, all I have to do when I get the ship done is attach the filling hose right here to this valve, then turn that valve over there and fill her up. You can come in here and watch me do it if you like. I'm telling you that's going to be a historic sight for this neighborhood. . . ."

It was undoubtedly a remarkable opportunity. But we never got a chance to take advantage of it. I saw Mr. Thompson several times during the next two or three weeks, but aside from his hydrogen-manufacturing plant he didn't seem to be making too much progress.

He explained all that. There had been a considerable delay in the manufacture of the gas bag. It had to be gastight, of course, and the people making it just didn't seem to get the hang of how you pasted six-ply goldbeater's skin into a large, continuous, gas-tight receptacle.

"They'll get it fast enough," he forecast cheerfully. "And when they do, everything else will happen in a hurry. I'll bind on the side strips—which ought to be delivered by that time. I'll hook up the engine. It's an apparatus they're putting together for me over on the West Side—nothing very complicated about it. It'll be done by then, too.

"There'll be sealed passages in the gas bag so's I can put in the cross struts for the propeller in the tunnel. That ought to take maybe one or two days. And then, you can see, everything will be easy sailing. I'll just have to connect up the basket and the controls and turn on the gas. Maybe you think I won't be glad to have the gas all ready!"

He was interrupted slightly by the opening of the front door and the passage of his wife wheeling a baby carriage filled with dirty laundry. She didn't speak to him.

"My wife," he explained after she had gone into the rooms at the rear. "Fine woman. She's just doing this little laundry work to help out. That's because we've put everything we've got into the airship. She'll get it back, of course, when I beat Santos-Dumont. He won't have a chance and I'll pull down fifty thousand dollars. She'll be glad then that she had this chance to help out."

There was some sort of mass meeting a day or two later at Schmidt's Hall to promote the airship. I didn't hear much of it because the doorman decided that twelve-year-old boys might cause a disturbance and interrupt speeches and otherwise mar the dignity of the occasion. The sponsors of the shindig were billed as the Lane Park and Lincoln Avenue Businessmen's Associations. It seems that not all their members came.

All was not lost, however. The next day Mr. Thompson seemed quite pleased with the whole proceedings.

"After paying for the hall," he said, "there was seventeen dollars and eighty cents left for the airship fund. I figured out that the seventeen-eighty was just about enough to buy some tough bamboo struts that I can fix up to be ready when they deliver the gas bag. And while I was out shopping for this material I ran across a great bargain in cigars. Got a whole box of them for two dollars and fifty cents. And, boy, it's a long time since I've tasted such fine cigars!"

The next step in the manufacture of the airship came that night. Mr. Thompson seems to have been careleses about smoking fine cigars near a hydrogen gas tank. They picked him up only slightly wounded in the middle of the Lincoln Avenue car tracks. The wreck of his shop and the rest of the building was scattered about him. His wife wasn't marked. She had been away somewhere delivering laundry.

The airship never got finished—not in our neighborhood— which seems a great pity. It would have been such a fine thing to look at, so much more interesting to look at than a five-wheeled automobile. I hoped for a time that Adams might take up the work of building an airship. But he never did. He seems to have been satisfied with his invention. In its commercial form it turned out to be the bull-wheel tractor, and the inventor made a lot of money in royalties on it. Funny thing, though, it never got such noisy acclaim as we gave it when we didn't even know what it was.

Chapter 36

The Badly Damaged Customer

AND then, of course, there were the saloons.

Historians have not been too careful in plotting the effect of these fine institutions on the growth of Chicago. They should be taken to task for their aloof attitude, their lack of simple understanding of what made the pioneer go in the way he did. Plenty of the city's best thinking undoubtedly was done in saloons. What came of it, I do not know. That a lot of our early architecture was of the tavern school goes without saying. Much that is revered in our art, music, oratory and politics stemmed from the same source.

Some of these institutions became famous landmarks before they fell down or the prohibition law discouraged them. There was the Relic House up on Clark Street at Center Street. The beer of the Relic was probably about the same as anybody else's. But the walls were certainly different. They were built of pieces of the slag that the Great Fire made out of the business district's best buildings— not much to look at but very historic. There were ten or fifteen small saloons over along Archey Road (Archer Avenue), each of which was the saloon that Mr. Dooley had run. There was a place out on Addison Street considerably patronized because "the car-barn bandits" had held it up. There were dozens of these drinker-ies striving to uplift the culture of Chicago by directing the customer's attention to subjects of science, folklore, progress, good conduct—things that would stimulate his mind while quaffing such things as the bartender could provide.

There was one odd saloon the policy of whose management seems to have been to render the customer unconscious as soon as possible. The percentage of profit in such an operation seems difficult to calculate. But it certainly was there.

So far as the visiting yokelry was concerned in the nineties, Chicago's principal attraction from the end of the World's Fair until the first years of the new century was not the Masonic Temple or Lincoln Park Zoo or the electric cars but this unprepossessing saloon on South State Street. The establishment bore the title of Heine Gebubler, a name much better known in the sticks of the Middle West than that of—let's see now—who was President in 1897?

Some of the lore that surrounded Mr. Gebubler's operations is still circulating. But it falls short of authentic history because it emphasizes the man's mechanical bents rather than the shrewd psychology with which he set a new style in what the trade laughingly calls entertainment.

Heine Gebubler had many imitators. Tex Guinan, with her frank greeting of "Hello, Sucker" to customers who were undoubtedly just that, was one of the best—although she never maimed anybody. Olsen and Johnson, with a stageful of pleasantries that included the wrecking of people's clothes, were following the Gebubler line when they stretched bad manners into a couple of years on Broadway. Currently a bad-tempered gent named "Toots" Shor has been packing them in by chasing them out. But we don't seem to have any of those geniuses in Chicago—not any more.

Let us not forget where the technique started. Heine Gebubler was the discoverer of the principle that the sturdy American likes

294

to get pushed around and called names. He established the dictum that the voice with the snarl brings in the profits. He weathered a bad depression by recognizing that the belt in the teeth is just as valuable a business invitation as the friendly handshake.

Heine is said to have been the coiner of the phrase "Nobody ever remembers you for a kindness and nobody ever forgets a kick in the pants." Whether he first thought up this idea or not, he was certainly the first one in these parts to put it into operation. He did everything to the customers that Olsen and Johnson ever did— with mechanical improvements.

He used to declare that his beer was as good as could be found anywhere in Chicago. And so far as can be determined, there was never any complaint about it, nor about his prices. But it is not for such things that his memory stays alive along the skid row that sprang up when lesser geniuses tried to carry on his great work. The beer may have been good, but there was some difficulty drinking it. In the circumstances colored water flavored with turpentine would have done just about as well. The tariff may have been right—but before you admit it you have to figure a fair price for sprained ankles, black eyes or spoiled clothing.

The customers came back to Heine Gebubler's not because they loved him but because they wanted to see somebody else subjected to his tender ministrations. Somehow it makes a dupe feel better if he is able to find out that he has some company in a half-witted world.

To the unprepared eye, Heine Gebubler's saloon looked like any other unpretentious German *Bier-Stube*. It had a long mahogany bar with a brass rail in front of it, a back-bar mirror frosted with epsom salt, and a few innocuous-looking tables and chairs along the opposite wall.

At the end of the bar a stairway led steeply to the second floor, on which, according to numerous placards, was to be found a free museum of natural wonders.

In one corner stood a "Motographoscope" machine. You worked it by dropping a nickel in the slot and peering through a little window and, theoretically, seeing some cinematographic wow like "Fun at Vassar," "Midnight in Paris," "Fire in the Harem," all "in natural motion." There were other slot machines providing Yucatan chewing gum, peanut candy and Sen-Sen.

If an entering patron had bothered to look, he would have noticed that all the men already in the place were standing in petrified stiffness along the bar. All eyes were fixed on the newcomer. And over the entire room hung an atmosphere of eager expectancy—as well it might.

The customer, generally an outlander, wandered up to the bar and generally ordered beer, which he was served in a large mug. With no trouble, disturbance or interference, he poured it down. Any of Heine's possible dupes could have walked out at that point. The house's attitude was that man, like a fish, must be played before you try to catch him. If the beer drinker turned back for more—which he generally did—he would learn something about how things happened in Gebubler's.

Nobody took a breath as he was served the second large mug. Nobody moved. Nobody closed an eye. In an instant everybody in the place would know what kind of customer he was. If he had been there before, he would pick up the mug in his left hand and drink it from the side to the right of the handle. If he didn't know his way about, he would usually pick it up in his right hand and drink from the side to the left of the handle. . . . And in no time at all the beer would have flowed through a slit in the glass down the front of his shirt.

If this wholesome pleasantry angered him, willing hands pushed him out into the street. If, as happened ninety-nine per cent of the time, he made the best of the situation and grinned sheepishly at the roaring mob along the rail, he was plied with fine wines,

liquors and cigars, praised for his good sportsmanship and generally fixed up for the next phase of his initiation.

By this time one of the less bright members of the Jukes family might have suspected that Heine Gebubler's simple saloon was strewn with pitfalls. But somehow the gull contrived to fall into them anyway—not all of them, perhaps, but many of them.

He might move from the bar with a couple of newfound friends to a table. If so, his chair was certain to collapse. If he spent a nickel to see the "Fun at Vassar" in "natural motion," water or soot would shoot into his face from the viewing window. The vending machines delivered April Fool candy and rubber gum.

The phenomena of the induction coil had been discovered by Heine Gebubler before such things had been put to practical use by anybody else. So the washrooms of his restful saloon were wired for electric shock in a variety of connections that need not be mentioned here. Gebubler was also the inventor of the collapsing washbowl, which had a way of dumping its contents onto the legs of the user. The soap, of course, was liberally laced with lampblack, and the towels disappeared into the wall when one touched them.

It is difficult to explain how anything else could happen to a customer except that at this stage of the proceedings he was probably too numb to care. At any rate, it is history that the victim who had come down through the gantlet from leaky beer mugs to electrified faucets nearly always went the rest of the way—up the stairs to the "free museum of natural wonders."

When he was halfway up, the stairs flattened out in a straight ramp down which the gull slid screaming into the mildewed blackness of the basement. He was rescued in good time, given much praise and more free drinks at the bar and tentatively elected to membership. If he showed the right spirit and held up his own obligations, such as buying drinks in his turn, all was well. If he hadn't yet picked up these rules, he was gently and cheerily escorted out. As he crossed the threshold some comedian with a slapstick smashed his derby hat.

Chapter 37

Ho! The Burning River

Never worry about the sights we saw in the Chicago of our childhood. We had neighborhood theaters which we could visit on Saturdays for a dime—if we had the dime. We could get a thrilling ride on the cable cars for half fare and investigate the whole town. We could sneak into high-powered and noisy picnics at Schmidt's Grove. We could get occasional rides in the grocer's wagon. We could attend about four circuses a year—or at least we could watch them come, stretch their canvas, take down the tents and go.

We were closer to nature in that golden age than the little hellions seem to be now. We liked to walk through the woods in the winter snows. It made us feel as Daniel Boone must have felt on similar walks—or at least we thought so. We had a sort of bird lover's society and we quested energetically for a look at our feathered friends. I don't remember that I ever saw anything on one of these journeys except a couple of robins, who were no treat to me, and the usual sparrows. We studied how the rain came down, and how the ice made patterns on freezing windows, and how the icicles formed on the eaves, and how the water left by the melting snow always seemed to be hurrying to get away somewhere. But,

299

of course, the big act of nature in Chicago was the burning of the river. That, I should say, was worth going downtown to see.

I don't wish to make it appear that this spectacle was rare enough to bring eager mobs in from the outlying suburbs. It may have caused something of a stir the first time it happened, though by the time I was eight or nine years old it seldom got more than a slim paragraph on the inside of the newspapers. But it was still something of a show, however commonplace.

The Chicago River, which brought about the building of a great city here instead of in any one of a dozen more inviting spots, was never much of a watercourse. Measured through all its branches, it has a length of maybe thirty miles. The French *voyageurs* called it a bayou—the sluggish outlet of a lake—which it undoubtedly resembled.

It was navigable by canoe for about four or five miles from its mouth. But five miles were five miles, and when the keel had gone aground in the mud it was possible to haul the canoe through a stretch of marsh and over the hump to the valley of the Des Plaines. The river was part of the shortest portage between the Great Lakes and the Mississippi Valley.

So Fort Dearborn was established in a bit of swamp near where the Michigan Avenue bridge was one day going to cross. And the traders came, and the fortune hunters, and the gullible people who believed the land agents' stories that the lake region was one day going to grow enough grain to feed the world.

Fort Dearborn vanished and a city took its place. The city dipped into a swamp and its foundations were below lake level. The sewers wouldn't drain and there were violent epidemics. When it became obvious that Chicago would have to alter its contours or die, the streets were raised seventeen feet. The sewers were revised.

When this engineering marvel had been completed the columnists of the day bragged that you were no longer in danger of drowning if you fell off a sidewalk into State Street. What they failed to add was that you were in no danger of drowning if you fell into the river. The waters was pretty well roofed by no end of odd matter that flowed from the elevated city.

A young engineer named Jefferson Davis, who escaped hanging to a sour-apple tree in the Civil War, had advised Congress in 1833 that Onion Creek, as the Chicago River was sometimes called, was really a river and worth improvement. As a result of his report, the Illinois-Michigan Canal, cutting across the watershed, had been opened for traffic in 1848. In the early eighties an attempt was made to pump water fast enough to create a backward current from the lake. But the town was growing too fast to benefit by any such makeshifts.

The city made some headway against typhoid epidemics by taking its water through a tunnel from a crib about five miles out in the lake. But meanwhile the river got slower and thicker and thicker and more putrid and more inflammable. Channels were dredged to accommodate the Great Lakes traffic, and factories of one sort or another had sprung up along the new line of wharves. Factory refuse, sewage and the muck from the stockyards all went into the river. A lock at the mouth of it—part of the Illinois-Michigan Canal pumping project—held the river motionless and as placid as a lake of tar.

Onion River is still far from being one of the world's most pellucid streams. But it has some flow now. And the crust has long been gone from the top of it.

Standing on the Madison Street bridge, one has a hard time envisioning the whole surface swept with fire—flaming like a burning prairie—with docks and bridge piers beginning to smoke and moored ships moving their screws and paddles to push the blazing tide away.

The fire department apparently developed some special techniques for taking care of burning rivers. The problem certainly was worth some thought. The best method, it was decided, was to shoo the flames away from pilings, piers, ships and such and let the inflammable flotsam burn itself out. Fortunately this didn't take too long. The blaze began to die down in two or three hours.

The burst of flame that we watched from a South Side bridge on that mellow spring afternoon in 1899 may well have been the last of its kind that Chicago was ever to see, for the opening of the sanitary canal in January 1900 restored the river to a more or less liquid consistency.

The fire was a weird exhibition, more memorable for the attitude of the crowds than for anything startling in the play of bluish flames across the water.

"Looks better at night," said an experienced river-fire watcher who stood next to me at the rail. "You can see it better at night, account of the dark."

Somebody behind me asked a policeman: "Is there water under that burning stuff?"

And the policeman answered wearily, "I wouldn't be sure."

Come to think about it, I wasn't so sure myself.

The spectacle lacked smoke and brilliance and flying sparks and uproar and fire engines and other things that make big fires memorable. There was some dramatic expectancy about it. This I thought was due to the policeman who wouldn't let anybody loiter on the bridge except those who could find a place at the rail. Every now and then he shouted directions about what to do when and if the pier took fire.

The skippers of ships docked along the river must have had a worrisome time. The screws of all of them were turning, the smoke drifting idly from their stacks. Without loosing their moorings more than enough to permit a foot or two of motion, they churned up the water and swung slowly out toward the channel and back again, keeping the fire out of harm's way. They didn't seem to be in much danger of burning, but nobody could tell. It was certainly hot out there in the middle of the river where the blaze was riding, and a shift of wind or heat-driven current might have sent some of the skippers on a dash to the lake.

The day was saved really by a tug that came along pushing a contrivance of sheet iron that looked something like a snowplow. This device rolled the fire ahead of it and actually mixed it up enough to toss a lot of sparks and a column of greasy, nauseating smoke.

"Well," said somebody, a little sadly I thought, "that saves the grain elevator."

I took another look to see the blaze being herded into the middle of the river. And then my grandfather took me home. So far as I know, the river hasn't burned since.

Chapter 38

O Capt'in! My Capt'in!

WHEN Grandpa Wilson came to our house in the spring of 1900 and announced that he was going to visit a friend on the lake front I consented to go along just for the ride.

From the time I first learned to walk I had traveled a lot with Grandpa Wilson, and while I set no particular store by his friends, save one who was raising canary birds in his kitchen, I recalled that they generally lived in interesting places.

Two or three times we had gone out into the wooded wilderness of Mayfair. We had explored Greyland Park, near where Milwaukee Avenue crosses Irving Park Road. We had visited an old lady who sold eggs in a forest west of Winnetka. We had journeyed to a farm on the Des Plaines River where you could have a fine time fishing for bullheads even though you never caught any. It occurs to me that Grandpa Wilson was probably in the real-estate business as a side line, but at the time it was a matter of no importance.

On this occasion we got off a cable car somewhere around Chicago Avenue and walked east. Michigan Avenue didn't amount to much in those days. It was just a sort of dreamy dead end that came to nothing where the river went by. A few blocks north, where Lake Shore Drive began, you could see the battlements of mansions on the Gold Coast—an imposing array of them. But the part of the street that Grandpa and I crossed wasn't much built up. Apparently it had no rating at all among the millionaires. There were a few homes in this backwash of quietude, some of them big, but in the main they were considerably less pretentious than the brownstone fronts you could still see on West Monroe Street. On the east side of Michigan Avenue a vast desert of sand stretched out to the lake. And that's where we went.

We followed a sort of path over the ridges past a little collection of shacks and so came to a queer dwelling place that looked like a stranded steamboat—as indeed it was. I might have been more impressed with this locality if I could have seen how it was going to look twenty years later—a crowded, bustling region of lofty skyscrapers, new hotels, clubs, hospitals, mansions and apartment buildings. But I was denied the vision. I stood wondering what Grandpa could possibly want in this forbidding, desolate emptiness.

Grandpa took his stance alongside the boat and yelled, "Hello up there!" Down a ladder at the side came a weird old man in a frock coat and a plug hat.

The man was tall and gaunt and old and dusty. He had sharp blue eyes, a face that looked like wrinkled leather, and an incredible, straggly mustache copiously stained with tobacco juice.

"Howdy," he said.

"Howdy," replied Grandpa. "This is my grandson." And so I was introduced to Captain George Wellington Streeter. The incident made little impression on me. I was hoping that we might be invited aboard the boat. But we weren't.

The two men talked earnestly for an hour or more about what the captain called "valuable proppity," and titles and foot values and other puzzling subjects. Then they shook hands and we trudged back to the car line. Not even the fact that we rode home in the grip car assuaged my bitter disappointment. I hadn't met anybody but the captain, who didn't talk to me. I hadn't seen anything because Grandpa had kept holding me by the hand.

A few weeks later my interest in Cap Streeter revived. The morning papers were filled with a story right out of the nickel novels—the sort of stuff a person with imagination and some status in a fourth-grade reading class could read.

There had been a battle on the lake front, this thrilling communiqué declared—a real battle with shooting in it, and people getting wounded by bullets and other people getting hit on the head with wooden clubs. And the central figure in that gory endeavor had been my old friend in the plug hat. Something dire had happened to him. He had been "ousted from the lake front," the paper said.

I asked my father what this news meant. His answer didn't clear my confusion.

"Streeter claims that the land out there is all his," my father explained. "A lot of other people say it isn't his, and those people got the police to chase him away from it."

"But who really owns the land?" I asked.

My father turned that question over in his mind. "My money would be on Streeter," he said finally. "But I don't think he can win. There's too much money and too much power and too many kinks in the land laws against him."

I let it go at that.

In the course of the years as a newspaperman I came to learn a lot about Cap Streeter and the Deestrick of Lake Michigan which to this day is called Streeterville.

The captain was one of the most remarkable characters who ever came to Chicago. He was born in Flint, Michigan, in 1837, the descendant of a long line of warriors who had fought with distinction in the American Revolution and the War of 1812. He emerged from the Civil War a captain after considerable battling on such

306

places as Missionary Ridge and Lookout Mountain. None of this surprised me very much except the fact that his captaincy had come from the infantry instead of the steamboat business.

He hadn't been associated with the roaring deep for too great a part of his life. His postwar activities were numerous. He promoted a small circus and toured for a while, with some success. He operated a museum in Louisville. Still wearing the ringmaster's costume that he favored to the day of his death, he put in a couple of seasons lumbering in northern Michigan. There was little in any of this to indicate his talents as an explorer. But, anyway, when he had finished his logging career he felt the urge to go down to the sea in ships.

He built a small steamboat, the *Wolverine,* and he ran it around the Great Lakes. When he sold out at a profit he went to St. Louis and bought a river steamboat which he called the *Minnie E. Streeter* in honor of his wife who presently deserted him. He did well hauling freight on the river for three years, then came to South Chicago and built another lake vessel. After another turnover he built a hotel and operated an omnibus line in Bedford, Iowa.

He was still restless. Bored with Bedford, he bought an interest in Woods' Museum, Chicago. He left it and went west with one "Dutchy" Lehman—later founder of The Fair store—to operate concessions at state and county fairs. He tired of this enterprise when the James boys held up the box office at the Kansas State Fair and killed a woman. He came back to Chicago and bought an interest in the Apollo Theater.

The captain was nearly fifty years old when, in 1885, he married his second wife, Maria Mulholland, of Belfast, Ireland. Maria was the niece of a prosperous Detroit shipbuilder and she steered her new husband back toward the sea. She was aided in her argument by information that had reached the captain about fortunes to be made running guns to revolutionists in Honduras. So he sold his part of the Apollo Theater to Mike McDonald, another worthy soul, and built his last ship.

Maybe it is a little wrong to say that he built it. He started with a wooden hull that he found in a South Chicago shipyard. It had long furnished provender for termites or teredos and was falling to pieces when Cap Streeter first saw it. But he didn't notice such things. His broad view was fixed on the Honduran revolutionists to whose aid he was presently to be flying. He took over the hull, patched it a little, fitted it with a secondhand boiler and engine, stuck a deck and a pilot-house on top of it and held a launching.

Mrs. Maria Streeter swung a bottle at it as it went down the ways and declared: "I christen thee *Reutan*."

Roatán is one of the Bay Islands of Honduras, and it may be that the captain wasn't quite sure of the spelling. But where the name came from doesn't seem to have made any difference in the ship's career.

The *Reutan* wasn't much of a craft. It was thirty feet long and looked top-heavy. But Cap Streeter was proud of it.

"She'll take any kind of weather the Gulf has to offer," he told his critics. "I'll try her out in a lake gale and you'll see what I mean."

The gale came on July 10, 1886. Cap and his wife were the crew of the *Reutan* on a trip to Milwaukee that day. They carried three passengers. The ship came to port after a harrowing voyage. The passengers returned to Chicago by train.

Well pleased with the test, Cap Streeter started home at noon. He had improved his costume by lashing a rope about his waist. This was a wise precaution, for he was washed overboard repeatedly and might have been completely lost if Maria had not been present to haul him back aboard.

An engineer whom they had picked up in Milwaukee was too frightened to get out of his bunk, so the Streeters had to tend the fires and the engine and steer the ship alone.

308

With the wind behind them they made a quick trip to Chicago. About 3:00 P.M. they crashed into a sand bar north of the river mouth and about 180 feet off shore. The *Reutan* was leaking in a dozen places and the voyage was definitely finished.

"I guess we'll just have to stay here," stated Cap Streeter philosophically.

The captain had never given much thought to the Gold Coast of the North Side before the *Reutan* went aground. But he was a shrewd opportunist.

The ship would never sail again, but it had come ashore in an upright position on a pleasant stretch of beach and offered many advantages as a home, including free rent.

The water between the sand bar and the shore was only a few inches deep. With a little shovel work the captain constructed a sort of causeway so that he could get to and from the boat without wetting his feet. In time he brought a collection of railroad ties with which he constructed a breakwater to keep the storms from coaxing his ark back into the water—and all of this without the permission of N. K. Fairbank, who thought he owned the land west of the sand bar.

How Cap Streeter occupied his time during the next several months is lost to the record. But who cared? Whatever he did, Lake Michigan was taking care of his destiny. The waves came in as usual. And they piled up quantities of sand along the captain's breakwater. In a year or so the *Reutan* was high and dry, and a considerable patch of yellow ground stretched from it to the east. Cap said afterward that he was surprised at this good fortune, and maybe he was; but surprise didn't keep him from taking quick advantage of his luck.

Chicago was in the middle of a great building boom. Rubbish heaps left by the Great Fire were finally being cleaned up, and immense quantities of debris were being hauled out to be dumped on the Northwest Side. Cap Streeter visited the hauling contractors and pointed out that for a decent fee he would furnish a dumping site much closer to town.

So the dump carts came to discharge their loads in Streeterville. Presently the captain spread out old brick, metal scrap, sand, cinders and nondescript odds and ends over the shallows. Farther and farther out into the lake moved the homemade beach. It extended northward from N. K. Fairbank's line past other holdings. But nobody seemed to notice what was going on until Streeter was sitting in the middle of about 180 acres of solid land.

Two years had gone by when N. K. Fairbank came riding across the sands in a fine buggy and a towering rage. He roared his protest and Cap Streeter chased him off the premises with a shotgun.

Fairbank consulted a lawyer and came away somewhat upset. The law governing riparian rights, it seems, was a trifle ambiguous. Streeter had an argument, the lawyer said—enough of an argument to make the outcome of a lawsuit dubious. So, for the moment, nothing was done about the matter. Cap and Maria sat snugly in the *Reutan,* and the lake went on building more beach.

In the early nineties Streeter hired a surveyor to map this land and lay out streets for a new subdivision. With the coming of the World's Fair in 1893 he went into the real-estate business. He chartered a boat to haul people to and from Jackson Park. But he made side trips to Streeterville and sold lots to the visitors. He did real well—too well. And that, perhaps, is what got him into serious trouble.

Owners of mansions north of Oak Street had been surveying the advance of Streeter's beach with considerable misgiving. They brought the matter to the attention of the Chicago Title and Trust Company, which had guaranteed the titles to their lots. In the summer of 1894 a half-dozen deputy sheriffs came onto the sands with eviction notices. Cap filled the legs of three of them with buckshot and they went away.

A week later came another invasion—a squad from the Chicago Avenue police station. Another fight threatened, but Streeter listened to the blandishments of a sergeant and was arrested on a charge of assault with a deadly weapon. Streeter pleaded his own case in court the next morning and was discharged. The judge accepted his plea that buckshot wasn't deadly and that the question of who owned the lake front wasn't the point at issue.

Cap did a brisk business selling lots for a month before the next delegation of deputies showed up. He peppered them from a foxhole ashore as they were trying to board the *Reutan* and they retired.

The newspapers announced his victory the next morning and Chicago laughed. But the captain was beginning to worry about his prospects. The public might hesitate to buy lots in an area given to gun fighting.

Streeter's next move is not well documented. Perhaps he had some good advice. Possibly not. At any rate, he put in the next few days at the federal courthouse and in the local libraries. He came up with an argument that kept scores of lawyers busy for decades.

It seems an engineer named John Wall had been sent by the United States government to Illinois in 1821 to run the state boundaries. In the Fort Dearborn area the line ran along the shore of Lake Michigan, which at the time was virtually at the east curb of Michigan Avenue. Acres of sand had been piled up by the lake before the coming of Streeter. But the official line of the east side of Illinois—and Chicago—had never been changed.

"We ain't Chicago," Cap Streeter declared. "We ain't Illinois. We're something new and outside. I claim this land as the Free Deestrick of Lake Michigan."

The Deestrick enjoyed prosperity, if not peace, for several years after that. There came a rover named Billy Niles to join forces with the Streeters and to take an appointment as "military governor." Settlers arrived to pledge allegiance to the new government, and a little village of shacks and outhouses went up to embellish the view of the expanding Gold Coast.

During this interlude there was one raid. While Cap and Maria were absent one night a gang of hoodlums came onto the sands, wrecked some of the shacks and took possession of the *Reutan*. The captain waited three days for the invaders to get sufficiently drunk. Then he went aboard with his followers and beat them into unconsciousness.

In 1899, the year before I first saw him, Cap Streeter called a "Constitutional Convention." He read a declaration of independence for the deestrick, declaring in effect that it was wrong to rob the poor. The American flag was run up while the crowd cheered.

That night the police made a surprise attack and arrested all the men they could find on a charge of illegal assembly. But nothing came of it.

A month later the police came back again—500 of them with Gatling guns and brass cannon "to suppress anarchy." After an all-day battle six inhabitants of the deestrick were captured. They were tried and acquitted.

Still the turmoil went on. Soon after our visit in 1900 an army of deputies came into the area posing as sight-seers and were accepted as such by the inhabitants, who did not know what sight-seers ought to look like. They captured the deestrick and burned down the shacks.

When the fire was over and the reserve police had gone away Cap Streeter returned by water with a boatload of armed followers. This force put up tents in the ashes of the shacks and remained in possession.

In the summer of 1901 Streeter and his wife went to Washington. On their reappearance in Chicago they produced what purported to be a warrant to all the land in the deestrick. It was signed by one Oak Smith as secretary to President Cleveland. It was obviously an invention and Cap Streeter was indicted for forgery.

While the case was pending there was another hoodlum raid on Streeterville. John Kirk, a onetime cowboy, was killed. Streeter, who was beginning to show signs of age, was indicted for murder, convicted and given a life sentence. Maria died a few weeks later.

That wasn't the end. Nine months after his trial Cap Streeter was given a pardon and returned to the deestrick. The war for the lake front settled down into a series of unimportant skirmishes.

Alice Lockwood Streeter, whom the captain married in 1906, armed herself with a meat cleaver and took to the life of Streeterville with gusto. As "Ma Streeter" she occupied a place in local folklore second only to that of her battling husband.

With sporadic interruptions by the police the captain did a good business in beer during the dry era. As governor of the Deestrick of Lake Michigan he repudiated the prohibition law.

It wasn't the kind of law that was suited to the deestrick, he declared. He held out until 1918 and the inevitable finish. Deputies, disguised this time as lot buyers, took the deestrick by infiltration tactics and burned down everything in sight, including the old *Reutan*.

Streeter and his wife went to live aboard an old houseboat tied to the Municipal Pier. They eked out a subsistence selling hot dogs and coffee.

Shortly afterward the courts finally got around to a decision on the matter of the Deestrick of Lake Michigan and denied all of Cap Streeter's claims to it. The captain seemed to be a little discouraged after that. He died at the age of eighty-four years on January 22, 1921. By that time thousands and thousands of Chicagoans knew that he had been here.

Chapter 39

Gold Bricks

THE Alaskan gold rush toward the end of the century made little difference to Chicago, which had been experiencing a gold rush of its own since the early forties.

Hundreds of adventurers went out to the Yukon, of course. But thousands of less energetic fortune seekers came streaming into the railroad stations to maintain the balance. The local effect of the great treasure hunt had little more than conversational connection with mines and miners. One refers, of course, to such things as the boom market in gold bricks.

It is hard to say at this late date where the gold-brick business originated. Certainly it antedated the shooting of Dan McGrew. The sick engineer who was so anxious to sell the brick seems to have taken to his bed before the forty-niners started their long trek to California. But daily newspaper reports from fabulous Alaska caused people to forget such details. The sick engineer didn't get any better, but for a time he did a business worthy of his accumulating talents.

Our high-wheeled-bicycle-riding neighbor, Willie Kress, had become a professional whose experience with shows and the like made him wise beyond his years. Ambitious, inquisitive and sure of himself, he should quite naturally have been one of the first men in town to learn about the gold-brick business and to see in it a chance for personal profit.

Unlike other crafty opportunists, he made no secret of his business. He talked—loudly and continuously.

"This-here engineer," he said, "he's got a block of gold, they tell me—solid gold—but he's got to sell it cheap."

"Why?" was the very fair question of Willie's listeners.

Willie seemed pained. "Well," he explained, "for one thing, this gazabo is sick. He's got to have doctors and a hospital. An' he's got to have money."

"Why doesn't he sell it cheap to a jewelry store where they make gold rings?"

"That's the story. Why doesn't he? Well, I'll tell you what I know about it an' what I think. It's this way: I'm just gettin' through with a meet at the Coliseum night before last when a fella comes up to me. His name's Fred. That's all I can tell you about him—his name's Fred. But I been seein' him around.

"He tells me that over to his boardinghouse there's this sick engineer. The engineer has just come back to town and all at oncet he gets sick. But he's got a sweet proposition, Fred tells me, a mighty sweet proposition.

"This-here engineer's been runnin' a donkey engine or somethin' up in Alaska, an' he gets holt of this block of solid gold. An' he cuts out, twenty-three, for Chicago. He wants to get his uncle to help him sell the gold. That's a good idea, Fred says, because his uncle's a jeweler. But the uncle has moved away. There ain't no trace of the uncle. He just sells his big jewelry store, takes the money an' cuts out. He don't tell nobody where he's goin'. So here's this engineer right up against nothin'. An' then, so help me, he gits sick.

"Now the way I figure it, this-here engineer stole that gold brick. That's why he's afraid to peddle it like you or I would. Somebody
316

might reccanize him an' he'd git pinched. So what I wanna do is raise maybe a couple hundred simoleons an' take it off his hands. It's worth thousands—maybe hundred of thousands—an' maybe your father'd like to go in with me."

My father didn't think too much of this proposition when I approached him with it.

"Willie is full of hot air" was his considered judgment. "And if there is any such thing as this gold brick he's yarning about, it's stolen property. So the best thing Willie can do is go ride his bicycle. They'll never arrest him for that."

Willie, however, was proof against that sort of argument. He borrowed some money or sold a share of the enterprise somewhere. He went with Fred to see the sick engineer and the amazing block of solid gold which the engineer kept conveniently under the bed.

"He was certainly awfully sick," Willie reported later. "Gee, I thought he was goin' to die right there! . . . He'd been sick an awful long time without no doctor. That was the trouble. So he didn't kick when I wanted to have the gold brick tested. We got a fella to do it right there in the building—an assayer, he was. A friend of Fred's.

"This fella—this assayer—he puts the acid on the brick an' gasps. 'This is it,' he says. 'By Jove, this is sure it! It's real gold—all of it—real solid gold worth maybe sixteen dollars an ounce.'

"And that ain't all. He drops some acid on the brick right there where I can see it. I know it's acid because I see him turn some brass black with it. But the brick doesn't turn black. Because the brick's gold, see. Just like they said, it's pure gold."

So Willie bought the gold brick. He never told me how much he paid for it. But it wasn't much. I knew that gold was worth a whole lot of money, but I knew that Willie didn't have it.

So the next day Willie got up early and hauled the brick to Peacock's jewelry store.

"Better idea to go to a good place first," he said. So he went and

317

showed the lump of solid gold to an appraiser, who gazed at it with no signs of enthusiasm.

"Haven't seen one of these things in a long time," the appraiser said. "If it's the kind I think it is, you've carried it too far." Then he got out a bottle of acid and a brush and took a swipe at the side of it. He watched unemotionally as the acid stripes turned black.

"Yep," he said. "Just what I thought. It looks mildewed."

"What'll you give me for it?" inquired Willie, who could never understand evil reports. "It's worth, say, eight, nine thousand dollars, ain't it?"

"Nope," demurred the appraiser. "It's old brass. An' the best Peacock's will give you for a piece of old brass this size at today's market price is about twenty-seven cents."

Willie picked the piece up.

"I'll get them fellas," he said.

But he didn't get them. The engineer had had a quick turn for the better after the selling of the brick. The sight of money seemed to have encouraged him. So he had moved to a sanitarium or a hotel or some other restful spot without leaving an address. Fred had moved, too, Willie discovered. And with Fred had gone the handy assayer who had been so deceived by the gold coloring of the brick.

So that looked like the end of the great fortune hunt. All the neighbors heard about it and made snide remarks about Willie. My father was more generous—which is to say that he was as generous as he had ever been to Willie. But he took the incident as the subject for a neat lecture.

"People who strive to get rich quick," he said in effect, "had better have some brains and some honest associates."

But there was one turn to the story that came about a week later. Willie, it seems, was still unconvinced. He took his brick up to Lincoln Avenue and Belmont to an old German jeweler named

318

Spraecke. Mr. Spraecke knew all about gold bricks and how to test them. He had the necessary tools. And he had also plenty of time. His diagnosis of the brick was just about what that of Mr. Peacock's assayer had been. But he went a little further.

"There should be a plug in this somewheres," he said. "They had to have a plug so's they could test it on real gold." So he swabbed the whole thing with acid and chortled when he saw one round spot of yellow emerging from a field of black.

"See what I mean!" he said. "We now take it out."

I don't know how much gold usually went into such a plug. I don't know the weight of the piece recovered by Mr. Spraecke. But it seems to have assayed more than thirty dollars which, I am well convinced, was more than Willie had been able to put out in the first place. From that day Willie was a new man, the first sage in town who ever made money buying a gold brick.

It is probably a little harsh to hint that Chicago was any more gullible than other American communities at a similar stage of growth. Wise New Yorkers had invested in a million dollars' worth of counterfeit Erie stock, privately printed by Jay Gould and Jim Fisk. Philadelphia strongboxes were filled with fake shares in the Comstock lode.

Other communities in other times had gambled in South Sea Bubbles, silkworms and Holland tulips. And, at any rate, a gold brick was something you could actually see. It looked like gold. It felt like gold.

The point of the matter is that Chicago, just struggling out of a slump that might have made the recent depression seem like prosperity, had seen a vision of hope in Alaskan gold and was justifiably impatient to cash in. Or, anyway, that is what the man says. Gambling and poverty have a closer connection than the textbooks on economics seem to indicate.

So the grifters who had come to town to take care of the World's

Fair trade lingered in a fertile field. The Willie Kresses bought gold bricks. Their wives and poor relations bought other things of similar worth.

A large portion of the housewife's time was occupied with running to the door to converse with some lad who was anxious to provide her with lottery tickets, secondhand diamonds or solid gold heirlooms at a considerable discount. Few housewives took advantage of these bargains. They didn't have any money, either.

There were guileful men with order books disposing of "surplus stocks of groceries, $2 with the order, balance on delivery"—which never occurred. And there was a continuous procession of minor operators putting out everything from brass polish made of soap and sand to tin rings supposed to keep the lamp from smoking.

Every household had a stock of spot remover that would burn a hole in anything it touched, pudding compound that turned out to be flour, brushes that shed hair like a collie dog whenever they met hot water.

Every bureau drawer was filled with "purchase coupons"—"pay the agent 25 cents; present this card with $2 and receive a barrel of apples, a set of chinaware, two dozen cabinet photographs or a handsome bedspread. . . ."

The fact that they were bankrupt to begin with is the only thing that saved a majority of Chicago households from further bankruptcy. But life was pretty complicated as it was. Not until years later were middle-class investors to come charging into the stock market to find out about margins. But there seldom was an era when even the thrifty had so great an opportunity for losing their savings.

You could buy pieces of Nevada mines at ten cents a share through direct purchase schemes advertised every day in the papers. You could get an entree with people who had schemes for extracting gold from sea water or even more improbable plans for lighting homes with electricity. And if you were smart, as you probably were, and shied away from the promoters and inventors, as you probably did, you had fine opportunities for putting your money into Wisconsin or Michigan land that generally turned out to be under water.

The world was filled with bogus insurance companies. And you could start a bank with about ten dollars capital and a sign over the door.

One searches the record in vain for an indication that the community was much disturbed by such things. The genius of the grifters was always a couple of steps ahead of the lawmakers, and during the mid-nineties nobody bothered to get too upset about it. The only people who could lose money to the grifters were those who had it and those who were silly with it. And times were too serious to permit much worry over such people.

Chapter 40

The Able Walker

THE boys were coming home from the Spanish-American War and movements were going on all over the country to erect statues to Admiral Dewey when my Grandpa Wilson, whose name you have heard before, took me out to Gaelic Park to have a look at the hero entitled Edward Payson Weston.

(I have forgotten where Gaelic Park was—if indeed I ever knew—except that it was somewhere in an unpopulated section of the Southwest Side.) But I have never forgotten Edward Weston. Memories of men of the hour, like Teddy Roosevelt and Schley and Sampson and Hobson, may fade. The statues of Dewey may be clouded by the hat he wore and may get torn down for filling stations, but to a lad raised by my grandfather—and a few of his relatives—the name of Weston will be green as long as mankind walks on two feet.

Came a Sunday afternoon. Once Grandpa, as was his custom, engaged to cart me off on sealed orders for some expedition that usually began with a ride on the Ashland Avenue streetcar. This time, however, he varied his routine. He arrived at our house in a livery rig—a sort of surrey with fringes on the top—and piled me into it.

I remember that I was unimpressed by the elegance of the turn-out. As a horse lover who rode every morning with the grocery man on his appointed rounds and every afternoon on the back step of the ice wagon, I had become a little blasé about tours in ordinary buggies. But I conveyed none of this critical thought to my grandfather. Mine not to reason why, not to ask about our objective until it was revealed to me as a sort of surprise.

I sat back in my fine plush seat and waited till I was given my cue.

"Where do you think we're going?" Grandpa inquired.

"Lincoln Park," I answered out of force of habit.

"Not this time," he assured me. "This time it's going to be different. We're going to see a great man."

Perhaps I looked pained. I certainly felt that way. "Who?" I inquired, just to make conversation.

"Who's the greatest hero in the country?" demanded Grandpa.

"Adolph Luetgert," I mentioned without hesitation. But that turned out to be the wrong answer.

"Not at all," declared Grandpa. "The greatest hero of them all is Edward Payson Weston—and a big boy like you ought to know all about him."

I merely sighed, because I had learned a long time before that I could never know all of my grandfather's friends any more than I could hope to know all the gnomes and pixies who seemed to be of the same tribe.

"Did he kill his wife, too?" I inquired, probably because the glories of Luetgert were fixed in my mind.

"He did not!" declared Grandpa. "He hasn't any wife—far's I know. He's a walker!"

"A what?"

"A walker—he walks—he's the champion walker of all the world!"

"What does he want to walk for?"

"Because he can do it better than anybody else!"

Well, there the secret's out. Edward Payson Weston was a walker who had walked faster and farther than any man, so far as there was any record to show for it, had ever walked before him. And this was a fact which, unexplainably, interested more of Chicago's populace than were concerned at the moment with baseball, football, tennis, croquet or horse racing.

Who first thought up the idea of including walking in the program of track meets—rather than rolling, crawling or hopping—it is difficult to say. But it seems to have been a good idea. In the nineties there were few more popular sports events—probably because all the onlookers knew all about walking, whereas they might have had some difficulty figuring how to pole-vault or put the shot. Each spectator could imagine himself in the hero's role—another Weston.

Judges of walking contests were pretty well respected. The difference between a fast walk and a slow run is not very large. The principal rule was that the contestant must have one foot on the ground at all times and that he must employ all of the foot in movement and not merely the toe or heel.

If you try this some time for speed, you may realize why it developed some new techniques. A sprinter's leg drive was of little use to a walker. What he needed was something like the legato movement of the skater. Weston walked with a glide in which his head and shoulders seemed to have no up-and-down movement at all.

Weston, of course, was the best of them, although a lad named Patrick O'Connor was pretty widely esteemed by enthusiasts along Archey Road. He was a prime showman who, long before Pyle's "bunion derby," recognized the value of newsworthy courses and spectacular termini.

"It is very simple," he observed. "You get more notices walking from the bottom of Death Valley to the top of Pike's Peak than you'd ever get from a snappy stroll across Lincoln Park." And he seemed to be quite right about that.

On the occasion when Grandpa and I drove out to cheer the great hero, Edward Payson Weston, he was traveling through Chicago on his way from San Francisco to New York with the aid of O'Somebody's Popular Cushion-Soled Shoes. He became quite a personage as Grandpa filled me in on the details of this momentous exploit. . . . Over the deserts he had come, and over the top ridges of the high mountains! He had been forced to find bridges over the broad rivers because the rules forebade his swimming. He had swung along through dust and snow, mud and sand and gravel—something like a courier of the Pony Express, I thought—replacing his worn-out shoes at relay stations along the way.

"He is a noble performer," my grandfather opined. "Walking is the finest form of athletics in all the world because everybody knows when you do it wrong. And with Weston it isn't only a sport but a fine art.

"I have always been a great one for walking myself. Not that I have ever gone in for these competitions. I have too much work to do to make a contract for a trip from San Francisco to New York. But some day, of course, I might try it. It might be worth the effort to get such a reception as Chicago is giving to this great athlete today. . . ."

Chicago, or as much of it as could be crammed into Gaelic Park and along the streets leading to it, gave Weston a reception all right—a reception that should have been heard anywhere between Racine and Momence. The roof of the world went off when he came striding through the main gate, his arms churning, his legs gliding, his whiskers in the breeze. It was an unforgettable moment as the roaring crowd stood up and the brass band started to blast "Hail the Conquering Hero." At any rate, Grandpa said that was what the band was playing.

He circled the track twice, amid a roar of hysterical applause in

which I joined without quite knowing why. It didn't seem like much of a job to hoof around the track, but Grandpa explained that this was very magnanimous of him. It damaged his record from San Francisco to New York by two or three minutes. Then, with a wave of his hand, he passed out through the main gate again, presumably on his way to the Atlantic.

There were other events after that. I forget what. We emerged to learn that the horses of Grandpa's livery rig had taken fright at the cheering and had lit out for parts unknown. Grandpa enlisted the aid of half the city police force, and our carriage was brought back about 6:00 P.M. We got home somewhere around eight o'clock and made explanations that were readily accepted by our worried relatives.

We might have left the gathering of the horses to the police, Grandpa admitted. He was experienced enough with runaways to know that the police were pretty good at that sort of business. And we might, possibly, have arrived in better time if we had taken a streetcar. But, he pointed out, the park was about a mile from Madison Street, and Madison Street had the only car line in the vicinity. The day was pretty hot, he mentioned, and a mile would have been a pretty stiff walk.

Well, who wouldn't remember the day Edward Payson Weston came through Chicago!

Mystery and Crime 7:

Everybody Knew Him

It is a popular belief that what everybody says must be so. Which makes one a bit hesitant to recall the story, now virtually a legend, of J.C.R. (or J.R.R.), the most mysterious man of mystery who ever befuddled Chicago's best minds.

Like the heir in the famous Tichbourne case, he was identified by an entire community despite the negative evidence of a calendar, and was as unanimously repudiated by his sponsors when they got tired of him. Had it not been for a lot of people bickering over the obvious, he would never have become an object of public concern and the mystery concerning him would have merited no more than a paragraph on page twenty-eight. "What everybody says" may not always be so, but it certainly makes trouble for lots of folks who don't deserve it.

Somewhere in the United States J.R.R. may still be alive, fed by the ravens or in some other miraculous fashion as he was thirty-eight years ago. He would be somewhat older than seventy years—and he would still be a man without a name. I don't think so.

It makes no difference. Alive or dead, he himself is only one improbability in a long series filed under his unverified initials. J.R.R. first became a person of importance to the press of the country when he was found unconscious on the railroad tracks near

328

Rochester, Minnesota. He had no right to be alive. His skull had been caved in over his right eye and had been fractured in three other places. A police surgeon sent him to the emergency ward of the Mayo Clinic purely as a matter of form. It would have been more logical to send him immediately to the morgue.

Right there the mystery started. No one was ever going to be able to say what had happened to this barely conscious man. It was possible, of course, that he might have been hit on the head by a hammer or some other sort of bludgeon. But, inasmuch as he had been found on a railroad right of way, there was a reasonable presumption that he might have fallen off a train.

That became the official theory of the case. There was nothing on his person to show his name or position in life. But the police didn't think this was anything worth worrying about. He was grimy, his clothes were torn and he needed a shave—all of which convinced the sleuths that he was nobody of importance and therefore the undoubted victim of an accident.

At the hospital he was taken to an operating room and there he was given immediate care. Whatever his status in the world that he was so near to leaving, he was interesting clinical material. The doctors trepanned his skull with considerable skill, picked splinters of bone from the battered area and patched him up again. Only after that did someone discover that his torn clothing was of good material and that what remained of his linen was fresh and clean.

"He will never be able to talk again," Dr. Will Mayo announced on the morning of May 14, 1913. "But he will live. I'm not able to guess why."

So the man lived, and presently was able to walk with an attendant in the hospital grounds. His speech, if it can be called that, was limited to formless gutturals. But one day, four months after he was found, he did manage to supply some clew to his identity. A nurse handed him a pencil and a bit of paper and asked him his name.

With a cramped hand he wrote first J.C.R. and then J.R.R., the signature by which he was presently to be known to all the world. After it he wrote a hieroglyph that looked like a simple geometrical design—a straight line with a semicircle above it. He never got much farther than that in his effort to tell about himself. In six months he had recovered entirely from the physical effects of his mishap. But all his efforts with pencil and paper produced only the line with the arc above it.

His responses to tests showed that he was improving mentally. He was quiet and friendly and apparently happy. The surgeons looked on him as a valuable specimen. Brain specialists from all over the Missouri and Mississippi valleys came to study his reactions. And he became a fixture at the hospital with prospects of remaining there well cared for until the day of his death.

It should be noted here that he was never allowed to wander by himself. There was always the possibility that he might annoy other patients. So while he had plenty of freedom of movement, there was always an attendant at his side.

The newspapers forgot about him for a while, but the local police, under stimulus of the hospital authorities, resumed their inquiry into the cause of his injury. The record showed that he had been found across the rails of the Chicago and North Western Railway at nine o'clock on the night of May 13, 1913. A passenger train, which would have cut him in two had he been there at the time, had gone over the tracks at 8:30. The conclusion was that he had fallen or been thrown from the train. But this remained only a theory. The records of the Pullman Company failed to show that any passenger had disappeared after surrendering his ticket, nor had any unclaimed baggage been found aboard at the Chicago terminal.

A tedious canvass of woolen mills and tailoring establishments produced evidence that the shreds of J.R.R.'s clothing had come from an expensive piece of cloth. The maker was located but he

330

was of little help. This particular pattern, he said, had been sold in large quantities all over the United States. J.R.R. might have bought his suit in Minneapolis or in Tucson or in New York.

So the case was officially forgotten. The man of mystery, unable to talk, unable to write, unable to share a confidence with anyone in the world, became strong and healthy and apparently contented.

He had no way of asking for anything he might need, from a cup of coffee to a cake of soap, no way of indicating what might be going on in the remnant of his mind, and hence no way of doing much for himself.

Then in the fall of 1914, as the nations of Europe were getting ready for war, the press associations took a recess from international politics and announced a matter of more important, certainly more mystifying, local interest. J.R.R. had disappeared from the Mayo Clinic in broad daylight.

This seemed to be the ultimate in puzzles.

Where had he gone?

How could he have gone?

Who, if anybody, was with him?

Why?

The world was still searching vainly for the answers when, eight hours later, came the astonishing sequel. J.R.R. had been found, well enough but panic-stricken and noisy, in the Chicago Union Station.

Here, of course, was a mystery that took all thought from the fact that an archduke had just recently been shot at some town called Sarajevo. Here was a mystery thriller much more interesting than a simple, forthright murder thousands of miles away in the Balkans.

The details of the case that trickled in from Rochester were difficult to believe. J.R.R. had been watched carefully all the day of his disappearance save for one half hour when he was supposed to be in his room. All the hospital personnel had been properly accounted for. He went out of the clinic with neither the money to buy a ticket nor the means to ask for one. He had gone into the blue during a few minutes when an attendant had turned her back. And though he had undoubtedly traveled from Rochester to Chicago on one of two trains arriving here about 8:00 A.M., no member of the train crews could recall having seen him.

When he was taken to Central police station an examination of his clothes showed that he had not ridden the rods or bumpers. This time he was clean, remarkably so. His linen was fresh. His hands and face had been recently washed.

On the supposition that somebody must have bought a ticket for him and put him on the train, reporters interviewed virtually every railroad employee who had been on the Rochester run that day. But nothing came of it. The obvious difficulty remained: the man by himself must obviously have attracted attention during an eight-hour trip; and if somebody had accompanied him, there seemed no good reason why he should have been left to his own devices in the Chicago Union Station.

People from Rochester came down to make certain that J.R.R. was really J.R.R. But they didn't indicate that they wanted him back. He was taken out to Oak Forest Infirmary, and the newspapers returned to their routine of reporting World War I.

Occasionally a line or two about him would find a way into print. Early in 1915 two women came to the hospital and asked permission to see him. They gave their names as "Mrs. Smith" and "Mrs. Jones" and said that they might possibly be relatives of J.R.R.

The elder was white-haired and about fifty-five years old, a woman of considerable dignity and appearance. The younger was possibly thirty-two. She was alert and pretty. Both were well dressed and cultured. Despite their names, they were granted an interview.

332

J.R.R. seemed to know them the minute he came into the room. And the recognition seemed to be mutual. The younger woman, "Mrs. Jones," threw out her arms, calling, "Jay! Don't you know me?"

J.R.R. for answer dashed forward and kissed her.

"He's Jay Caldwell," she told the attendant. "I knew that the minute I saw his picture in the papers. That mark he makes is the brand of the Cup and Saucer Ranch."

The attendant, when he took J.R.R. back to his own quarters, was certain that the mystery was solved. When he came into the front office five minutes later he was surprised to find that the two women had gone. They never came back.

From that time on J.R.R. put in much of his time watching the gate as if expecting a return of the visitors. The attendants refused to share his hope. So they were considerably surprised at the end of the year when Mrs. Iles Pitkin of Chicago arrived at the hospital.

"He is my son," she said. "I'm sure of it now. I've been waiting for a message from beyond. You'll find a scar shaped like the letter X on his back below the right shoulder. There are two red spots on his knees—scars from a fire. There's a muscular knot on his left hip. The hair on his head is black and gray. But the hair on his chest is red. . . ."

"She couldn't have guessed it," decided the superintendent. So J.R.R. was identified as J. R. Robart, son of Mrs. Pitkin by a former marriage, and duly installed in Mrs. Pitkin's home. He had a gala home-coming. He was interviewed by reporters, which is to say they asked him all sorts of questions and he smiled in answer. Photographers took new pictures of him.

The turmoil of the war could be set aside for the moment while the populace rejoiced in the fact that sweetness and light still prevailed in the muddled world. A lost lamb had been found and Chicago was well pleased.

It looked as if J.R.R. presently would be no more mysterious than any other South Side householder. But that wasn't the way things went with J.R.R.

When the newspapers had finished their interest in the case, Mrs. Pitkin and her newly recovered son went away from their home. A week later they came into court in Dickinson, North Dakota, and filed suit on behalf of J.R.R. against Jay Caldwell, Sr., a wealthy rancher. They asked for $125,000.

"We intend to establish," their attorney told the local press, "that J.R.R. is really Jay Caldwell, Jr., son of the defendant. We shall prove also that this Jay Caldwell, Jr., before his disappearance from Dickinson in May 1913, owned half the Caldwell Ranch."

J.R.R. circulated freely about Dickinson after that and it began to look as if he might have a good case. Mrs. Mary Caldwell Ryan, sister of the man who had quarreled with his father and vanished from Dickinson, accepted him in public as her brother. Virtually everybody in the community was convinced that Jay Caldwell, Jr., had come back to claim his property. In the face of this evidence Mrs. Pitkin admitted that J.R.R. was not her son. Simultaneously Jay Caldwell, Sr., was loudly vocal on a similar theme.

"He's not Mrs. Pitkin's son? Well, he's not mine either!"

And he was bitter about his daughter.

"Mary Ryan would identify Jack Johnson as Jay Caldwell if she thought it would annoy me," he said. "And anyway, alive or dead, Jay hasn't any estate. When I sold him a half interest in the ranch I took back his notes for the purchase price—ninety-six thousand dollars. And they haven't been redeemed. Also, Jay was an inch taller than J.R.R. He was blond and J.R.R. is dark. Jay never looked like this man—not a bit."

The case came to trial just about the time the United States was getting into the war and so was given little space in the newspapers.

J.R.R., accompanied by Mrs. Pitkin and a brace of lawyers, in-

334

troduced strings of witnesses to establish his identity and to show that animus had existed between Jay Caldwell, Sr., and his son.

The defense case was simple. It consisted of a few newspaper clippings, true copies of the Associated Press dispatches and a file from the local office of the Western Union. All of this, as laid before the jury virtually without comment, showed that Jay Caldwell, Jr., had been alive and transacting business in Dickinson on May 16, 1913, three days after J.R.R. had been picked up from the North Western Railway tracks in Rochester.

Mrs. Pitkin didn't give up. She returned to Chicago, denied the suggestion of reporters that she had engineered the flight of J.R.R. from Rochester. Her lawyer made a few more useless motions in the Dickinson court. Then, like so many other characters in the case, she vanished.

J.R.R. remained in Dickinson as a sort of guest of the Ryans. In 1930 he was missing for a few days and caused a remarkable hullaballoo when he turned up in a hospital in Denver. He got away from there after a week and has never been heard from since. He is one Chicago institution who certainly managed to get away from the old environment.

PART VIII

TIME'S VISTA

Chapter 41

Und So Weiter

Well, anyway, look at the matter long or short, that gives you some idea of what living in Chicago has been like. Chicago, the pundits of the nineties declared, "is an independent miracle—vigorous, powerful and uninhibited. It takes the risks and it needs no advice." And I guess it hasn't changed much. Today they might say of it that it is old and cautious and sits in the wreckage strewn by its quick, vast growth, needing plenty of help. But critics were always loose with words.

It was a great place for trial and experiment, for the adaptation of design and materials and for progress without profit. And since the days before The Great Fire, when it was "a city of sham and shingles," it has continued to be so described. It may have messed up its beautiful surroundings and confused its inhabitants and shocked the distant readers of the newspapers, but nobody can say exactly that it has been standing still.

Financial panic came to the town as to other places in 1893. At approximately the same time Chicago invented the Union Loop—the circle of elevated roads about the business district. Economists say there was no connection between these two items—the panic and the Loop—but they certainly had an engaging juxtaposition.

339

The "Loop" was probably the greatest and most annoying of all Chicago's inventions. The State Street merchants had learned early about the instability of cities. In a short period the roaring mercantile district of Chicago had shifted from the vicinity of Halsted and Lake streets into the swamp nearly a mile east, the place where horses foundered and only strong men would dare to walk. It had remained there nervously while the town was lifted seventeen feet, and State Street was paved, and the so-called rapid transit was developed, and tall, gray buildings began to reach up into the sky.

There was growth on the edges of this downtown district. Even in the middle eighties the new city was feeling its way north and south and west. The dealers in dry goods and similar stuff realized suddenly that their magnificent real-estate holdings might turn out to be a bad investment. There should be some way, they thought, to stabilize the market sites, to stop this wasteful rambling toward Evanston and Englewood and Oak Park. So they raised their voices and got some skillful help. Elevated tracks were built in Wabash Avenue, Van Buren Street, Wells Street and Lake Street. Trains from the North, South and West sides were routed around them and about a square mile of downtown was fixed to become the highest-priced real estate in the world.

These worthy merchants and their elevated-railway associates have been gathered to their fathers. But they builded well. Their businesses went on for almost sixty years with increasing prosperity as the city grew and the congestion of the Loop approached ultimate stagnation. Casual investigation of the subject makes you tip your hat to these people. Their nurturing of the country's second city from a business area smaller than that of Keokuk, Iowa, was a feat never seen by the world before, nor, fortunately, since.

Once the Loop was established the city's growth had to go up instead of sideways. In quick order old skyscrapers were torn down to make room for newer, more efficient ones. Thousands upon

340

thousands more people came into town. More streetcars stumbled in to carry them—more busses, more taxicabs, more private cars. It got so that a person who had nothing to do but walk the street was a poor insurance risk.

It was a roaring city, in which respect, also, it hasn't changed a a bit. The blight began to show up south of Twelfth Street—now Roosevelt Road—and west of the river and north of Kinzie Street. Modest residence districts took on a new character as slums. But no one noticed such minor matters—not then.

The town continued to be the source of remarkable news stories. In 1900 the new drainage canal, which linked the Great Lakes and the Mississippi River by a direct water route, was opened. The stationary, inflammable Chicago River suddenly began to move. With a churning current such as hadn't been seen in these parts since the end of the glacial period it turned away from the lake and went romping through a cut across the old "divide" toward St. Louis, which had arranged a welcome of public meetings and howls of protest and writs. The water continued to flow, and Chicago's typhoid menace was virtually out of existence in 1905.

On December 30, 1903, some 596 people, most of them women and children, were killed by a flash fire in the Iroquois Theater. It was afternoon. The asbestos curtain wouldn't work. Flame from a floodlight leaped to a mass of scenery. Somebody opened a stage door. The draft from this source sent a blazing gust out over the audience. The lights went out. Iron gates across stairways from the galleries were locked. So were outlets to the fire escapes. Exit doors swung inward instead of outward, so that when the crowd of screaming children piled up against them they did not swing at all. There have been few such disasters in the history of the United States.

There was no mourning for the last cable car. It took its final trip in 1906. But there was a wild reception for the first electric car to run over the old tracks. Newspapers from as far away as

341

New York sent special correspondents to report this gladsome event.

That same year the Chicago Cubs won the National League baseball pennant. The Chicago White Sox won a similar prize in the American League. The White Sox won the World Series four games to two; and nothing like that has happened in Chicago since.

In 1908 a group of high-minded citizens under the leadership of the younger John V. Farwell banded themselves together as the Commercial Club and produced the Plan for Chicago. Somewhat belatedly the haphazard expansion of the community had been examined. A dream for its future orderly growth had been carefully studied. The "Plan," printed in book form, was one of the most interesting proposals for civic beautification ever issued. It is still an influence, though the vision of a straight, clean river, beautiful buildings, parks, avenues and bridges is still far, far away.

Bill Thompson was elected mayor in 1915. He was to be pretty active about the town till 1931. He closed the saloons on Sunday, amid the bitter protests of the drinking classes, in his first year.

Thompson was an active lad with plenty of political savvy. All during the time he served as mayor the Germans of Chicago were an important voting group. Most of them spoke German. Most of them were cheered by Germany's war successes. All of them took a dim view of war as an institution. So, in the summer of 1917 when an organization called the People's Congress of Peace was barred from holding a convention in Wisconsin, Minnesota or North Dakota, protesting American participation in the war, it received an invitation to meet in Chicago. Whether or not Thompson had authorized the invitation, he did nothing to stop the meeting.

Governor Lowden interfered with an angry demand that the mayor abide by the Illinois law against such assemblages. Thompson replied by calling on his chief of police. So, with police pro-

342

tection, the People's Congress of Peace held their meeting. It was all over when the militia sent by the governor arrived.

The war was over in November 1918. The troops began to roll back in the spring of the next year. There was a vicious race riot in the summer of 1919; it grew out of some sort of bathing-beach wrangle. The Volstead Act, enforcing prohibition, was passed in October 1919, and the community passed into what many trained observers called "a new era." Murders arising from the hooch business of the "new era" totaled 399, more than one a day, for 1928.

Whatever the world may have thought about Chicago's liquor traffic during the years of prohibition, conditions weren't much worse here than anywhere else. By the end of 1920 it was possible to get a drink anywhere in the United States except the lobby of the main hotel in Cedar Rapids. Bootleggers didn't have to come to Chicago to be killed. The coroner was just as busy in New York, Philadelphia, Butte, or Pishwaukee, North Carolina. New York's East River was paved with masonry made by encasing a hooch-trade rival in a barrel of wet concrete. The commercial profits—and hazards—of this business were naturally just about the same in one town as in another. But Chicago seems to have been a little noisier about it. It is interesting to note from the point of time where one may look backward over the work of liquor re-form, from 1919 to 1932, that very few Chicago people ever saw an act of violence or even an act of impoliteness. It sounds odd, but there it is.

Frederick Stock took over the direction of the Chicago Symphony Orchestra in 1905. He became one of the country's great conductors. There had been grand opera in the city since the time of the Civil War. The Auditorium Theater had been built for opera, and the elite of the town had gone there regularly in season from 1889. Ravinia Park had become one of the most popular summer concert spots in the United States.

The opera company transferred from the Auditorium to the new Civic Opera House by Samuel Insull eventually died. The wrangles over who was to lead the Symphony Orchestra took the matter out of local music notes and put it on the front page of every paper in the country. Chicago talked loudly in other things besides the beer business.

The city's first moving-picture house of the supercolossal type was finished in 1917. It was greatly admired for an architecture hitherto unviewed by anybody in what has been called the "civilized world." Never had there been such a magnificent combination of Gothic, Greek, Roman, Assyrian, Babylonian, Egyptian, East Indian and Chinese conceptions. Every couple of hours the lights were turned up so that you had a couple of minutes to look.

For the rest of the time you might as well have been sitting in an unplastered tunnel; but no matter: you knew what magnificence was veiled out there in the dark.

These theaters of the gorgeous-gorgeous school were immensely popular until television came along the other day. They spread out over the city and far into the country and didn't do the local theater much good. The time came when to get into a drama such as *South Pacific* or *Oklahoma* you would have to make your request for seats six months in advance. Always Chicago was Chicago, the same old highly cultured place with a lot of new slants.

Until the Second World War began the finest exhibitions of comedy and tragedy were presented in the courtrooms. There was the case of a fortuneteller, for instance, a thin, sad-faced woman with a deep and earnest belief in her own powers. One night she forecast that the husband of a friend was about to meet with a regrettable—and permanent—injury. Then she killed him so the friend could not complain that she had been in error.

There was the case of "The Heirs of Sir Francis Drake," who had bought a couple of million dollars worth of shares in his nonexistent estate at ten cents apiece. There was a lad suspected of

344

having poisoned his ward with typhoid germs; and a woman physician convicted of having murdered her daughter-in-law in an effort to get some insurance money for her son. There was Alphonse Capone, who was sent to prison for income-tax violation, which seemed a strange end for a murderer. And then we had Samuel Insull and fifteen or sixteen of his associates who faced a judge and jury after the collapse of the Midwest Utilities Corporation. All were acquitted, which seemed fair enough. There was no testimony in the trial that could have been understood by anybody but a certified public accountant.

Not only the surviving bootleggers but the entire city was rich when prohibition ended. It was doing a few of the old-time magnificent deeds—such as laying out a north and south drive, contriving some new sewer systems and pumping stations and building a few excellent bridges. New skyscrapers were beginning to rise amid the bones of the old in La Salle Street and Dearborn Street and in the backwashes along the river. But nothing was being done to care for the day when there would be too many automobiles for the present street system. Nobody seemed to be aware of the presence of the automobile—not enough, at any rate, to recognize it socially. The city was more dignified than in 1899, perhaps. It was grayer and a little slower, and more conscious of its long white whiskers. It seemed, perhaps, a little dazed.

On February 14, 1929, the whole population of Chicago turned its mind to prohibition once more. A couple of machine-gunners disguised as policemen rode up to a garage at 2122 North Clark Street in what seemed to be a squad car. They strode in and exterminated seven men, five of whom had been active participants in the hooch business. Of the remaining two, one had been a garage mechanic, the other a not-too-innocent bystander. This wholesale execution became known popularly as the St. Valentine's Day Massacre. The man whom the raiders had been most anxious to remove had come late for the meeting. He escaped the bloodshed and hid himself out for a week at St. Francis Hospital, complaining bitterly about a bad cold. That, too, one suspects, is the sort of thing that everybody believed would happen in Chicago.

The stories went on, a sprightly grist. The newspapers stayed in business.

Prohibition went away on December 5, 1933. The old saloon came back by washing the laundry signs off its windows and opening the front door. The bootleggers, for a while, stood around looking sheepish. They then took a hand in gambling or the running of brothels or the sale of soft drinks at gun point. There has been no lack of interesting activity in the town, and, certainly, no lack of ex-bootleggers and racketeers.

It's still not such a bad place, as big cities go. Like all of them, it's overcrowded. It is difficult to get around in. And the percentage of hokum in the speeches of the people who run it is getting almost too high to bear.

It is changing its shape. The Loop is still extant, its lofty office buildings still planted firmly in their high-priced real estate. But you get indications that the merchants, after a sixty-year fight for decorum and stability and moblike congestion, are getting tired of it all. New shopping centers are being constructed on the outlying edges of the town. New skyscrapers are jutting up out of what was good pastureland just before the Second World War.

A brave group of rehabilitators who, unfortunately, lack two or three billion dollars are fostering a movement to overcome the long developing blight of the near South Side. They have made considerable progress in that section. Thousands of people have gone out of trembling shacks into decent modern homes. But there is still plenty of blight, and the movement away from the old Loop may add to it. We may some day see a new Chicago consisting of a ring of new municipalities well outside the city limits of what constituted Chicago in the days of John H. Kinzie. And who will say that that isn't just the development any far-seeing traveler would have forecast over a dish of tea in the ferryhouse of Mark Beaubien?

As for the people who remain in this pulsating environment—well, somehow, they are the same, too. They may not be able to ride high-wheeled bicycles. They may not be able to judge the heat or the timing of an old kitchen range. They may not know how to cook delicacies out of such ingredients as apples, flour, cornstarch and cinnamon. But they have come to the right place, and they seem to know instinctively what to do in it.

The other day a motorman on the Northwestern Elevated overheard the broadcast of a Cubs' baseball game as he was leaving his station on the way south. He had been signaled to go at a crucial moment. The game was tied. The Cubs seemed to be on the verge of winning it. So he brooded over the situation, block after block.

In due course he came to the Addison Street station. And as he pulled up to a stop he heard a wild burst of cheering from the ball park. It lifted him out of his seat and he knew he could stand the strain no longer. So he unhooked his control, opened the door, stepped across the platform and walked down into the street. A moment later he was in the bleachers. I don't remember how the game came out. But the nice feature of this episode has nothing to do with the game, anyway.

The elevated line was tied up for something like forty-five minutes while the management looked around for a new motorman. The old motorman, whatever his name, is one of this city's best people. He has the true spirit of the pioneer, the initiative, the purpose and the flair. And, of course, he couldn't live anywhere else.